Unpretentious Valour

An Autobiography

by William McKane

Published by CR Print
in association with
William McKane

First Published October 2008

First Edition

ISBN 978-0-9560683-0-9

Foreward

I often wondered what the last day would be like. I walked out through the Tally Lodge at the main gate, past the army guard force watchtower to the car park. After being checked by the squaddies on duty at the extern gate, I drove my car out of the Maze for the last time. It was all over! I had served more than 24 years as a prison officer in Northen Ireland's Maze prison. But more than that, my total service in the Ulster security forces now spans over 43 years.

For some time I thought that when I retired I would write a personal memoir of my life, events, incidents and experiences. This is my story. It is not in any sense a chronological history of what became known as 'the troubles'. It is a story designed to revive the public interest in the bravery of the men and women of the Northern Ireland security forces, who have borne unremitting dangers and difficulties with commendable steadfastness~ and to pay tribute to the unpretentious valour of some of those who died, and whose very memory became an embarrassment to the government they served.

This is a story of faith: faith in God, faith in myself and faith in my friends and colleagues. It is a love story about a young boy from a small village in County Down and a young girl from South Armagh who were brought together as the result of a brutal, sectarian, terrorist campaign. But most of all, this is a story about service, loyal service, to my Queen, my country, and the British Crown.

Chapter 1

I was born on the 8th November 1939. The youngest of three boys, my two brothers were born seven years and three and a half years earlier. We lived in a small cottage at the end of a long winding lane, near the village of Donacloney in County Down. My mother Annie (nee Burns) was a mill girl. She was reared in a house on the main street of the village, where she had lived with her parents and one brother William, who was two years older than her. Uncle Willie was my godparent, after whom I am named. He also worked in the factory as a cloth-passer and remained there all his working life until his retirement in 1968. He died in 1987 at the age of 87 years.

My father Abraham McKane was a weaver, although at various times throughout his life he worked in the Belfast shipyard. He was the seventh son in a family of ten, most of whom I never met because they had emigrated before I was born. Of all my uncles I would most liked to have met are the two who fought in the Great War 1914-18, my Uncle Wesley who served with the Australian army, and Uncle Samuel John who served with the 36th Ulster Division at the Somme. Both survived the war and lived to an old age.

The cottage where we lived had four rooms, one of which was a weaver's shop which contained a handloom from an earlier time when weaving linen was a cottage industry throughout Northern Ireland. There was no electricity or running water, the domestic water supplied by a large pump with a cow's-tail handle that sat in the front garden. The water was conveyed to the house in two white enamel buckets, which were placed on a bench beside a jaw-box sink in the small scullery.

The dominant feature in the kitchen was a gaping open fireplace with a hob on each side, and a crook and crane that swivelled a kettle or pot over the fire and allowed it to be raised or lowered to whatever temperature was required. This was the house where my father was born in 1895 and where, for generations before him, people scratched out an existence on a few acres of land. At the back of the cottage, about a mile-and-a-half to the South, we could see the impressive facade of Donacloney Presbyterian Meeting House. Its black sculptured stone enclosed with dark yellow brick gave a commanding aura to a superb place of worship. This was our church where my mother and father were married and where we attended services and Sunday school. About a mile in the opposite direction we could see the high, red brick chimney of Donacloney factory, an imposing and much loved landmark in the district. Donacloney is still a busy linen manufacturing community, founded by the Liddell family in the early eighteen hundreds, although weaving linen has been carried on in Northern Ireland for centuries. The community has grown around this sprawling red brick factory, which is built on the banks of the river Lagan, Northen Ireland's principal river, and nestles in a wide valley among the sweeping fertile hills of County Down. It was at the close of the 17th century that the finer skills of the art of linen weaving were introduced by Huguenot exiles, who settled in Ulster after they were driven out of France.

They say memories of early childhood usually involve a trauma, and mine was no exception. I was about three and I was playing at the back of the house with my inseparable companion and faithful friend, an Old English sheepdog called Gyp, when we decided to explore the back field. It was a long field of grazing pasture, surrounded on three sides by hedges and sloping down to a narrow drain at the bottom. We walked for some time and, as we approached the drain, suddenly a water hen scurried in the reeds. With one spectacular dive Gyp splashed into the water and caught the bird in his teeth. As if in the same movement he returned, clambering out onto the bank where he left the bagged foul at my feet. I lifted the water hen and we started for home. On arriving back at the house, we walked round the gable and into my mother, who had been conducting a search for us. She immediately exclaimed with a broad smile,

" Where on earth were you?"

I produced the water hen from behind my back, held it up by the legs and said:

"Gyp taught a wee watee hen."

There are many things I do not recall from those early childhood days, but I remember vividly my mother hugging me and saying,

"Lony days! Lony days!"

Much discussion took place that night when my father came home from work and the family was gathered together. My keenest memory of that day is of feeling important, and being the centre of attention, and seeing how much they all loved and cared for me.

Chapter 2

In the autumn of 1943 we left County Down and moved to Lurgan in County Armagh, into to a small two-up, two-down kitchen house at Number 15 Charles Street. Charles Street is situated in the Lough Road area of Lurgan. Behind the busy fayade of the main road, on either side lay a veritable warren of streets, rows of terraced houses, built when the town and country planning service was little more than in its infancy. Gas street lamps were still in vogue, and I remember watching with fascination as the lamplighter, who travelled around the district on his bicycle, would use a long rod to open the globe of each lamp and turn the brass catch which would light up the area. We lived near the railway station, which was convenient for my father to travel to Belfast, for he had started to work in the shipyard again. He did not talk much about his work at that time but sometimes in later years when he was in a nostalgic frame of mind, he would recall his earliest experiences in the 'yard'. And with a distinct sense of pride he would say, "I worked on the ship that Lord Kitchener went down on."

It was not until researching this book that I discovered the name of that ship. She was HMS Hampshire. The Hampshire spent four weeks in Belfast in January/February 1916, for slight repairs, between service at Scapa Flow. Soon after she left Belfast, she was detached from the Grand Fleet for the special duty of conveying Lord Kitchener and his staff to Russia. The circumstances surrounding the sinking of the cruiser, even to this day, are not clear. But what is known is that on the 5 June 1916, as she sailed near the Orkney Islands in Scotland in bad weather, she struck a mine and went down with the loss of almost all on board except for a few members of the crew who swam to safety. As my father was born in 1895, he would have been a young man of about 21 years of age when he worked on the Hampshire. The death of Lord Kitchener, the premier soldier of the British Empire at the time, was set in verse by Robert Seymour Bridges, when he penned the words:

Among Herculean deeds the miracle
That massed the labour of ten years in one
Shall be thy monument. Thy work was done
Ere we could think thee; and the high sea swell
Surgeth unheeding where thy proud ship fell
By the lone Orkneys, at the set of sun.

(Courtesy of Lord Bridges)

Belfast shipyard was the Cape Canaveral of the world's shipbuilding industry, the birthplace of the Titanic and many other great liners from the turn of the century through the inter war years. It was at this period that my father worked on the construction of another famous ship, HMS Belfast. A cruiser of the Southampton class, the Belfast was launched by Mrs Neville Chamberlain, wife of the then Prime Minister, on the17th March 1938, the only surviving example of the great fleets of warships built for the Royal Navy in the first half of the twentieth century. The Belfast served with distinction in both the Second World War and the Korean War. This magnificent vessel is presently moored in the Pool of London near Tower Bridge and is in the charge of the Imperial War Museum. HMS Belfast is an enduring reminder of the reality of naval warfare in the twentieth century and a befitting testament to Britain's Imperial epic.

One exciting event in my boyhood was the arrival of American troops in Northern Ireland. A large company of them was based at a country estate near my home. They were part of the military build-up of allied forces in preparation for the 'D' day landings. They were the first soldiers 1 had ever seen in my life and it was the first time 1 had seen a black man. Sometimes they would parade from their camp to the town centre, which took them past the end of our street. To me they seemed so tall in their green battledress that they looked like firtrees. The black men among them had shiny faces and my brother used to tell me they had to be polished every morning.

The war years were a time of great trepidation throughout Ulster, and the war effort had taken a determined sense of urgency. My mother took a part-time job in a small stitching factory that made shirts for the army and RAF. Sometimes she brought work home with her to be folded and pinned, and at times piles of shirts were stacked all around the place.

As the youngest in the house, it was like living in a house full of parents, who all saw it as their duty to keep the developing lad right with advice and all kinds of instructions and warnings, not to mention an odd clip round the ear, just to make sure he was paying attention.

Both my parents were devout Christians and the sense of family was very strong. When I picture my mother, she is wearing an apron, bustling around the house, always in motion, cooking, washing and ironing. My father was strict but quiet, totally opposed to drunkenness or any other kind of unruly behaviour. He was an industrious man who worked hard whilst my mother coped. As I look back on my life, I am aware that my father was my potent role model. He used to sing hymns, his favourite being 'When the pearly gates unfold'. It was not so much what my parents said that shaped my outlook on life. It was the way they lived their lives. When the values are correct, the children will follow those standards and principles. They actively discouraged us from taking any interest in politics. They never even voted at election times.

Although the neighbourhood was dull and drab, most of the houses were warm and welcoming. It was a reflection on their occupants, whose pride showed in improving the dwellings to the best of the tenants' ability and to the limit of their finances at the time. The people were modest and would have given you the bite out of their mouths. It was a normal practice in the street, for neighbours who would run short of provisions about mid week to come to the door looking for the loan of a cup of sugar or a wee jug of milk to tide them over to the weekend. It was while living in Charles Street that I started my school career. I was enrolled in the Model Primary school, Brownlow Terrace, and with my brother and some other children in the street we would walk the short distance each day.

The war ended, and young as I was, I have stirring memories of that period of my life. I remember assembling with all our neighbours and friends in the street for a gigantic celebration to mark the occasion. Streamers of red, white, and blue bunting were strung across the street. Tables were set out end-to-end and covered with Union Jacks, and although rationing was still in force, the parents were able to provide plenty of sandwiches, buns, sweets and lemonade. However, once the excitement was over, life returned to much the same as it was before, and the following year we were on the move once again.

Chapter 3

A secret dream of my parents had always been to own their own house.

And in order to achieve this we moved to Hill Street, which they perceived was a more desirable neighbourhood. Although only about a half mile away, when we arrived in our new district we discovered that all metal railings and fences had been demolished and taken away to be melted down for the war effort. I recall clearly a huge water tank at the street corner bearing the words, 'Emergency Water Supply'. This was to be used to extinguish fires in the event of an air raid. Beside the tank there was a large red brick air raid shelter with a reinforced concrete roof. Small air raid shelters were also constructed in some back gardens but other families depended on the cubby-hole under the stairs for protection from a potential attack.

Hill Street was a long street of two rows of terraced houses that rose, as its name suggests, to a hill in the centre. There was a repeating pattern to the streets that connected Hill Street to its parallel, Sloan Street. They were the same distance apart that, if looked down upon, would have made them look like the steps on a ladder. They were Edward Street, New Street, James Street, Mark Street, George Street, Ann Street and Union Street. Jerry-building after the First World War had necessitated using a common design, which resulted in all the houses being virtually indistinguishable, the consequence being a street of terraced houses in a huddle of streets, with an enclosed yard behind each house. The neighbourhood was nicknamed 'the marrow bone'. My mother and father started to attend Union Street Gospel Hall and my brothers and I enrolled in the Sunday school. Each Sunday afternoon we would walk the short distance from our house to the Hall and sometimes we would meet up with other boys who were also going to the Sunday school. One of them was Drew McCandless. Although about six years younger than me, Drew was a tall lad with clear dark eyes and a calm face. It is a sad fact that as the years went on I lost contact with many of my childhood friends, although I still have a warm spot in my heart for those long ago days, when the older children looked after the younger ones and there was real friendship amongst us all.

On almost every street corner you would find a confectionery shop which kept an endless supply of sweets, ice cream and soft drinks. One such shop was at our house, Number 43 Hill Street, and was managed by my mother. It had been a small front parlour of the house and had been converted into a shop long before we took up residence. An L-shaped counter took up most of the floor space and there were shelves all around the walls. A front door allowed entry from the street and a second door led into the living room. There was an outside toilet at the bottom of the yard, and when you wanted to have a bath, a zinc tub was brought in and placed in front of the fire in the kitchen. The hot water was carried in kettles and saucepans from a copper gas boiler in the scullery.

I had comparatively free access to sweets whenever I wished. Such a privileged position effectively meant that, from an early age, I acquired plenty of friends and soon became a trusted member of a 'gang'. I soon learnt to handle the demands of the group as we invented deeds of daring and escapades which would help to establish my position among my friends. Included in the gang were: Jim Harra, Billy Cordner, Bobby Bentley, .lim Hewitt, Jack Stewart and some others whom I have not seen since those early years.

The change of address also meant the change of school and I started to attend Carrick Elementary School, where I would acquire a basic primary education. In later years, I would turn out to be a better student, but such academic progress could not have been predicted at this stage where my standard could only be described, at best, as basic. My brothers had similar educational accomplishments. To me, the only difference in the change of school effectively meant that instead of turning left leaving the house in the mornings, we turned right. As we walked up the street we would meet some of our schoolmates and we would all walk along to school together. In James Street we would meet up with Norman Kendall, who was a couple of years younger than I and the main topic of conversation would soon turn to football, especially when we would meet up with another good pal of mine, Tom Taylor. Tom was a fair-haired, clean-cut young lad about a year younger than myself. He was a good footballer and played for the school team. The school football team was coached by Mr Alister Black, who was also my class teacher at the time. A keen disciplinarian, Mr Black served with the RAF in the Burma Campaign during the War and therefore believed in a meticulous code of behaviour from his students.

I was not much of an athlete, though I enjoyed street games like rounders and cricket. The game of rounders was played to a similar principle as baseball, with a bat and ball and between two teams. The game of cricket called for some improvisation, which entailed the drawing of a wicket on a gable wall with a piece of chalk, and we would play as if it were an international match at Lords.

One summer when I was about eight or nine, my parents rented a small cabin at Groomsport, a seaside village near Bangor in County Down. It was my first holiday and was all the more poignant to me, now when I look back on it, as it was the only time I was ever on holiday with my mother and father.

In 1950 Britain was at war again, this time in Korea. Not that I recall much about it as it seemed to be less significant than the Second World War and therefore generated less interest on a global scale. But like all twelve-year-old boys, warfare holds a certain fascination particularly when they have no perception whatsoever of its horrors. The Korean hostility ended in 1953 with the signing of an armistice, and it was a couple of years later that I met a man who had served with the Royal Ulster Rifles in that war. His name was Billy Hanna and he was awarded the Military Medal for outstanding courage in the face of the enemy.

I left school in 1953 at the age of fourteen and started to work. My first job was as a delivery boy in a home-care and hardware shop. For anyone starting his first job, it is a daunting experience and was none the less for me as I walked into the three-storey high, Victorian building. The shop was a large, square room with a high, oak-panelled ceiling, from which tin mugs, billycans, hurricane lamps, and an assortment of other such items hung in bunches like grapes on a vine. Wooden shelves lined the walls from floor to ceiling and were packed full of electrical fittings, nails, and tools of all descriptions. There was a timber yard at the back of the shop, and stores that contained bricks, sand, cement and other building materials. When delivery lorries would arrive in the yard, it was part of my job to help the yardman unload the supplies. It was heavy work, but what turned out to be an even more burdensome task for me was the delivery of the materials to the customers. The merchandise was stacked onto a handcart and I had to push my burden to its destination. Sometimes there was five or six hundredweight in the cart, and I used to wonder if they needed a donkey rather than a delivery boy.

Chapter 4

One evening in the late summer of 1953, the news headlines were taken up with reports of an attack on an army camp in Essex which had been carried out by an organisation that up to that time I had never heard of. It was the Irish Republican Army (IRA). In follow-up searches after the raid, police arrested three men, one of whom was a 31-year-old Dublin man called Cathal Goulding. A leading member of the organisation at the time, Cathal Goulding would later become Chief of Staff of the IRA. Over the following three years similar attacks were carried out in other parts of England, as well as in Northern Ireland. The object of these raids was mainly to acquire arms and ammunition in preparation for an all-out terrorist campaign against Northern Ireland. Although they enjoyed some success, the attacks were mainly a disaster for the IRA.

For the next couple of years after I had started work, I began to pay attention to some of the older boys in our neighbourhood who had joined the Ulster Special Constabulary. This was a part-time auxiliary police service that had been formed in the 1920s. The Specials, also fondly known as the B Specials, or the B men, were organised throughout the six Ulster Counties, and were under the control of the Inspector General of the Royal Ulster Constabulary. Each county was under the command of a County Commandant, and within each county the force was divided into districts. As I watched these men from time to time, in uniform on their way to the drill hall, I decided to enquire about joining. I was told that the minimum age limit was 18 years, but when I became 17, I enrolled and gave my age as 18. I am not sure why I joined the Specials. Maybe it was growing up during the years of the Second World War, and later the Korean conflict, but there is one thing sure, I always had a keen interest in police work, from reading Sherlock Holmes books during my school days, to the Scotland Yard cases of the time. Or perhaps I saw joining the USC as hopefully the first step in a police career, but certainly the sight of those men in their uniform made the police an attractive prospect for me. Maybe the glamour of the uniform had something to do with it too. All these images were fixed into my mind during those most impressionable years. But maybe it was someone else who inspired me towards a career in the police. He was a young policeman called Harold Cobb. I cannot say 1 knew him very well; it was probably more of a passing acquaintance. A keen amateur gardener, Harold used to grow more produce than he needed for his own family, so he would arrive at our house with some lettuce and tomatoes for my mother to sell in the shop. Harold was about the same age as myself and when he was on duty his uniform was always neat and tidy. He looked the typical policeman from the top of his head to the soles of his feet.

My first stage in joining the Specials was that I had to visit a Justice of the Peace to swear an oath of allegiance to the Queen and to uphold the law. I placed my left hand on a large Bible, raised my right hand and repeated the words after the JP. As far as I remembered the words of the oath went something!

like this:

'I do swear that I will well and truly serve our Sovereign the Queen in the office of Special Constable, without favour or affection, malice or ill will, and that I will, to the best of my power, cause the peace to be kept and preserved. Prevent all offences against the person and properties of Her Majesty's subjects; and that while I continue to hold the said office I will, to the best of my skill and knowledge, discharge all the duties thereof, faithfully according to the law. So help me God'.

The day soon came when I reported to the Sergeant Instructor at the drill hall to be issued with a pair of black drab looking trousers, a tunic, a webbing belt with a brass buckle, and an oversized cap with a badge in the front. The tunic was of the First World War army style with a high turn down collar that made it look somewhat out of date. The regular police uniform was similar, except for the jacket that had an open neck and was worn with a shirt and tie. However, the USC were later issued with a more modern uniform befitting the force. As soon as I got home I went upstairs to my room and put the uniform on. I looked in the mirror, and I have to say I liked what I saw. The uniform gave me a sense of self-reliance, something I had never experienced while I was growing up. I felt distinctive.

The drill hall was in a small cul-de-sac off Connolly Place, where I had to attend one evening in the week. The hall was a long hut structure of corrugated iron sheeting. There was a .22 rifle range at the back end of the hall, where we had target practice and weapon training. We also attended lectures on some aspects of law enforcement, especially the Special Powers Act, which provided anti-terrorist legislation. These activities were called 'drills' and included weapon and uniform inspections as well as marching in military formation. As I attended the drills and got to know the other men in the platoon, I discovered that the discipline, the structure, and the camaraderie gave me a feeling of belonging. I found a sense of selflessness within the organisation that reminded me of the caring atmosphere within my own family.

Each platoon was fully mobile with a Crossley tender, which was driven by a regular RUC man, and used to convey them to the rifle range or to shooting competitions that were organised between districts and counties. Moreover, they were mainly deployed in patrolling their own local areas, and sometimes they used their own cars for this purpose. They would set up vehicle check points (VCPs) on main roads, and monitor the movement of known terrorists. road patrol were made up of a sergeant and about eight constables. They would walk along the side of the road, facing oncoming traffic, and spaced out in pairs about ten yards apart. The Special Constabulary were particularly suited to the work they had to do, as the members of each platoon were made up of farmers, labourers, factory workers and people from all walks of life. They were the eyes and ears of the community, and a vital intelligence gathering source for the Crime Special (CS) department of the police. The CS was the predecessor of the Special Branch, the centre of the intelligence-gathering network throughout the Province. I was not long in the B Men when I met a man who impressed me from the start. His name was Tommy Cush. A tall, well-built man, he was about five years older than I was, and, although quiet and not easily upset, there was something about him that commanded deference. We became good friends and any time I had a problem, Tommy was there with a word of advice.

In early 1956 the IRA decided to start an all-out armed campaign against Northern Ireland, but a number of dates that had been set for the spring and summer had to be cancelled for various reasons. However, by December the inevitable happened and a number of bomb explosions, particularly in counties Fermanagh and Londonderry, ushered in a terrorist campaign that would continue for the following six years. The IRA reverted to tactics of ambush, assassination and arson, with bomb explosions at railway bridges, electricity pylons, telephone kiosks and the like. When the IRA campaign started, the RUC was under recommended strength. As a result, and in order to strengthen the police, some members of the USC were mobilized to take up full time duty. The viciousness of the IRA campaign caused a deep sense of resentment in the general population and a determination to resist the onslaught. More and more Special Constables were mobilized, and by the end of 1958 there were long waiting lists of men wishing to join the Specials, many of whom were exservicemen who had experienced action in terrorist campaigns in other parts of the world.

I applied to be mobilized and was accepted. I was instructed to report to Bessbrook police station on the 1 sl April 1959. When I told my parents that I was going to be mobilized, they were quite excited about the prospect of me becoming a full-time constable. But when I told them I had been posted to South Armagh, they became rather apprehensive about the whole idea. However, the 1 st April soon arrived and a policeman in a Crossley tender picked me up at my home. I put my suitcase in the back of the truck, got into the passenger side, and we headed off for Portadown police station, where it had been pre-arranged that the Bessbrook Crossley would collect me. At Portadown my transport was waiting for me, and as the two drivers had a chat, I transferred my case to the other truck. "This is Clark Houston, Billy," the policeman said as he introduced me to my new colleague. We shook hands, and after a few more pleasantries we started out for Bessbrook. Clark was clean-cut and tidy and spoke with a broad Belfast dialect. There wasn't much conversation on the journey, but he continued to dart suspect glances at me from beneath the shiny black peak of his hat. As we approached the village of Jerrettspass, he told me that we were entering the Bessbrook police district and were only a few miles from the station. We took a right turn off the main road, and about a half mile further on we stopped at a level crossing. "This is the White Gates," said Clark. "It's the main Belfast-Newry line." When the train passed, the gates opened, and we continued on to a crossroads called Kid's Corner. Then to a steep hill called The Doctor's Hill, which led to the Millvale Road, and on to the Orange Hall

Corner where we turned left and drove into Fountain Street, the main street of the village. Even the names struck a chord with me they gave a quaint air to the place. It was a charmingly old-fashioned village that had many similarities with Donacloney, in that it was also a busy linen manufacturing community. It didn't strike me at the time, but I was entering a village that I would later consider to be my second home, and its people would always be held in very high regard by me. The village had grown around the Yarn Spinning Mill and Linen Weaving Factory of the Bessbrook Spinning Co. Ltd. The mill was a large granite building, renowned to be the largest of its kind in Ireland, and founded by the Quaker family of Richardson. Situated in the South of the Orchard County of Armagh, Bessbrook lies close to the border with County Down and the Kingdom of Mourne, about two-and-a-half-miles from the busy market town of Newry and about eight miles from the border dividing Northern Ireland from the Irish Republic.

The Crossley came to a stop outside the police station. An imposing twostorey, white pebbledash structure, the front door was fortified with a sandbag emplacement, and over the door was the traditional blue lantern bearing the RUC crest. We got out of the truck and Clark took my case out of the back. 1 followed him to the door, and he lifted the brass knocker and let it fall once. We could hear the dull echo inside, and a pair of eyes appeared at a small observation window. Without a word being spoken, we could hear the clinking of a security chain on the inside, and the door opened. "Hallo, Hughie, this is Special Con. McKane, Special Con. McConnell," said Clark as he glanced back at me, and we walked into a wide tiled hallway. 1 stepped forward and shook hands with the constable, who smiled broadly and said, "Welcome to Bessbrook." He was the station orderly. A door to the left led into the guardroom, and a door on the right had a small sign, which read, 'Station sergeant's office'. Clark knocked and opened the door and as he did so, a tall, well-built man walked slowly out of the office. He had thinning grey hair, and tattoos on his arms and the back of his hands. I had the opinion he had been in the navy, although he was a man approaching retirement. Without uttering a single word, he looked at me for a time as though to scrutinise every detail about me. "This is Sergeant Young, the station sergeant," said Clark as he glanced at me over his shoulder. When he finally spoke, he explained that I would be detailed station fatigues for a couple of days to allow me to get to know the other men and familiarise myself with the routine of the station. He turned on his heel and walked slowly back into his office. It was a dry reception from the station sergeant, not a single word of welcome. Clark immediately lifted the case and said, "I'll show you to your room". I followed as he went up a wide mahogany staircase that lead to an "L" shaped landing and a narrow corridor from which there were doors into rooms on either side. A door at the end of the corridor opened into a large dormitory with a row of single, metal-framed beds on each side. At the head of each bed sat a small table and beside that a large wooden locker with double doors. A long table took up much of the centre space, surrounded by about a dozen chairs. "This is your room. We call it the 'field', because of its size," said Clark as he set the case on the floor. "Just pick a vacant place and it's yours." Some of the beds were already made-up; their occupants probably out on duty. As Clark left me, I chose a comer bed, opened my case and started to put my things in the locker. I looked around the big room that would be my abode for the next three years.

The duty of station fatigues effectively meant the cleaning of the corridors and offices, and also assisting the cook in running errands to the shops. The cook was a Mrs Lockhart. A small, white-haired motherly figure, Minnie was responsible for the kitchen, not only for the cooking but for all the expenditure and accounts, a task she performed with enthusiasm, as she had served for more than thirty years in the job.

Bessbrook police station was the district headquarters for the South Armagh area, which consisted of six out-stations in the towns and villages of the district. They were Forkhill, Cullyhanna, Crossmaglen, Newtownhamilton, Camlough and the Newry Armagh force. The Newry Armagh force was responsible for the part of the town that is situated west of the canal in County Armagh. Although much of the South Armagh countryside is hilly and rugged, it boasts of some of the most spectacular scenery in Ireland.

The Bessbrook station had a transport pool of one district car, a Land Rover, an armoured personnel carrier (APC), and a small armoured brengun carrier, which was on loan from the army. This vehicle we were told, was used in the desert during the war with Montgomery's eighth army. Later when I became a reserve driver, the vehicle I most enjoyed driving was the district car. An Austin Westminster, it was a luxurious vehicle that truly lived up to its name.

As the days passed, I started to pick up the day-to-day running procedure of the station and got to know the rest of my colleagues. The full complement of the station was one District Inspector and one Head Constable, four sergeants and thirty-four constables, half of whom were mobilized Specials. The single men had to live in the station, and there was plenty of banter as we were all in the same age group. All the married men lived in or around the village, but the Head Constable lived in married quarters, which was a detached building but still part of the station complex. Apart from the normal beat patrols in the village and immediate area there were bicycle patrols, when two constables would cycle to other areas of the sub-district. Then there were the border patrols, which were carried out in the Land Rover and APC. The object of these patrols was to check on the out-stations and to set up VCP's on roads leading across the border. The border patrols were normally carried out in late evening or at night and were about four or five hours in duration, which meant we had to take flasks of tea and sandwiches for a meal break. There were also early morning border patrols, which we called 'risers' because we had to leave the station about 5.30 or 6am. There was one 'riser' each week, which was the established practice. It took place each Thursday, when we had to escort a Mail van from Newry carrying pension money, as it made deliveries to all the Post Offices in the South

Armagh area. The IRA had frequently targeted Post Office delivery vans in the border areas, and armed robberies were carried out to finance their terrorist campaign.

When mobilized the pay was the same as the regular police, so I could soon afford to buy a second-hand car, and I decided on an Austin A30 because it was small and economical to run. The car gave me some independence and meant that I was no longer reliant on public transport to get home on my rest days or leave days. Apart from the normal days off duty, the single men could also apply for a four-hour pass, but they had to be back in the station before midnight. It became an unofficial practice that in the morning, when we finished a night duty, we would apply for a four-hour pass from 8pm. This effectively gave us a full day off, which was a satisfactory arrangement provided everything was OK at the station. But we always left a contact phone number, and at any rate the rest of the lads would have covered if anything had gone wrong.

After a few months, my stay in Bessbrook was interrupted when I was temporarily transferred to Newtownhamilton, where I replaced a constable who had his leg broken whilst playing football for the district team.

Newtown, as it was locally known, is situated in a remote mountainous area of South Armagh, close to the border with the Republic. It was early autumn and the countryside was a fresco of yellow gorse blossom, and some whitewashed cottages capped with weathered thatch gave a tranquil air to what appeared to be a peaceful country scene, a scene that could easily have given a false sense of security. The full complement of police in Newtown was one station sergeant and eight constables. Although I enjoyed the friendliness of the people and the rural area, I was glad when my tour of duty ended and I was posted back to Bessbrook.

In order to counteract the IRA's campaign, the police decided to form a Reserve Force comprising regular policemen and mobilized Specials, to be deployed in border areas as a quick response to possible IRA attacks. The Reserve Force was self contained with its own vehicles and armed with a selection of small arms, pistols, rifles, stenguns. It was well trained in antiterrorist techniques, and all personnel had to attend periodic refresher courses to maintain a high standard of policing. The training base for the Reserve Force was at Ballykinlar in Co. Down. There all mobilized Special Constables were trained whether they were deployed with the Reserve Force platoons or used to reinforce police station garrisons.

As the IRA campaign continued, the anti-terrorist methods deployed by the police improved, and perhaps through painful experiences they became more efficient. A numerical colour code was introduced to protect the security of the patrols in the South Armagh area. The scheme designated a colour of either green, red or blue, followed by a number. Green patrols were VCP's on main roads. These would remain on the same road, although they would move location from time to time. The number following the colour indicated the location of the patrol on the road. For example, Green 2 could have been a bridge, or Green 5 a road junction. Red were foot patrols along the border road during the hours of darkness. The object of these patrols was to check the movement of suspicious persons and vehicles crossing the border. Blue patrols were vehicles, which were used to set up checkpoints on minor roads along the border. This was a flying picket type of force designed to support the foot patrols. Sometimes the foot patrols were made up of as many as sixteen men an RUC sergeant, seven or eight RUC constables, and the remainder mobilized USC men. The entire patrol was spread out in twos, about thirty yards apart and with the sergeant and a constable in the centre. These two men would have red torches to signal oncoming traffic to stop, and would only step out of cover when necessary. When a vehicle was stopped, only the sergeant would approach it, to check the identification of the occupants, whilst the remainder of the patrol remained in concealed covering positions. This kind of patrol tactic made an ambush or a surprise attack from a vehicle by the IRA very difficult. As a twenty-one-year-old I found this kind of patrol duty an exciting experience.

One dark night we were dropped at a location somewhere in the South Armagh countryside, and we had to walk to a pick-up point near Moyra Castle, in the Forkhill district. For some distance the road ran parallel with the main Belfast to Dublin railway line, before it merged and ran under the line at Kilnasaggart Bridge. Kilnasaggart Bridge is situated right on the border with the Republic, and the railway embankment slopes down on both sides of the line to low-lying fields surrounded by dry stone walls. A bleak and isolated spot. I was carrying a large box-shaped radio receiver, which was on loan from the army and fitted with a long, standard aerial and earphones. My position on the patrol was in the centre of the formation along with the sergeant, who was on detachment from the Newry Armagh Force. We had walked for some time and were approaching the bridge when the man at the point passed back word to the sergeant that he thought he heard voices on the line, coming from the direction of the bridge. We immediately took cover and the sergeant made his way to the point to investigate. We all lay quiet for a while, as one of the men said he thought he recognised the voices. When the sergeant made contact with the pointer, he flashed his torch on and off a few times towards the bridge. Suddenly out of the darkness came a number of responding signals from a red torch, at which the sergeant went slowly forward in the direction of the bridge. Keeping under cover as best he could. After a few minutes he returned, and passed the word along that everything was all right, as it was a Reserve Force patrol and they were now approaching along the railway embankment. This was the only time in my experience in the security forces that, due to a failure in communications, a very serious mishap could easily have occurred and could have resulted in loss of life through friendly fire.

Chapter 5

The Easter weekend of 1961 was the forty-fifth anniversary of the Easter rising in Dublin and, because of the continuing IRA campaign greater security precautions were considered necessary. All police stations along the border Counties were put on standby against possible attacks, and in Bessbrook some local USC men were brought in to reinforce the station over the weekend. Since my arrival in Bessbrook I had became good friends with a regular called Brian Maguire. Brian had served in the Irish Guards, and on leaving the Army had joined the police. He and his wife lived in Camlough, where he was originally stationed before being transferred to Bessbrook. We were on duty together on the Tuesday, and during our tour he told me that his wife had dropped him off at the station that morning because she wanted the use of the car, and he asked me if I would give him a lift home when we finished. I said I would, and by the time our stint was complete it was late evening and we started the two-mile trip to Camlough. When we arrived, he invited me in for a cup of tea, and I followed him as he opened the front door and proceeded along the hall towards a small kitchen at the back of the house. As he entered the kitchen he suddenly said, "Willie, here's a young girl I'd like you to meet. Her name is Delta Cromwell." I slowly stepped forward and we shook hands. "Pleased to meet you," she said "How do you do." I replied. We sat down and were handed a cup of tea. As I glanced at Delta I thought she was most attractive, but a little bit shy. As we finished our tea, Betty asked me if I could give Delta a lift home on my way back to the station as she lived in Bessbrook. I said I would, and as we drove back to Bessbrook very little conversation passed between us. I stopped the car outside her house, and as she was leaving I asked her if I could see her the following evening. She agreed, and as I headed back to the station I couldn't believe my luck when I thought about the relationship that was starting. I thought Delta Cromwell was beautiful, intelligent and refined. I enjoyed being with her, and as the weeks went by we saw more and more of each other. I have to say I became infatuated with her, and when I was on duty I couldn't wait for the hours and minutes passing till I would see her again. There was one thing I was sure of, even from that early stage in our friendship, and that was that if she would have me, Delta Cromwell would be my wife.

The security authorities in Northern Ireland continued to review precautions along the border counties. One such scheme was to seal the border in the event of an IRA attack inland, and to block all possible escape routes. In South Armagh a rapid reaction strategy was devised to set up roadblocks along that section of the frontier. The plan was code-named 'Teleprinter', and it also took into account attacks on targets in adjacent counties as well as Armagh. The Bessbrook station had to provide roadblocks at specific locations along the border, and in order to attain the greatest possible speed in our objective, practice call-outs were organised at all hours of the day and night. The plan also provided for small mobile columns of part time USC men in their private cars to proceed at high speed to the scene of the attack. At the time IRA units travelled to the Republic to under-go training programmes in the use of firearms, bomb making and up-dated terrorist techniques.

I decided to invite Delta down to Lurgan to meet my parents and we arranged the visit for Sunday afternoon, 12th November. I was granted a leave day which permitted me to be off duty until midnight. I looked forward to spending a pleasant evening at home with Delta and my family.

Sunday the 12th November 1961 was the fourth anniversary of a bomb explosion at Edentubber near Carrickanon border post on the main Belfast to Dublin road on the Southern side of the border in County Louth. Five IRA men died in the blast that took place in a cottage that was owned by one of the men. It was being used as a bomb factory when something went wrong and all the explosives in the house suddenly detonated. The force of the explosion completely wrecked the cottage and the blast was heard for miles around. Civic Guards who arrived at the scene afterwards carried out a search of the area and recovered the body of the man who occupied the cottage. Some distance away two more bodies were pulled out of the wreckage, and were so mutilated that their identity could not be established at the time. Some 70 yards from the actual seat of the blast a fourth body was found lying in a field, and a further search of the debris uncovered the fifth body. Pieces of human remains were scattered across the fields, and some fragments of their clothing along with pieces of flesh were hanging on the hedges.

The mutilated bodies of the five victims were taken to the morgue at Louth County Hospital in Dundalk, where they were identified mainly by pieces of clothing and rings and personal items found on them. The five men, one from Newry, one from Bessbrook, and the other three from the Irish Republic, were later removed from the hospital to St. Patrick's Cathedral Dundalk for Requiem Mass. In follow-up searches the following day, police found four Thompson sub-machine guns and some hundreds of rounds of ammunition.

Before leaving the station that Sunday morning I had talked to some of the men, who told me they were going out on a mobile that day. They were to meet-up with some of the men from Forkhill station, and then set up a check-point in the village of Jonesborough. Jonesborough is situated on the side of a hill that overlooks the main Belfast to Dublin road, only about one mile from Edentubber. Where the devastating explosion took place four years before and where each year a memorial parade is held by the IRA to commemorate the deaths of their five comrades.

Hill Street was a quiet neighbourhood on that Sunday afternoon, even though the sun was shining and it was rather warm for early November. I stopped the A30 outside number 43, and Delta and I walked up to the front door, which was opened by my father. As we entered the house, I introduced Delta to my parents, who welcomed her warmly and we were ushered into the sitting room where we all engaged in polite conversation. My brother had recently bought a second-hand black and white television set, and after tea we returned to the sitting room to watch the evening news. The TV was switched on and as the news report commenced, a map of Northern Ireland appeared on the screen, with an arrow pointing to South Armagh and the name Jonesborough. The words of the newsreader sent shivers down my spine, as he said, "One policeman has been shot dead and three others wounded in a border ambush in South Armagh." I watched with disbelief as the report continued with a photograph of one of the men from the Forkhill station, and the words "Constable William John Hunter, who was murdered in the attack". Of the three men wounded, one was another regular RUC constable from Forkhill called Samuel Gault, and a regular Constable and a Special Constable from Bessbrook. I knew them all very well, particularly the two Brook men whom I had served with since I was first mobilized. There was a cruel irony in that Samuel Gault would have an appointment with the IRA, some quarter of a century later to the very day, during the poppy day massacre at Enniskillen in 1987.

It was late and the village was quiet as we drove into Bessbrook that night. I stopped the car at Delta's house, and as we arranged to meet the following evening, I left her and drove to the station. Not surprisingly, most of the men were still up sitting talking in the guardroom, and the focus of conversation was the ambush. As I poured myself a cup of tea from a large teapot that was brewing on the stove, the men started to tell me about the incident. It was an eight-man patrol, and they set up a VCP in Jonesborough to check vehicles crossing the border to attend the commemoration at Edentubber. The gunmen were hidden behind a cemetery wall near Jonesborough Parish Church, an elevated position overlooking the checkpoint where the police were standing. Just before 2pm they opened up with a volley of machine gun fire, and the four policemen were hit. The rest of the patrol immediately returned fire, but didn't claim any hits as the raiders were concealed behind the stone wall. The Special Constable who had received a bullet wound to the right thigh, which was bleeding profusely was helped by the Bessbrook Head Constable, who had been touring the locality in the district car and had arrived at the scene shortly after the attack. The Head Constable removed his tie and used it as a turnique to control the bleeding until medical assistance arrived from Daisyhill Hospital in Newry. As police reinforcements arrived, they combed the immediate neighbourhood on the Ulster side of the border, and as the Guarda poured into the area, they systematically searched the Republic side. A number of spent shells were found at the scene where the IRA men had positioned themselves, and later police found a full Thompson sub-machine gun magazine at the side of the church, where ironically the customary morning service had been held about two hours earlier. The terrorists were believed to have entrenched themselves in the cemetery some hours earlier, and after the attack they were seen running across the border into the Republic. Meanwhile, the crowd that had attended the commemoration ceremony at Edentubber paraded back to the main Dublin road, lead by a brass and reed band from Drogheda. The ceremonies concluded with the playing of the 'Soldier's Song' on the roadway less than fifty yards from where the ambush took place.

An inexcusable mistake made by the authorities when they were organising the VCP in Jonesborough that afternoon was that on each anniversary of the Edentubber explosion a road check had been set up in exactly the same spot. Therefore it was not difficult for the IRA to assume that history would repeat itself, giving them plenty of time to organise the ambush.

A few weeks later two regulars arrived in Bessbrook from the RUC training depot at Enniskillen to replace the two wounded men. One was a man called Gerry Cathcart. A Belfast man, Gerry was quiet and kept himself to himself. He was a keen footballer, who had played for a local Belfast team before joining the police. He played for the police district team, and always took an active part in sport. When I left the police in 1963, 1 lost contact with Gerry, until I read about his murder some twenty years later in 1983.

Although the early 1960's were plagued with atrocities committed by the IRA murder gangs, the serious crime rate in Northern Ireland remained low in comparison to the other regions of the UK. But the brutal murder of a 19-year old girl stunned the province, and was talked about in police circles for years.

The sad story began in the early morning of January 28th 1961 . When a man who was exercising his dogs along a quiet side road near the village of Damolly, on the outskirts of Newry, found a lady's black shoe lying on the roadside, about one hundred and fifty yards from a small cottage occupied by a family called Gamble. A short distance further on he made another discovery. It was the matching black shoe, but lying close by in a ditch he also found a black silk scarf. He continued on to the junction with the old Belfast road, where he met a friend who was working at the gate of a field. The two men engaged in conversation, but did not attach any significance to the scarf and the articles of footwear. As they parted company, the man in the field started to search for a hammer he had left there the night before, but was unable to find it. It was then that he began to connect the lost hammer to the scarf and shoes, and as he became concerned, he went back to examine the articles. As he lifted the scarf he observed a blood stain on it. He immediately left it down and dashed to the Gamble's home.

The man returned to the scene with Mrs Gamble and one of her daughters, and as the mother examined the scarf and shoes, her daughter found a black handbag nearby. Mrs Gamble recognised the articles as belonging to her daughter Pearl, and the last time she had seen the items had been the evening before when Pearl was wearing them as she left the house with two companions to go to a local dance. A deep feeling of apprehension gripped Mrs Gamble as she realised that Pearl had not yet returned home. On the previous evening her two friends had collected 19 year-old Pearl at her home and they set off for a dance in Newry.

When the Newry police were informed, the situation began to take a dramatic turn, and a widespread search of the area was carried out and more articles of clothing were found. Blood stained overcoat, a black belt, a brush and comb, and a light grey skirt, all of which were scattered over a wide area. Police also later found a bloodstained handkerchief and a button.

Large numbers of police with tracker dogs and civilians took part in the day - long search of the fields surrounding the location, and by late evening the naked body of Pearl Gamble was eventually found. Partly concealed in a clump of whins, her body was mutilated, and had extensive throat and head wounds, which had been caused by a knife or similar sharp instrument, and there were a number of stab wounds to the front of the body. The body was later removed to the Royal Victoria Hospital in Belfast, where the State Pathologist performed a post-mortem. Later Pearl's body was taken to Banbridge Hospital where the Coroner opened an inquest, which was adjourned after formal identification.

In continuing searches over the following days, police used grappling irons to drag the Clanrye river in Newry, in a bid to find the murder weapon and articles of blood-stained clothing which may have been dumped by the assailant. The searches became what were up to that time one of the most concentrated murder hunts ever launched in the history of policing in Northern Ireland. Three miles away from the scene of the crime, the Bessbrook police were briefed to be extra vigilant in the course of their normal duties, and to look out for discarded clothing or a possible murder weapon. Eventually a man's gabardine coat and a blue suit were found in the Newry River, and within days a man was arrested. He appeared at a Special Court in Newry and was remanded in custody to appear at Belfast Custody Court. He was Mr Robert McGladdery, a 24-year-old ex-waiter from Damolly village. He had lived only a short distance from the cottage where Pearl lived with her parents, five sisters and one brother. McGladdery was charged with the murder of Pearl Gamble, and when the trial opened in Belfast it received national headlines as the' Pearl Gamble Murder.'

The trial opened with evidence from the two girls who accompanied Pearl to the dance on the evening of Friday 27th January 1961. One of the girls told the court how she saw Pearl dancing with Robert McGladdery at least twice, and that he had been wearing a light blue suit and black shoes. Mrs Gamble testified that she had left the key in the front door, so that Pearl could let herself in without disturbing the rest of the household. She stated that she got up at 5 am to make breakfast for her son and another daughter who left home at 6 o' clock to start work in a Newry factory. Mrs Gamble also stated that she had noticed Pearl's absence but was not unduly worried, assuming that her daughter had stopped the night in a friend's house. During the trial a legal clause was invoked which prohibited a considerable part of the evidence from publication. Throughout the lengthy hearing McGladdery protested his innocence, but on the 16th of October the jury returned a verdict of guilty, of the wilful murder of Pearl Gamble. Lord Justice Curran who had presided throughout, then sentenced Robert McGladdery to be hanged, and fixed the date of execution for November the 7th. An appeal was immediately lodged, which failed, and his execution was re-scheduled to take place in the Crumlin

Road Prison, Belfast, five days before Christmas on December 20th. Realising that all efforts of gaining a reprieve were now exhausted, McGladdery sent for a Newry police sergeant who had befriended him some years earlier and taken him to gospel meetings. The evangelist visited him in the condemned cell, where he confessed to the murder of Pearl Gamble and requested that his admission of guilt should be made known. On the 20th December 1961 the law was duly carried out and Robert McGladdery was hanged. He was the last person to be executed in Northern Ireland.

The IRA's campaign of violence stopped as suddenly as it had begun, and in January 1962 they called off their terrorist offensive. This was followed in February by a statement from the organisation explaining their decision. The declaration stated, The IRA has ordered the termination of its campaign of resistance to the Crown Forces which was started in 1956. All arms and other materials have been placed in dumps, and all active service volunteers withdrawn. The statement ended, "The Irish Resistance Movement renews its pledge of eternal hostility to the forces of the Crown, and calls to the Irish people for their increased support, and looks forward with confidence for the final and victorious phase of the struggle for the full freedom of Ireland.' There is no doubt that the IRA was defeated. The whole campaign had been futile from the start. The main feature that brought the terrorist onslaught to an end was the lack of support from the general population. The Nationalist community had quickly become, at best, apathetic and at worst, openly hostile to the IRA's activities. However, it was the most serious challenge to the security of Northern Ireland for more than 30 years. The IRA's actions had at first, to some extent, fired the Republican spirit both north and south of the border. The fact that the Irish Government reacted firmly against them did little to lessen our fears in the Security Forces, as it was in fact the latest attempt in a sustained campaign to undermine the existence of the Province. From the IRA's point of view the whole campaign was a total disaster, as its members became divided and demoralized.

As a direct result of the 1956 IRA insurrection, six policemen were dead and eighteen wounded; the USC had twelve wounded and two soldiers of the regular army were also wounded. Six IRA men were killed and six wounded in actions with the security forces. The total casualties on both sides were twelve killed and thirty-eight wounded, and there was a total of six hundred and five terrorist incidents of which two hundred and seventy one were classed as minor. There were thirty-one attacks on police stations, all of which were repulsed by the police, who were exemplary and must take most of the credit for the defeat of the IRA. At the same time, the Specials provided first class intelligence and an endless reserve of manpower as support and backup for the police. The IRA's February proclamation made it clear that its subversion was by no means over but merely suspended, probably until another suitable situation would present itself for them to exploit, a situation which would indeed present itself a mere six years later. Security precautions by the police and Specials did not cease immediately but continued on for the best part of a year, although patrols and road checks were gradually run down. The numbers of mobilized men were progressively reduced and I found myself on the list. Later that year I was demobilized and I went back into civilian employment, although I remained in the part time B Men, who were now mainly deployed with drills and weapons training.

Chapter 6

I drove up to Bessbrook three times a week to see Delta. On a Saturday night we would have gone to see a film in either the Savoy cinema in Newry, or the lveagh in Banbridge. On a Sunday we would have gone for a drive in my car along the County Down coast, and sometimes stopped for tea in a restaurant. Sometimes we would have spent the evening at Delta's home with her father and mother. I would also have seen her midweek, usually on a Wednesday night when we would go for a drive in or around the South Armagh area.

One night we decided to go for a drive around Camlough Lake, which is situated about a mile outside the village and sits snug and tranquil between Camlough Mountain and Slieve Gullion, the two highest peaks in County Armagh. 1 drove the car off the main road into the Ballynalack Road that runs the length of the lake and rises along the lower slopes of Slieve Gullion. We stopped in a small lay-by that overlooked the lake and gave us a panoramic view of the valley and Camlough Mountain on the far side. The road was lined on either side with low dry-stone walls topped with clusters of gorse and purple heather that snaked along the winding course of the road. We had parked for some time, and darkness had descended when I started the car and tried to drive out, but as the wheels turned they skidded on the grass and caused the car to slide sideways towards the stone wall. We decided to get out and try to push the car onto the road, but this exercise proved impossible, as the car was too heavy for us. There was nothing else for it, but to walk to the nearest farm house and try to get help. So we locked the car and started to walk along the dark lonely road, hoping to find someone, somewhere, who could help to get the car back onto the road. We had been walking for some time, and as we rounded a bend in the road, we could see the glint of the moon on the lake far below. To the right, a pine forest stretched high up the mountain with the treetops silhouetted against the moonlit sky. Suddenly, as the road declined we could see a light in the distance, and kept up a brisk pace as we headed in that direction.

Two large, round, whitewashed pillars sat on the left-hand side of the road, indicating the entrance to a farmyard. The light shone from a window of the house, and although it wasn't a full moon, there was light enough to partially illuminate the yard as we made our way across the surface that sloped with the contours of the hill. I knocked the door and we stood in the silence for a few moments. Then there was a rustling sound from the back of the door, and a woman's voice asked, 'Who's there?' I explained my car had got stuck in a layby about a mile down the road, and I needed help to get it out. I could hear the low mumble of voices and the sound of hobnailed boots on the floor, as a man's voice asked me my name. 1 told him, and the door opened slightly as he peered out at us. The door slowly opened revealing a small, stout man in his late 50's. He invited us in, and as I followed Delta into the hall I could see the inquisitive expression on his face. We entered a large farmhouse kitchen and the woman directed us to be seated at the table, as she moved a kettle to the side of the open fire. We introduced ourselves and soon we were all engaged in conversation over a cup of tea. He explained that the only form of transport he had was his car, although he had a team of horses for working the farm, as the land was spread out along the lower foothills of the mountain. It stretched for about a mile along the lakeshore, and was too rugged a terrain for a tractor or any other type of machinery.

As we finished our tea, he stooped down and laced his boots, put on a big heavy overcoat and cap, and I followed him as he made his way out into the yard. The car was parked in a high shed with a lean-to roof attached to the gable wall of the house. A single light bulb hung in the centre of the ceiling, lighting up the whole interior and the contents of the shed. Bales of hay were stacked at the back, and farm implements were placed along the sides of the shed. A few chickens that were roosting in the hay were suddenly disturbed by the light and the intrusion. A large, black car was parked in the entrance. I do not remember the make, but it certainly was a vintage model, with headlights that sat on the front mudguards and running boards under the doors, that extended along the sides from the front mudguards to the back. The man climbed in behind the wheel, turned on the ignition, pulled the starter, and immediately the engine started up with a constant purring sound. He put her into gear, slowly released the clutch pedal, and the car started to crawl out of the shed; it came to a stop in the yard, where his wife and Delta had joined us, and we all got into the car. The car moved at a snail's pace, up the hill out of the yard and onto the road.

The moon was shining bright, and there was a cool breeze blowing up from the lake when we arrived back to where the car was stuck. We got out and I hitched one end of a rope around the front chassis bar, and tied the other end to the towing hitch on the farmer's car. I got into my car, released the hand brake, and as he drove slowly forward the rope tightened and the A30 rolled slowly out on to the road. As I untied the rope from the two cars, all four of us had a last chat on the roadside before we thanked them for their help, and I drove down the mountain onto the main road again. The next Sunday we returned to the farmhouse, where Delta saw the woman and left them a cake and some pastry for their kindness. That was the last time we ever saw the old couple. I was always careful about where I parked the car after that.

I proposed to Delta and she accepted. We got engaged the following Christmas. It was Christmas 1964 and on the Saturday before, we took the day out to Belfast to purchase an engagement ring. The first shop we visited was a well-known jewellers in Royal Avenue, where Delta selected the ring she wanted. To celebrate the occasion we had a meal in a nearby Chinese restaurant, before starting back for home. We were married on the 7th September 1966 in Bessbrook Presbyterian Church, and the reception was held in the Roxborough House Hotel, Rostrevor. The weather was excellent and the hotel setting was splendid. My chief memory of that day was of seeing the two families coming together. They were all from the rural community and with similar working-class backgrounds. We lived in Bessbrook for about a year and a half, and our daughter Joanne was born on the 8th December 1967, in Daisyhill Hospital, Newry. I then bought a house near Lurgan where we have lived ever since. We became good friends with a couple who lived in the district, Bobby and Gretta Ferguson. They were members of a recently formed congregation of the Free Presbyterian Church, and one day they invited us to a service the following Sunday. The Free Presbyterian Church is puritanical in its austerity and has sound Calvinistic theology in its teaching. We decided to attend the service, which was held in a red bricked building (originally a schoolhouse) in George Street. There were no pews; the hall was set out with rows of steel tubular-chairs and an organ played at the side of the pulpit. Psalms were sung with great fervour and I thought it somewhat surprising that hymn tunes were often used. We enjoyed the fellowship of the assembly and decided to become enrolled as members.

In 1966 the security forces in the Republic were carrying out a search when they found documents which seemed to be an IRA plan of action for the future which included a great deal of social disruption in both parts of the island. The find was taken very seriously by the government in the South, and the Minister of Justice read part of the plan in the Dail, and explained in detail what it entailed. The Justice Department withheld the remainder of the documents, which related to IRA training tactics, from publication. In May of the same year, newspapers in the North published those parts of the documents that related to Ulster. In essence it was planned to make an armed stand similar to the 1956 Hungarian rising, or to that made in Dublin in 1916. It also envisaged the intervention of the government of the Irish Republic in support of the IRA, and their making an appeal to the United Nations to intervene.

The documents were alarming to the Eire Government as they also contained plans to infiltrate trade unions, Irish language and cultural organisations and even religious bodies of all persuasions in the Republic. University students were to be 'indoctrinated' as was illustrated at that time in the South, when students were used as pickets in strikes and demonstrations. In effect, whenever an excuse arose for a public protest, the IRA planned to capitalise on it and exploit the situation to the full. The IRA propaganda committee in Dublin, in an effort to discredit the documents, said that they only represented suggestions for future policy and that it was obvious the IRA was not strong enough, at present, to attempt anything so ambitious. Nevertheless, the documents showed how the IRA strategists were thinking at the time, and particularly with the experience of the past thirty-five years, security precautions were increased, and once again the USC were deployed. However, as the Easter weekend passed off without incident, attention was directed to the border and patrols and roadblocks were used, particularly on roads leading across the frontier.

In 1967 the IRA political wing Sinn Fein tried to organise itself throughout the Province, in the guise of Republican Clubs, but this front organisation was banned by the Ministry of Home Affairs. At about the same time an equally sinister development took place, when it became clear that an organisation was being formed in Loyalist areas, which was designed to thwart possible IRA activity. The organisation became known as the Ulster Volunteer Force, although at the time it was a small, and for the most part an inefficient group. An ominous development on the Republic's side of the border occurred when a splinter group from the IRA carried out a number of bank robberies. The name of the group was the Saor Eire Action Group. In August of the same year, I heard a name that brought back memories of the time when I was on the police in South Ammgh. The 'Chief of Staff of the IRA, Cathal Goulding, came to Londonderry, where he attended a meeting which discussed the formation of a Civil Rights Association.

The IRA had clearly decided that their best course of action was to create disorder through a civil rights campaign in Ulster. A decision no doubt encouraged by world events. 1968 was a year of disorder and threatening revolution in many parts of the world. There was a world-wide revolt of youth against the Vietnam War, with riots in cities across America, including Washington. In January-February the Communists launched their 'Tet' (New Year) offensive, which devastated American morale and, in conjuction with the anti-war movement, forced President Johnson to start winding down the war. Serious riots broke out in London. Simultaneously, violence erupted in Paris when left wing students fought with CRS riot police in the streets of the Latin Quarter. There were also student riots in Rome and Berlin. Much of the disorder was, in all probability, fostered by the death two years earlier of Che Guevara, the guerrilla revolutionary and former lieutenant to Fidel Castro, who was shot dead by troops in the Bolivian jungle. Che Guevara was a hero figure to a whole generation of youth.

In the summer, riots broke out at the Democratic Convention in Chicago, and in September the insurrection against Communism in Czechoslovakia was crushed when Warsaw Pact armies were sent in to prevent, what was termed, a 'counter-revolution'. The 'Prague Spring', As it became known, was led by a former Communist party chief, Alexander Dubcek.

In the same year, a Jordanian Arab gunned down Senator Robert Kennedy, and Martin Luther King, leader of the black civil rights movement in America, was assassinated in Memphis Tennessee. All this was taking place against a backdrop of violence during black civil rights marches in America, which had already been inflamed by the murder of their charismatic leader.

The comparatively recent inception of television in the UK as a widely available media meant that we could watch these international events unfolding in the comfort of our living rooms. It was in this global atmosphere that the first civil rights demonstration in Northern Ireland was held. It was a march from Coalisland to Dungannon in County Tyrone, and it went off peacefully as it had been re-routed to avoid a loyalist area. A second march was organised in the city of Londonderry, but the march was banned because it went through a Loyalist area. The marchers defied the ban, with the inevitable consequences - a clash with the police, which developed into a riot that continued for two days. This was the start of a period of riots and disorder, which spread to other parts of Londonderry, as well as Belfast and some other towns throughout the Province. At the same time Republican propagandists launched a vicious campaign against the police and USC, with allegations that they had been responsible for some of the disturbances. Allegations that were later strongly reputed by the Scarman Tribunal, that was set up in 1969 to report on the violence and civil disturbances in Northern Ireland. The tribunal summed up by stating, 'There is nothing to justify any general criticism of the USC, when they performed riot duty.' However, the Labour Government believed the propaganda and in August, when the Northern Ireland Cabinet met the Prime Minister in Downing Street, they were astonished that the first item on the agenda was the disbandment of the Special Constabulary. The Government's decision was carried through, and the last day the Specials were on duty as a force in Northern Ireland was the 31 st Marsh 1970.

That was the closing chapter in the history of the Ulster Special Constabulary, a force of dedicated men who were prepared to discharge a dangerous and arduous duty for the whole community in Northern Ireland for little reward. A force that was slandered by a vicious propaganda campaign that, unfortunately was widely believed in the UK Mainland. However, the disbandment of the Specials solved nothing, as the IRA flourished and were greatly encouraged by their demise. With the benefit of hindsight, it was an act of folly, which gave the green light to the IRA and caused a serious escalation in their terrorist campaign. The ferocious brutality of the rioters that followed the marches, with the use of petrol bombs, home made napalm cocktails (a mixture of sugar and petrol in a milk bottle), and finally firearms, illustrated there was something more serious under the surface than simply protests about civil rights. Such violence was unique to Northen Ireland and did not raise its head, to the same extent, anywhere else in the world.

At the time some newspapers claimed that the Specials were poorly trained in the use of firearms. This type of false infomlation was contradicted when a rifle competition between various branches of the UK security forces was held in 1968. Nineteen teams drawn from the regular army, the RAF, the Territorial Army, the RUC and the B Men took part. The Hamiltonsbawn Sub-District of the USC from Co. Armagh, were the outright winner, winning the Queen Victoria Trophy. The runners up were Comber and Ballygowan Sub-Districts, both from Co. Down. It was the first time since 1897, when the competition began, that a team other than an army team had won the Trophy. To take the first three prizes was a remarkable achievement for the Specials. The result of the competition made manifest the skill and expertise of the USC in their use of firearms.

Two new forces were established to replace the USC, the Ulster Defence Regiment (UDR), and the Royal Ulster Constabulary Reserve (RUCR). The UDR was formed as a regiment of the regular army, with seven battalions having a total strength of 1,236 men. This was raised to 4,100 and at a later date the regiment's numbers were increased to10,000 by the addition of three further battalions.

The IRA now resent the UDR and the Army, who have done their best to be accepted in all quarters. If there had not been a terrorist organisation called the Irish Republican Army, it would not have been necessary to have an auxiliary police force like the Ulster Special Constabulary. At the time of writing this book, it is evident how history has repeated itself once again. As a result of the same type of Republican propaganda, the Patton Commission has been set up to reorganise the R U C.

The RUC Reserve was to be an unarmed force of 1,500 strong, but this figure was soon raised to 2,500 and its members were permitted to be armed if necessary. All former Specials were encouraged to transfer into the new forces, and many did. At the time, I was working in an optical factory, and some of my work-mates who had been in the B Men joined the Territorial Army. They asked me to join. I thought it over and decided to give it a try.

It was the 5th Battalion, the Royal Irish Rangers, with Battalion Headquarters in Armagh City, and 'C' Company, which was a rifle company, was based in the T A centre not far from my home. The company had only recently been formed. And I soon discovered that 1 knew many of my new comrades, although there were some younger men whom I did not know, but when I got talking to them, I found that I knew their parents and had even gone to school with some of them. Although the history of the Rangers outdated the Specials, the T A had many similarities with the USC, in that their main activities were weapons training and military exercises, most of which took place at the weekends. Summer training camps were organised on the mainland, and we would have to travel in battalion strength. All the trucks were loaded with equipment and we sat out in convoy for Belfast, where we embarked onto an army transport ship, proceeded to Liverpool and then on to the army base, usually on the East coast of England. The experience certainly broadened my knowledge of life in the army, and with the sudden influx of men into the company came the prospect of promotion for the more senior men, and I was upgraded to Lance Corporal.

The Regiment was first formed on the 1sl July 1968, at a time when most of the old 'Regional' Regiments were being amalgamated. The Rangers are an amalgamation of the Royal Inniskilling Fusiliers, The Royal Ulster Rifles and the Royal Irish Fusiliers. These three regiments had previously been combined in the North Irish Brigade, but the 'Brigade' system was abolished, and under the new organisation the Rangers (at the time the only line regiment in the British Army), became part of the King's Division. The Royal Inniskilling Fusiliers, unofficially known as the 'Skins,' date back as far as 1689. The Royal

Ulster Rifles, unofficially known as the' Stickies,' and The Royal Irish Fusiliers, unofficially known as the 'Faughts,' were formed during the Napoleonic wars, 1789-1807. On formation the regiment consisted of three regular battalions, but later the third battalion was disbanded. The 1st Battalion was stationed at Catterick and the second at Gibralter. These two remaining battalions were not, each in itself: a direct successor unit to the old regiments but each inherited, as a 'cross section', the entire history and traditions of all three.

In 1969 the 2nd Battalion left Gibraltar after a successful two-year tour, and came home as part of the Strategic Reserve. At the end of the year both battalions were once again under orders to go abroad, and the 1st Battalion went to serve with the British Army of the Rhine, and the 2nd Battalion moved to Bahrain. As the Rangers continued to serve, it is certain that the regiment did, as did its predecessors, worthily uphold the finest traditions of what The Great Duke of Wellington referred to as 'that best of all instruments: the British Infantry. '

Although the 5th Battalion was initially limited to the two rifle companies, and as a Home Defence unit was denied support weapons, this was set to change as more NATO role, T A Battalions were required. This was seen as quite an achievement, against the background of growing competition, since the fonnation of the seven volunteer battalions of the Ulster Defence Regiment.

Even though the Rangers were now under the control of NATO. This did not exclude them from a possible IRA attack, so precautions still had to be taken. As the Lurgan T A centre, was also occupied by the 2nd Battalion, UDR, so both companies were responsible for the security of the base. The UDR mounted guard during the daylight hours and the Rangers, accompanied by a UDR unit, were responsible for night guard. The guard system was that two men would take up sentry duty in a sandbag emplacement (sanger), at the front gate, whilst others would patrol the camp area, making sure all was secure and orderly. The remainder of the guard force would rest until it was time to rotate the duties in a two-hour (stag) method. It was a good arrangement, that allowed everyone to get some rest, as we all had to go to our place of employment the following day.

The Headquarters in Armagh also had to be guarded, and at times, particularly at weekends, a shortage of men meant men from 'C' Company were asked to fill in. It was on the Headquarters guard force that I met Sergeant Hugh Mc Ginn, who was the sergeant in charge. He was the 5th Battalion's weapons training officer. Hugh was a married man, and had been a member of the Territorial Army for over 20 years. Shooting was his abiding interest and his earliest success in marksmanship was in 1965, when he was a member of the 5th Battalion Royal Irish Fusiliers team which won the Queen Victoria Cup for the first time. Hugh was an annual competitor at Bisley and widely known and liked in the shooting fraternity.

There was a great deal of light-hearted rivalry between the companies, as considerable importance was put on personal fitness and military skills. We were encouraged to take part in cross-country manoeuvres and orienteering. Football teams were raised and we all took part in inter-company competitions.

The Headquarters night guard procedure was much the same as in 'C'-Company, with an outside unit patrolling the grounds, and a sanger at the back wall of the camp overlooking a graveyard, which did not inspire confidence in the night-guard during the quiet lonely hours. A rest area with cooking facilities allowed each unit to have a break before rotating their two hour stag. A famous antic sometimes deployed by the IRA was occasionally to fire a single rifle shot some where on the outskirts of the city, and the echo would reverberate in the silence of the night across the whole area, the object evidently being to keep the security forces on a constant state of alert and create fear in the general population. However, we soon realised what they were playing at and totally ignored their subterfuge.

It was whilst on these temporary guard duties that I came to know Trevor Elliott. Although Trevor was slightly younger than I was, he had joined the Battalion before me and like myself, he enjoyed the activities and the comradeship that the T A offered. He was a drummer in the Regimental pipe band, and we all enjoyed marching to the tunes they played. Perhaps one of the best-known and loved of all Irish marches is Killaloe, which was adopted as the Regimental march of the Royal Irish Rangers. A lively tune, it reflects the pride of the Irish infantry soldier and is played at all formal parades. The T A band carries on the long tradition of the Irish Regiments.

I changed my job and started work in a Courtaulds factory about a mile and a half from my home. The firm specialised in the manufacture of fabric, from man-made fibres through a knitting process. They produced dressmaking material, curtain material, and even upholstery fabric for export. But the main outlet was the UK home market. The firm had adopted the Continental 12-hour work-shift system, which meant we had to work three 12-hour shifts one week and four the next. This in turn gave us three rest days off one week and four the next. As a result, the majority of the men in the factory had part time jobs to occupy them on their days off. One day I met an old schoolmate, Billy Cunningham, who had joined the RUC about ten years earlier. He told me there was a major recruiting drive on for part time Reserves, especially for men with some experience in police work. I talked it over with Delta, and I decided to apply for the Reserves. I knew I could do the job, but what was more important to us at the time was that I would be detailed duties on my days off from my regular employment and the extra money would come in useful.

I had to resign from the T A, which was an unhappy decision to take because I had now to say goodbye to all my friends. In my time in the Rangers I had graduated to the rank of lance corporal, which was the very pinnacle of my achievement in a short but memorable military career.

In 1992 The Army Bill provided for the merger of the Royal Irish Rangers, and the Ulster Defence Regiment, and in July of that year The Royal Irish Regiment came into existence with the amalgamation of the two regiments. The six thousand strong Ulster Defence Regiment battalions continued to operate in Northern Ireland, and the two former Royal Irish Rangers battalions of 900 soldiers would serve both in Ulster and abroad.

Chapter 7

The troubles had escalated in 1969 to a point of almost civil war, with the death of the first policeman to be murdered in the present campaign, 29 year old Constable Victor Arbuckle, who was shot and killed on the Shankill Road in Belfast, probably by Loyalists. Citizens Defence Associations were set up in both communities as a form of protection against each other. It was at this time that the Eire Government, who had appointed three Cabinet Ministers to be in charge of Northern Ireland policy, was approached by prominent IRA figures from Belfast, requesting help from the South in the form of arms and ammunition. After a number of such contacts, a meeting took place in Bailieborough Co, Cavan, between the Republicans who were seeking weapons, and representatives of the Irish Government who were willing to supply. The go-between was an Irish Army Intelligence Officer, Captain John Kelly. Soon large amounts of money were crossing the border, in quantities of £1,000 to £1,500 per week. The money was laundered through bank accounts in the south, and distributed to IRA units in Belfast and Londonderry. However, when it was realised that the finances were going to the traditionalist Marxist/Leninist IRA, the Dublin Government set about creating conditions that would eventually cause a split in the organisation. With the intention of establishing a Northern Command to divert potential IRA activities from the Republic and intensify their terror strategy in the North, a further £30,000 was allocated to the dissident wing of the movement to finance the printing and distributing of a new newspaper, 'The Voice Of The North', which would take the place of the Marxist regular news-sheet. 'The Voice of the North' was a very different publication than anything seen before, in that it proclaimed green sectarian nationalism instead of red Marxist revolution.

At their convention in a Dublin hotel in early 1970, the pressure within the IRA had reached breaking point. The Marxists wanted to recognise the legality of the Dublin Government, while the dissidents advocated defending Nationalist areas of Belfast from possible Loyalist attacks, a notion strongly opposed by the Marxists, who saw any form of intervention in the current strife as a sectarian act. A point emphasised repeatedly was that the IRA did not exist solely to defend one community from another, as the whole history of Republicanism from Wolfe Tone was to advance the unity of the island, a view strongly expressed by their leader Cathal Goulding, when he said, "What happens when we shoot a Protestant? They'll shoot one of us! Then we'll retaliate, and all the time we are drawn into a bloody sectarian war and away from our socialist objectives." The Marxists' objectives were the overthrow of the capitalist governments on both parts of the island. With the benefit of hindsight, the wisdom of his words has been borne out, in the events of the past 35 years. This was a man of vision. Cathal Goulding had the welfare of all the people at heart. A true Irish patriot. Sadly, the Gouldingites were ostracised and the two factions finally parted company. The Marxists became the Official IRA, and the dissidents became the Provisionals. The money supply from the south, which was going to the Marxists, stopped for a few weeks, and when it started again was going to the Provisionals. The split in the IRA soon worked its way onto the streets, with the Provisionals gaining control of almost all Nationalist areas except the Lower Falls district of Belfast.

The Irish Government decided to assist the formation of the PIRA in a more tangible way. A disused army camp, 'Fort Dunree ' on the Inishowen peninsula in Co. Donegal-ironically, a former British military training base during the First World War-was fitted out and made ready for occupation. Units of the PIRA were taken to Fort Dunree and trained by Irish army instructors in the use of firearms and tactics of urban terrorism. 'Military street fighting'. At the same time plans were being hatched to invade Northern Ireland, the scheme being for the Republic's army to cross the border and go into the West Bank of the Foyle at Londonderry, and to make a second encroachment across the border at Newry, where they would rush to the nearest junction with the MI, and drive up the motorway to Belfast. The order was given. 'Prepare for incursions into Northern Ireland,' and Irish Army units were moved up to the frontier. This operation was carried out in such haste that gas masks fell off the backs of army lorries and littered the road for miles. But the plan had to be scrapped when they checked their equipment and discovered that the total ammunition in their possession would only keep them supplied for three days.

After a sensational gunrunning show trial in the Dublin High Court in October 1970, the Prime Minister sacked the Ministers responsible for Northern Ireland policy from his govermnent. The case revealed that the Cabinet Ministers along with accomplices bought a large quantity of guns on the Continent, which were to be smuggled to the PIRA in Belfast. £30,000 from a secret fund set up by the Finance Department in Dublin was used to acquire the weapons, but when the consignment was on its way to the Republic the conspiracy was blown. Some of the accused were acquitted on the grounds that the attempted arms importation was not illegal because it had been authorised by the Ministry of Defence. The scandal left the Irish Government in crisis and forced them into the real world, where they had to face realities. The most disgraceful episode in the history of the Irish State caused the Government to rethink policy regarding the PIRA, who were no longer characterised as latter day Robin Hoods with their merry men. Today, more than 35 years after the events, there is no doubt about the Irish Government's complicity in the formation of the PIRA. But even to this day the full extent of their involvement is not clear. In a documentary programme screened on Ulster Television in 1997, one of the Eire Government Ministers in charge of Northern Ireland policy in 1969, Mr Kevin Boland, described his Government's tactics at the time, and said. "It was decided that if a local resistance could be encouraged and equipped with a minimal amount of material, the trouble in the North could be kept going for ever." After seeing the programme I wrote to my MP Mr. David Trimble about the Eire Government's involvement in the conspiracy. However,

Mr Trimble, in his wisdom, did not think it worthwhile even to reply to my letter.

In the summer of 1970, the first gun battles took place in West Belfast between the IRA and the army, and after a 'no-warning' bomb attack at a Belfast bank, 30 people were seriously injured. On the 6th February 1971, Gunner Robert Curtis of the 32nd Royal Artillery died in a burst of machine-gun fire from an IRA gunman. The murder took place in the New Lodge area of Belfast. Robert Curtis was the first soldier to die in the present terrorist campaign and the first British military casualty in 50 years. By coincidence, about two months later the IRA man who murdered Gunner Curtis was himself shot dead in an exchange of gunfire with the army in Belfast. It was a strange irony that the street where he died was named Curtis Street.

But it was the invention of the car bomb as a weapon of mass destruction that elevated the IRA to the level of the most savage terrorist organisation since the Third Reich. This fact was brought home to me personally on the 21st July 1972, when the PIRA detonated 26 car bombs around the centre of Belfast, killing 11 people and injuring 130. One of the car bombs exploded at Oxford Street bus station, where seven of the victims died, including two soldiers who were clearing the area at the time. The ages of the casualties ranged from a 9year-old boy to a 70-year-old woman, and the task of identification was seriously hampered because of the severe mutilation of the bodies. I learnt later of a distant relative, who was returning with her husband from holiday on the mainland. They were waiting at Oxford Street for a bus to take them on the final part of their journey, when the car bomb exploded. They were not actually injured by the blast, but the shock of seeing people blown to pieces had a lasting effect on their health. On the evening of the outrage we watched the television news programme, and were horrified to see firemen sweeping up and collecting some of the bodies that were so badly dismembered, they were put in plastic bags. The 21st July 1972 became known as 'Bloody Friday'.

On joining the Police Reserve I was posted to Gilford, which was quite convenient, as I had only to drive about five miles to my duty station. The full complement of police in the Gilford station was two RUC constables, two full-time Reserves and ten part-time Reserves. Like many other Police stations of its size in the Province, it was a limited opening station. This meant the station was closed from 9 pm to 9 am the following morning. The Portadown Police covered the policing needs of the town during the night. Portadown Police Station is the district headquarters of' J' Division.

The RUC Reserve did not constitute a separate force, as the Specials did but they were at all times under the complete control and direction of the RUC, and performed duties locally to assist the regular police. All the new recruits into the Police Reserve in 'J' Division had to attend training courses, which were held in an annexe to the rear of Tandragee Police Station. 1 also had to serve a probation period, during which time I was trained by RUC instructors and was required to attend a specific number of training sessions each month. To my surprise, the sergeant instructor who took the class was none other than Harold Cobb, who had recently been promoted and was appointed lecturer. I soon got to know many of the other Reservists and discovered that one, Richard Baird, was employed in the same factory as myself, although we worked on different shifts and therefore only knew each other in passing. Richard was stationed in Banbridge, where we frequently met, particularly on Court days when I was on duty at the Petty Sessions. All part-time Reservists had the opportunity to apply for full time duty, in which case they would serve on a three-year contract basis and carry out normal police work.

I did not let the security situation worry me too much but I tried to take sensible precautions to protect my family and myself against the IRA. I realised the constant danger that all members of the security forces lived in from day to day, when a former colleague was murdered at his work. He was Ivan Vennard, a postman, and he was shot dead on the evening of the 3rd October 1973 as he was collecting mail from a sub-post office in the Kilwilke housing estate in Lurgan. Witnesses to the murder said that two young men, one of whom was armed with an automatic pistol, walked up to Ivan and shot him at point blank range. As he fell to the ground they pumped another four bullets into his body, killing him instantly. A married man with two young boys, Ivan was a member of the local Ulster Defence Regiment at the time. I knew him when I was in the T A. He had also served for 12 years in the Royal Artillery and had served two tours of duty overseas, one in Aden during the terrorist insurrection there, and one in Cyprus with the United Nations peacekeeping force. Less than a year before the murder, a police Land Rover patrol was ambushed in the estate and a constable who was on his way to deliver a Christmas present to a young girl was shot dead.

The Gilford police district covered a large rural area of Co. Down and Co. Armagh, and to help us patrol the area the station was supplied with a car. It was a two-tone silver and grey Ford Escort, with no markings to indicate it was a police vehicle. At times when there was no available driver, the senior constable would ask me to take the car out, which was unofficial as only designated drivers who had passed a police driving test were allowed to drive police cars. He finally suggested that I should apply for the police-driving test, and although I was a reserve police driver when I was mobilized some ten years earlier, I had to go through the driving test again. An Inspector from the motor transport group at headquarters arrived at the station one morning to put me through the test. As I drove out of the station compound with my scrutiniser passenger beside me, I decided to keep to the roads that were familiar to me. When we returned, I parked the car in the compound and as we walked towards the station, the instructor handed me a document confirming I was successful and was now a reserve police driver.

As the days went on, 1 enjoyed driving the car because it allowed me to travel around the district and meet people. A typical day on duty began at

8.30 am when I arrived at the station that was opened by the senior constable. He lived in the married quarters, but could gain access through a door dividing the two parts of the station. After attending to the morning mail and any complaints that had been left for us, we locked the station and left on mobile patrol of the district. One of the senior constables was always in charge, and sometimes one or two of the other part-time Reserves would accompany us. One morning as we were driving slowly through the town, a man and his wife were walking along the street, and he flagged us down. The constable who was with me knew them and as I stopped the car he said. "Hello Bob, morning Mrs Harrison." "Hello Francie," came the reply in unison. He told us he had applied to join the part time Reserve and had been accepted. He was told that he would be posted to Gilford, but he was in the UDR and had to wait for the transfer papers coming through. Occasionally we would call into Portadown station and meet some of the men there whom we would accompany on duty to the Petty Sessions. It was on these Court days that I met two full time Reserves, Jim Wright and Andrew Baird. Jim was a local man and a member of the Salvation Army, which he had attended for more than thirty years. He played in the band, but it was his singing that won him his greatest reputation, with his soft baritone voice. A kindly and helpful man, Jim had released two LPs. of his Gospel songs, which according to their sales were a 'phenomenal success'. He was very popular in the Portadown area and his bearded face made him instantly recognisable. He was known as the 'singing policeman'.

Andrew too was a Christian and belonged to Craigavon Baptist Church, where he played an active part in the Sunday school and in community relations groups with young people. He and his wife ran a 'Good News' club for children from the neighbourhood, in the garage of their home. Among the children who attended the club were three whose father was the MP for the area, Mr Harold Mc Cusker.

Bob Harrison arrived and took up duty in Gilford, and as we worked together I got to know him very well. Bob was a married man with two of a family. He worked as a male nurse in Bannvale Special Care Hospital, just outside the town, and when we were on duty together he would talk about his work, how he tried to educate the patients, the more talented of whom he took delight in training to contribute to various forms of entertainment, especially singing, as Bob and his brother Thomas were gifted singers. They had displayed their natural singing ability in Gilford and the surrounding district. He sang in the choir of All Saints Parish Church, at Tullylish, and frequently sang a solo portion at the Harvest thanks-giving service or on other special occasions. An extremely popular singer at weddings, in the weeks that followed he would sing at the wedding of a fellow member of the Reserves, in Gilford Parish Church. He also took a keen interest in the Boy's Brigade. His son was an officer in the same BB company.

One tour of duty that has remained a memorable experience to me was when we went to Belfast for weapons training. There were about eight or nine of us, all Reserves, and we headed off in two cars. The weapons training centre was in the now disused rope works factory, in East Belfast, where all kinds of rope was manufactured for the ship building industry in the past. The Special Patrol Group, who were in charge of all weapons training, took over the building and the workshops were renovated into offices and classrooms. One long shop was converted into a fully equipped indoor firing range, complete with sandbag emplacement and target point at one end. An interesting part of the day came at lunchtime, when we were all put in Land Rovers and taken to the canteen at Castlereagh Holding Centre. The centre was the focus of attention in the early 1970's, due to spurious allegations that were made against the police. I found my visit to be an experience, even though it was only to get a bite of lunch.

Wednesday, 16th October 1974 was a wet morning and it had been raining most of the night. As I made my way into my work I found that the main topic of conversation among the fellas was about a major riot and fire in Long Kesh Prison. The riot had started about 6 0' clock the night before, when four prison officers in a republican detainee compound were beaten up by a number of prisoners. Three of the officers were taken to hospital, where it was found that one had a fractured skull. As other warders went into the compound to arrest those responsible for the attack, they too were set upon and the rioting escalated until it engulfed all the republican compounds, where about 15 huts, as well as the prison hospital and kitchen, were burned to the ground. Fifteen prison officers were injured, and the army had to use CS gas and rubber bullets to prevent the IRA prisoners breaking out through the perimeter fence. The mass orgy of destruction sparked sympathetic protests in other jails in the Province, the worst of which was in Armagh women's prison where the governor was seized and held hostage by female prisoners. The riots spread to Magilligan prison in County Londonderry, and in the early hours of the morning there was a spate of highjacking when armed youths rampaged through some parts of Belfast and Londonderry, as well as some other towns.

As I listened to the account of the trouble, and later saw the prison in flames on the evening TV news that night, it all gave me a spur, and I thought of joining the Northern Ireland Prison Service. The sudden out-break of the troubles in 1969 and 1970, and the opening of Long Kesh internment centre and prison in September 1971, created a serious short-fall of prison staff in Northern Ireland. As a result there was a wide-spread advertisement campaign in all the local newspapers and on TV for prison officers. So I wrote off to the prison service headquarters at Dundonald House in Belfast for an application form, which I received a few days later. But I did not return the form at the time as I decided to stay in my job at Courtaulds and in the part time Reserves, which I enjoyed so much.

When I arrived home from work on Monday 7th July 1975, I was upset when Delta told me it had been on the news that there was a bomb explosion at Carrick School and a policeman was killed. Later as I watched the TV news, the full story began to emerge. The policeman who died was Detective Constable Andrew Johnston and it was thought that he was an innocent victim of the blast, because the bomb had been intended to kill the school principal, my former teacher, Mr Alister Black. Mr Black had been elected to serve in the Northern Ireland Constitutional Convention, which was established only two months earlier on the 1st May. He was a representative of the recently-formed Vanguard party, and had been headmaster of Carrick School since 1953. A second detective constable, Mr Harry Beattie was seriously ill with head injuries, as too was the school caretaker Mr John McConnell. It later emerged that Mr Black came within seconds of being the victim, when after a reported break-in he had gone to the school, accompanied by the caretaker and several other police officers. He started checking to ascertain if anything was missing and began opening the drawers of his study desk. After looking in the first drawer, he was advised to leave the rest to the CID. As the CID men arrived Mr Black left the scene, and soon afterwards the second drawer in the study desk was opened. This triggered the explosion, killing the detective instantly. The principal's study was completely destroyed and extensive damage was caused to the school building. Soon after the blast a statement from the Vanguard party said that the movement was clearly of the opinion that the bomb was meant for Mr Black, who had in the past received threats from the PIRA. Mr Black's son Philip was a member of Craigavon Borough Council at the time. Detective Constable Johnston was married with a fifteen-month-old daughter. He was a native of Belfast and had joined the police five years earlier.

Every Friday morning we had to escort a car from the wages office of a local factory to a bank in Banbridge to collect the payroll for the mill. On Friday morning, the 31st July, I was detailed to drive the car on the escort, and as we tailed the car on the journey the senior man told me that he was short of men to cover the annual band parade that was to take place in the town that night. I volunteered to stand in for the duty, and he told me to take up point duty to control the traffic at the corner of the Lurgan-Portadown roads, at the top of the town. When the escort was complete, it was the normal procedure for us to patrol around the district but at the same time keep in close contact with the station until the mill's wages were paid out. As I returned to the town for the band parade that evening, I parked my car opposite the Woodlands housing estate, close to the corner where I was to take up duty. This would enable me to go home after the parade without actually driving through the town. Each year when the band parade was held in the town, twenty or thirty bands from all across the province would take part and a large number of spectators from neighbouring towns would arrive to give their support. The Portadown police were always required to supply a number of men to help us to divert traffic around the town and to assist in crowd control. As I took up duty at the corner, a grey Ford transit minibus with about ten constables on board approached from the Portadown side, and I directed it down the main street towards the police station. Little did I know but only a few hundred yards away from where I was standing, the IRA were setting up an ambush that would later demonstrate the depths of depravity to which they could sink.

It was a warm summer evening, and as the parade formed up on the Banbridge Road, the main street became thronged with on-lookers lining both sides of the road. The bands paraded through the town to the Woodlands, where they turned and made their way back. The light was beginning to fade as the crowds dispersed, and I waited for a while until calm had descended on the area. It was about 9.30 p.m. when I drove off and made my way home. Shortly after arriving home, I was in the garden, when I heard the sound of police sirens on the Giford Road. I rang the station to see if anything was wrong, and it was then that I heard about the atrocity. When the band parade was over, the Portadown police had left the station in the minibus. As they did so, another minibus of the same model and make was driving out of Gilford on the main Portadown road. This vehicle contained a group of about a dozen pensioners who were on their way home after attending a bingo session in Banbridge. As the minibus drove past the entrance to Bannvale Special Care Hospital and approached a sharp right hand bend, a hail of rifle and machine gun fire struck the vehicle. One eighty-year-old man was shot dead and several others were seriously injured, including the driver, 42-year-old James Marks, who was shot in the head. The pensioners who survived the attack were all suffering from severe shock when the police minibus arrived on the scene only seconds after the shooting. The police immediately took charge of the area, administering first aid before getting ambulances and help. At daylight the following morning we searched the area and followed the tracks of the gunmen who had made their escape from the ambush point, which was behind a stone wall, through fields that sloped down to the river Bann. The tracks continued on the other side of the river through fields that rose up to the Stramore Road where, as we discovered later, the get-away car was waiting .. As the IRA had monitored police activity in the area on previous occasions, particularly when there was a band parade and extra police were required, the ambush was clearly a case of mistaken identity, with the old people's bus being taken for the police vehicle.

The systematic slaughter of the innocent by the sectarian murder squads of the Provisional IRA continued, and within four weeks the IRA would perpetrate a massacre that would shock the world. I was on a rest day from the factory on Tuesday 2nd September 1975, so I reported for duty to the station early that morning as usual. When I walked into the station, one of the younger Reserves told me that his girlfriend had rung him early in the morning to tell him she had a relative murdered in a shooting incident in South Armagh the night before. As we listened to the news bulletins, we became aware of the full horror of the outrage. It had taken place at an isolated Orange Hall near the border, outside Newtownhamilton where an Orange Lodge meeting was taking place. Four Orange-men died in a hail of machine gun fire, and seven others were wounded when gunmen burst through the door and opened fire.

The attack took place at 10 o'clock at Tullyvallen Orange Hall. The lodge meeting had been under "way for some time, when the front door burst open and two gun-men sprayed the inside of the hall with machine gun fire. As more gunmen on the outside of the building fired automatic weapons through the windows, the Orange-men threw themselves on the floor, and one of them, an off-duty member of the security forces, drew his weapon and opened fire. This courageous action undoubtedly saved the lives of some of those in the hall.

The men who died in what became known as the Tullyvallen Orange Hall Massacre were James McKee, a 70-year-old retired farmer, and his son Ronald who was 40 years of age; Mr John Johnston, who was also 70 years of age, and 40 year old Nevin McConnell, who was the manager of Newtownhamilton livestock mart. All four men lived locally, and the members of the lodge who survived the attack raised the alarm. Ambulances rushed the dead and injured to Daisyhill Hospital in Newry, while some of the more seriously wounded were airlifted by army helicopter to the Royal Victoria Hospital in Belfast. As the security forces began to search the area, a suspicious package was found outside the hall, and an army bomb expert defused the device, which was a two-pound booby trap bomb. Two days later a fifth man died of his injuries in hospital; he was William Herron who also lived locally. Later when traces of blood were found on fencing about one hundred yards from the hall, it was discovered that one of the terrorists had been shot in the stomach. Survivors of the slaying described later how, just before the shooting started, the lodge had decided to stop meeting in the hall for the time being, for fear of such an attack. It was to dangerous,' one of the survivors said. The murders were carried out in a most brutal and cowardly manner, for the sole purpose of instilling fear and terror in the hearts of the Protestant people in the South Armagh area. The following day the shooting was claimed by the South Armagh Republican Action Force, a flag of convenience for the Provisional IRA.

During my time on the B men in Newtownhamilton I often patrolled that area of the border on my bicycle, and got to know many of the local people. I was on duty at socials and dances in the district, especially at harvest time and during the winter nights. The last time I was on duty at Tullyvallen Orange Hall was at a dance in 1960 when the hall was reopened after renovations. Although there was an IRA campaign going on at that time, it was not conducted with the same vicious sectarian hatred as the present terrorist action. Who would have thought that in those more peaceful times, such a massacre would take place in Tullyvallen only fifteen years later. It was a naked sectarian attack, that showed clearly the savagery of the IRA death squads. On the 1st September 2000, a quarter of a century after the killings, I attended a memorial service in Tullyvallen Orange Hall, in memory of the five men who were so mercilessly murdered. The five good and honest men who were so abruptly robbed of life that night were symbolic of a typical cross-section of Protestant rural Ulster. At the service in the hall the survivors of that evil night

25 years ago and the loved ones of those who perished gathered to remember them. That night I saw the wood-grained table that the men sat around and which undoubtedly saved some of their lives, because to this day it bears 17 bullet holes from the indiscriminate shooting. Ironically, there were 17 lodge members at the meeting that night. The master, secretary and chaplain died in the first burst of gunfire.

After having second thoughts about joining the prison service, I returned the application form to Dundonald House and soon afterwards I received an invitation to attend an interview in Rosepark House, Upper Newtownards Road, Belfast. The meeting took place at 2.20pm on Wednesday 9th September 1975, and as I made my way into the waiting room a few minutes before the set time, I found there was one other applicant waiting to be interviewed for the job. I sat down and a few pleasantries passed between us, as an office door opened and a young man walked out.

A secretary sitting at a desk near the door asked the second chap to go on in and, as I was left alone, I felt a little bit nervous. The interview was quite brief and a few minutes later the office door opened and he walked out. The secretary called, 'Next please,' and I got sharply to my feet and walked into the office. On the far side of the room, three well-dressed men sat behind a desk with their backs to a window. The one in the centre spoke with a County Antrim accent and had a distinct military bearing. "Thank you for coming, Mr McKane; have a seat." A chair was precisely placed in the centre of the office, and as I closed the door behind me they scrutinised me carefully and continued to eyeball me as I walked to the chair and sat down. They each in turn asked me a number of questions about why I had applied to join the service, and about what I expected the prison service to be like. I told them I had no idea what the job would be like, as my only perception of a prison was what I had seen in films. I was surprised when one of them asked me about my financial situation, and in particular if I was in debt or had any money problems.

When I told him I was not in debt he asked if I knew why he had asked the question in the fIrst place. I replied that I did not know, and he explained that if a prison officer owed a lot of money, and the prisoners knew it, it would make him vulnerable and in danger of being compromised. It was a danger that had not crossed my mind, but as far as I was concerned the problem did not exist. One of the interviewers spoke with an abrupt tone and asked awkward questions. He would set a scenario and then ask me what I would do in that particular event, at the same time knowing perfectly well that I did not know what the inside of a prison looked like, and therefore I hadn't a clue what I would do in a particular sequence of events. I thought he was testing my temperament and trying to unsettle me, so I kept calm and answered his questions as best as I could. As the interview came to an end, the man in the centre, who seemed to be in charge, spoke quietly and said that they would be in touch with me. As I left the office, I was quite happy that the interview had gone very well for me and I had answered all the questions with confIdence. A few days later I received a letter of notification of my success and acceptance into the service. The communication invited me to report to the Crumlin Road Prison Belfast, at 9 am on the 20th October, to commence a one-week induction course for the prison service, and to bring an empty suitcase with me as I would be supplied with a uniform and would need the suitcase for my clothes.

On Monday morning, the 22nd September, I reported to Gilford station for duty as usual. As I walked into the station, one of the men told me that there was a report that a bomb had exploded in Portadown, and that some police had been injured. When we switched on the transmitter, there was heavy radio traffic and it was clear that the blast had occurred at the security hut in Church Street, which controlled the town's sealed-off zone. A few moments later the phone rang. It was a sergeant from the Portadown station, and he spoke to the senior constable and told him about the bombing. He said that two constables were badly injured in the explosion, and had been removed to Craigavon Hospital; and as every available policeman in the station was engaged in searches of the area, they were short of men to mount a security guard at the hospital. As he put down the phone, the senior constable turned to me and told me to go home and change into civilian clothes, and report to the hospital to take up guard duty with the two constables. It was only when I arrived at the hospital that I was told the names of the two men. They were Andrew Baird and George Barlow. Although both men were members of the full time Reserve and I knew Andrew, I only knew George very slightly.

Both men were still in the operating theatre, where they were under-going emergency surgery. There were some very distressed people in a small waiting room beside the theatre and as I sat down I heard that both men had lost limbs in the blast. It was only then I realized, that one of the women was Andrew's wife, who was being comforted by other relatives. After about an hour one of the surgeons came out of the theatre, sat down beside Mrs Baird and spoke to her in a calm tone of voice. As he left, Mrs Baird became even more distressed, and in the conversation that followed I learnt that Andrew's legs had to be amputated. One of his arms was also shattered and he had sustained several deep lacerations. In the days that followed, Andrew remained in an unconscious state, regaining consciousness for one brief moment when he muttered a few treasured words to his wife, who kept a regular bedside vigil.

Andrew's life ended on the afternoon of the 14th October, when he slowly passed away still in a deep coma, 22 days after the IRA bomb exploded. Accompanied by some of my colleagues from Gilford police station, I attended the funeral, where the mood was one of deep sadness, along with the determination of all of us to press on and to defeat the IRA murderers. Andrew was the first policeman to be murdered by the IRA in Portadown. Although George also suffered serious wounds to the lower part of his body, he survived the bombing but succumbed to his injuries and died about a year later.

It was not the circumstances I would have wished for when leaving the Reserves. But once again I was on the move from one branch of the security forces to another. I handed in my gear to the senior constable at Gilford station, said good-bye to all the men, who wished me all the best, and I left the Police Reserve, ready to embark on my new career in the Northern Ireland Prison Service.

Chapter 8

I will never forget the first day in my new career. I parked my car in one of the little side streets that ran off the Crumlin Road, and made my way towards the prison, carrying my large, empty suitcase as instructed. It was 9 0' clock on Monday morning, the 20th October 1975, and a cool autumn breeze blew off Belfast Lough towards the north of the city. Belfast, like any other industrial city at that time of morning, hummed with activity and as I turned a comer, the large building came into sight. Along the road, there were blocks of Victorian town houses, and beyond those were the geometric-shaped streets of terraced houses.

Her Majesty's Prison Belfast was a grim, forbidding-looking place, which stood amongst the well-known landmarks of the city. There has always been a certain amount of mystique surrounding prisons, and to me this was all the more true because I had no idea what to expect. Surrounded by the traditional high walls, its dark, granite stone with sandstone cornices and sills were dulled with the grime of the years. Characteristic of its age, its massive solid steel gates had a small wicket-door to the side for pedestrians. As I knocked the door, a face appeared at an observation window. I could hear a key being inserted into the lock, and as the door opened a prison officer said, "Come in!" As I walked in, he asked my name and marked it off a list on a clipboard. I was then directed into a guardroom, where I met some other men who were also waiting with their empty suitcases. I sat down and a few more arrived, making up our number to twelve. Then a grey haired man in uniform came in. He was wearing glasses, and had two silver bars on his shoulder, which were the insignia of his rank. As he took off his hat and sat down, he said, "I'm principal officer Hamilton, the training PO here in the Crum and I will be taking you for one week here in Belfast. Then you will do two weeks training at the prison officers training college at Millisle." He continued to brief us on the course for the week, and as he finished he said, "Our first priority now is to take you to the stores and get you kitted out in uniform."

We all filed after him as he walked out of the room and turned left. An officer opened the gate that gave us access into an open yard. When we were all in, he locked the gate behind us, and we paraded after the PO as he carried on down a narrow alley between the high perimeter wall and the main prison block. At the end of the alley we turned left and we filed through a wooden door. It was a large square room, with racks stacked to the ceiling with clothing; on one side grey denim trousers and jackets worn by the prisoners, and on the opposite side black trousers, tunics, shirts, ties and hats that were worn by the prison officers. Three prison orderlies stood behind a long bench in their grey denim garb, and as each of us told them our garment sizes, they grabbed the uniform and stacked it on the bench. I collected my gear and made my way between the racks, where there was a minimum of privacy, and began to change into the new uniform. As I did, I couldn't help but look at the orderlies who were the first prisoners I had seen in the jail. Although they were probably only serving a few calendar months, which was a short sentence by any standards, but to the perspective of a recruit into the prison service they were hardened prisoners who needed to be watched! Once we were all togged up, the PO told us to leave our suitcases in the store and follow him into the main prison block. We were taken to the reception area first, where a photographer photographed each of us for identity purposes, and we were then provided with an identity pass which allowed each of us into the prison. But before our tour of the jail would start, the PO suggested that we follow him into the officers' mess, where we would have a coffee break.

As we sat with our coffee in the mess, Mr Hamilton, who was a friendly, kind-hearted man, gave us a quick run down on HMP, Crumlin Road. "The prison was designed after the model of Penton ville prison in London, and was opened in 1845." As he continued to give us a history lesson about the building, its inhabitants and the hangings over the years, I began to think that my new employment was going to be a bit of a culture shock. As we walked into the main hall leading to the circle area, the first thing that struck me was the smell. Prison smells were everywhere; I had never been in a prison before and therefore had never smelt prison smells. They were by no means foul smells; a kind of mixture from a large number of people all confined together, and cooking odours which permeated up from the kitchens and went through the whole prison. The PO walked to a door and shouted, "glass door, please!" This was somewhat surprising, as the door was of a heavy wooden construction and did not resemble glass in any shape or form. But as I learned later, the door had been called the glass door for years, and no one knew the reason. Eventually an officer opened the door and we filed through into a central area. From here you could look down the length of all the wings in the jail, simply by moving slightly. There were three, long halls which fanned out from the central hub like the spokes on a wheel. A, B and C wings rose to three storeys high, known as the ones, twos and threes preceded by the letter of each particular wing. Steps led down underneath A wing to what was known as 'The Base.' This was where the sex offenders, informers and child murderers were kept for their own protection. The high openness of each wing was broken by heavy wire mesh netting that was strung across each landing, supported by iron railings on either side. The PO explained that this was a safety net in case someone decided to deny the courts their sentence and jump! Such safety apparatus was typical of many other such establishments on the mainland.

It was the prison sounds that stand out in my memory: the continuous rumble that echoed throughout the landings of each wing; the clang of gates and grilles opening and closing; the boom of heavy cell doors being shut; the ceaseless jingle of the keys that the officers used; the shouts of orders and the rattle of boots on the iron gantry and stairs. As the PO continued to describe the prison and its routines, I could see what he meant when he said it was like a typical Victorian-style prison. The cell doors on either side of the landing got smaller as they retreated into the distance, like the rails of a railway track on a picture. On each landing it was a repeat of identical lines of cells. A steel staircase dog-legged up to meet a steel gantry that connected the landings on either side. As Mr Hamilton continued his explanation, we proceeded into 'A' wing and I began to see for the first time the inmates and their accommodation. Each cell had a bed, a small table and chair, a tin locker and a plastic chamber pot. The cell doors were made of steel and had an observation slot about eye level. On the wall beside each cell door there was a cell-card that bore the name, number and sentence of the occupant. Each cell was about six foot wide by eight foot long. The solid concrete walls were painted a dull beige colour, with a steel-barred window set high at the back of the cell. As we left the wing, I felt I was glad to get out of the place, but our tour continued into other parts of the prison. The afternoon was spent in a makeshift classroom, in a building outside the prison that was originally the married quarters for the prison staff. The training PO lectured us on the use of our batons, whistles and keys, and stressed the importance of keeping our keys hooked onto our key-chains. The security of the prison was paramount and he continually emphasised the point. One sentence he quoted day in and day out was, "The security of a prison is only as efficient as the people who operate it!" At about 5pm we were stood down and told to report for duty at 8 0' clock the following morning. I collected my suitcase and headed for home. As I got into my car and drove off, after spending my first day in the Crum, I mused on my new surroundings and on some of the people I had met. I did not know if I was going to be happy in the prison service, but one thing that I was sure of, it was going to be different from any job I had ever worked at before.

Tuesday morning I reported to the training office and was detailed to the landings for some 'hands on' experience. I was introduced to the class officer of the landing, the officer in charge, who asked me to accompany him at unlock. When all the prisoners were counted and the numbers returned to the circle and the Chief Officer was satisfied that the prisoners were present and correct, he then shouted out the order 'Unlock!' And immediately the officers on all the landings started unlocking the cells simultaneously. I walked along the landing with the officer as he opened each cell. An inmate would appear carrying his water gallon and plastic pot, to start the daily morning routine of his ablutions. He would quickly walk to the recess, empty the contents of his pot into the slops-sink, wash the pot under the tap, fill up his water gallon with fresh water and return to his cell. He would tidy his cell and wash himself before parading to the dining hall for breakfast. As the days passed, I used to wonder how they felt, especially the lifers, who had nothing to look forward to but the same melancholy procedure day after day. It was amazing how quickly I learned the everyday practice of the landings, and as long as I could stand the smell, I thought I could cope with the job 'OK.'

On the Wednesday I was detailed court escort duties to Belfast Crown Court. The Court was on the opposite side of the Crumlin Road from the prison, and a tunnel under the road connected the two buildings, and led from the prison into the dock in the courtroom. I accompanied another officer to the cell of an IRA prisoner in 'B' wing, to escort him to court. He had been charged with a number of bombing offences, including the Europa Hotel in the centre of the city. The Europa was the largest hotel in Belfast and wasn't long built at the time. By the end of the troubles the Europa had the unenviable title of the most bombed hotel in the UK. The trial had been in progress for a few days, and Wednesday's sitting was to be the summing-up of the evidence and sentencing by the judge. The other officer led the way, with the prisoner behind him, and I took up the rear. We went down a staircase and along a narrow corridor at the side of 'D' wing-visits and the legal-visits area, where barristers and solicitors interviewed their clients. We came to a grille manned by an officer who, when he had checked our identity, opened the grille and we walked though. I suddenly realised we had entered the tunnel under the road. It was higher than I had expected, about eight feet high in the centre with a rounded ceiling sloping down at each side to a concrete wall. You could not see the end of the passage, as there was a bend for a short section in the middle. The inside was painted white and lit by bulkhead lights that were attached to the ceiling, and heating pipes ran along the side. A grille manned by a prison officer indicated the end of the tunnel, and as we walked through, the grille-officer changed the prison numbers on a blackboard. This was the point where the prison precinct stopped and the courtroom started. The area widened out into a holding chamber, with holding cells along the side. We put the prisoner into one of the cells beside a flight of concrete steps, and the officer leaned over and spoke quietly to me, "Them stairs lead up to NO.1 Court. Do you want to go up and see the set-up?" "Yes, that would be interesting," I replied as I started up the stairs. At the top, a short landing led to a wooden door and I turned the knob and walked through. To my surprise, I was standing in the enclosure of the dock. Although the court was not in session, there was a considerable number of people present, all engaged in muffled conversation. The dock was in an elevated position above the well of the court and about level with the judge's chair on the opposite side. The entire chamber was painted in pastel colours brightened by the light from four fluorescent lights. A number of barristers in their black gowns and white wigs sat in the well of the court. To the right were the press benches, and to the left, witnesses in the case sat along with the police. The public gallery rose up behind the dock and gave a clear view of the whole interior. I returned down the stairs to the holding area to await the start of the trial. A few minutes later we were asked to bring the prisoner up to the dock, as the court was sitting, and we started up the stairs with the prisoner between us. As we entered the dock, the prisoner sat down, and my colleague and I sat on either side of him. A few minutes later the Clerk of the Court called out, "All stand!" We all stood up and the judge entered at the side of the bench. Then when he sat down, everyone in the court sat down. The judge started his summing-up by making reference to the evidence from the police Scenes of Crime officers and army bomb disposal officers. The deliberation went on for hours, but finally the judge gave the verdict and sentenced the bomber to twenty years' imprisonment. When the penalty was announced, I felt a bit nervous as I glanced at the prisoner to see how he had taken it. He remained motionless, but gazed across the court as if he could see into the past. The judge spoke again: "Take him down!" Immediately we stood up and I walked out through the wooden door, followed by the prisoner and the officer. The prisoner was locked in one of the holding cells while we waited for the warrant and documentation, before returning to the prison through the tunnel.

Friday was my last training day in the Crum, which was taken up with a classroom session in the morning, and the afternoon was spent with a final tour of the jail that ended with a sombre visit to the death cell and the gallows. As we gathered around the cell door, the PO explained the procedure for an execution. The prisoner was placed in the cell a few days before the sentence was to be carried out. Against one wall of the cell was what appeared to be a large, wooden locker with double doors. In fact the locker concealed an adjoining door that gave access to the scaffold, and a few moments before the penalty was to be carried out, the locker doors were opened and the prisoner was led through into the execution chamber. There was absolute silence as the PO demonstrated how the rope was placed around the prisoner's neck in order to give a clean break. Each member of the group seemed to be self-absorbed with the discussion as we left the hanging cell and returned to the more comfortable surroundings of the class room, where we finally received our instructions to report to the Prison Officers Training School at Millisle on Monday morning. On my way home that evening as I reflected on the past week in the Crumlin Road Prison, I thought that in all my previous experiences in the security forces I had learnt the unwritten rule, to listen carefully and say very little. But in my new surroundings I was rapidly learning to adapt an even more guarded approach and analyse everything very carefully and say nothing.

The Northern Ireland Prison Service College consisted of two portacabin type buildings, which had been constructed on the site of the Borstal institution at Woburn House, on the outskirts of the village of Millisle in County Down. As I drove through the gates, I was directed past the main Borstal building, along a narrow road that led to the prefabricated portacabins. A principal officer who was standing at the door, marked my name off a sheet of paper and told me to go into the kitchen and have a cup of tea whilst waiting for the rest of the squad to arrive. The buildings were comparatively new and were laid out like campus acconunodation. Between the two blocks there were squares of closecropped grass, bordered by narrow, tarmac paths. The area lay in a quadrangle, that opened at one end to a drill square, where we paraded each morning for inspection by the college governor. I enjoyed the marching and the discipline, particularly in the mornings for the Governor's parade. A small, aloof man, he would stand on his office steps as we marched past, like Napoleon inspecting his troops.

When we were all gathered into the classroom, the principal officer began our training course with a routine lecture on prison security. The established practice of the training courses was classroom lectures each day which concentrated on the law concerning the treatment of offenders whilst in prison, the discipline and control of inmates, their reception, transfer and discharge, and their work, education and recreation. The daily lectures were interrupted on the Wednesday afternoon of each week, when we had to parade in the gymnasium for lessons on elementary physical training. The gymnasium was a large, oblong room with wall-bars along the side. On the opposite side was one large, glass window that looked out into the forecourt and car park. A badminton court was marked out on the pine floor, with the side line about six feet out from the walls. Basketball nets were fixed on boards high at either end of the room, and an alcove to the side led into a shower room and toilet area. Stacked in one corner were racks of dumb-bells, and against the back wall were two weight benches. We were equipped with trainers and heavy white Karate Gi suites, and when we had changed into the gym kit, we were divided up into six pairs for lessons in self-defence and unarmed combat. To my consternation, my mate for the exercise was a tall, well-built man with hands like navvy shovels and a vice-like grip that would have taken your breath away. The physical training instructor (PTI) demonstrated various defensive modes of arm locks and holds designed to incapacitate a would-be attacker. The difficult part of the exercise came when I had to struggle with my opponent and try to put him down with an arm lock. I had no mission. His strength and fitness over-powered me every time and he slung me about like a wet sock! I was glad to see my visit to the gymnasium over, and I could only hope that 1 didn't run into a violent prisoner with the physique of Roy. I became a good friend with' Big Roy', as we called him, and we were posted to the Maze, where we served together for years.

We visited the Borstal on the Thursday and got a tour of the grounds and complex. The large residence was built in 1834 and sits in a 17 acre site. It fronts on to the County Down coastline at a point of outstanding beauty. It was purchased by the Northern Ireland Government in the 1950s and was converted into a Borstal, with the first inmates being committed in 1953. About the same time, 14 houses were built as staff living quarters. Although most of the land was leased to a local farmer, to the rear of the main building there was a walled garden of about two acres, where the Borstal boys trained in the art of horticulture and cultivated a range of flowers and vegetables each year. The house was, and still is a listed building and therefore is protected from any form of structural change, or alteration to its early Victorian architecture.

As we entered the building, the housemaster took us around the rooms and explained the procedure of the institution. I was struck by the cleanliness of the place. The large rooms were dormitory accommodation and the floors were polished to a very high shine. A table with a few chairs sat in the centre of each room and along the sides, single iron-framed beds gave an almost barrack room appearance. Each bed was stripped, with the sheets and blankets folded into an 18-inch square and placed in a neat bed-pack. The Borstal boys were dressed in black army style jackets, black trousers, blue shirts and black shoes that were spit-polished. A small, rectangular piece of cloth was sewn on the right sleeve of each jacket, which indicated the grade of the inmate. It was an open Borstal and the boys had a certain amount of freedom in the grounds of the school. In the years that Wobum House was a Borstal institution, the numbers of boys that absconded was minimal, in comparison to Borstals on the mainland. The Borstal system ended in 1980, and soon afterwards Woburn House became the Prison Officer's Training College.

In the final week of our training we had to visit the Maze prison for one day's practical experience in prison work. It was 8.00am when I arrived at the main gate of the Maze. I went into the tally lodge to be photographed, and I was given a day pass. The place was thronged with traffic-day staff reporting for duty and night guard staff going off. I drove in through the gate for the first time and came to a stop, behind a long line of cars, at a black and white striped barrier. As I parked my car in the car park, close to the army camp, I surveyed the place with astonishment. The Maze was a small town of corrugated iron fences and high concrete walls topped with coils of razor wire. They were still constructing the high, outer walls and the whole place resembled a gigantic building site. It was swarming with activity, with companies of soldiers on their way to the firing ranges and others on their way to the mess for breakfast, whilst army vehicles were leaving the camp to patrol the north Belfast area. When I met up with the PO and the other men in the squad, we proceeded through the gate lodge into the prison. We went through a series of gates, each one manned by a prison officer who requested, "Pass please?" And we produced our day passes as we filed by. We arrived at detainee visits, which had been burned down in the riots a year earlier and had been replaced with a row of porta-cabins, which were all joined together like the carriages of a train. The end cabin was the PO's office and as we went in, he welcomed us to the Maze prison and detailed us to our posts for the day. I was detailed 'visits runner' and had to accompany an experienced officer called Herbie. A new man in the job knew nothing and had to be shown everything, whereas the more senior men knew everything. Visits runner basically meant that we had to wait until a prisoner was called for a visit. We would then be given a chit bearing the name, number and the compound where the prisoner was held. We would go to the compound and collect the inmate and bring him to visits, where he would be allocated a 'box' (visiting cubicle). Whilst this process was taking place, an officer would be collecting the visitors in a minibus at the visitors' car park, and conveying them to the visits area.

We were not waiting long, when Herbie was called and handed a chit by the book man, whose task it was to record all movements of prisoners and visitors. Herbie grabbed the chit and we were off. I followed him as we left visits and made our way into Phase 1, which held the detainee compounds.

Herbie talked fast and continued to explain that there were six Phases in the Maze altogether, and where we were going. Like an accomplished chauffeur, he pointed out the places of interest to admire and the potholes to avoid. "When you are taking a prisoner to visits, always walk behind him, so that you can keep an eye on him." The advice was endless. "If you are on gate duty, always keep the keys on your key chain so you can't lose them." "Always keep your baton strap out of sight of the cons, otherwise they will know by the newness of it that you are a new recruit." It was all sensible stuff but even at this early stage in my career, I could not help contrasting it with the inadequacies of the service. But I have to say I took Herbie's advice to heart, because he spoke with such fervour that you would have thought the entire Western Defences depended on it.

When we arrived at the compound, Herbie spoke to an officer who was standing in a sentry box at the compound gate, and told him the name and number of the prisoner he wanted. The officer shouted the details into the compound, whilst Herbie went into the PO's office, a small wooden hut that sat at the side of the compound. He returned in a couple of minutes with the prisoner's security book, which contained all the details about the prisoner, including his photograph. Every time the prisoner left the compound, it had to be recorded in the security book dates and times when he left the compound and returned. Herbie compared the photograph with the prisoner and when he was satisfied it was the right man, he gestured to the officer that it was all right to let him out. The gate officer opened the pedestrian gate, stepped inside and locked the gate after him. It was an airlock system, in which there was a passage between two gates that was covered on the sides and top with heavy mesh wire, the theory being that a prisoner would be unable to dash out of the compound, as both gates were never opened at the same time. Beside the pedestrian gate there was a set of longer gates on the same principle, except these were vehicle gates to allow a tractor or small van into the compound. Between the gates the inmate was given a rubdown search, and as he walked out we followed him to the visits complex.

On arrival at visits, the prisoner was given another rubdown search and Herbie handed the chit to the book officer, who gave him a metal tag with the number 7 on it. Herbie said, 'Number seven,' and the prisoner walked along the corridor, past the open cubicles on each side until he came to one with '7' over the door. He walked in and sat down behind a small plywood table that had two chairs on either side of it. Herbie hung the tag on a nail at the side of the door, opened the security book and entered the date and time of the visit. The visitors arrived and we remained in the corridor outside the cubicle, where we observed the prisoner until the visit was over. Then the procedure was reversed and the prisoner returned to his compound. In the afternoon I reported again to visits and teamed up with Herbie, and we were soon on our way to bring another prisoner to visits. As I walked past one of the compounds and encountered some of the people who populated the Maze prison, I was beginning to feel my way through my strange and new environment. It was here that I saw for the first time some of the men who had dominated the terrorist organisations over the years, some of whom were a legend in their own communities. I also met the other prison officers, who were generally very friendly and helpful with every new recruit into the service.

We arrived at the compound, collected the security book and the prisoner was called. He was a tall, bearded figure, with a mass of unkempt hair that made him look rather like a nutty professor. As he walked out of the compound, I looked closely at him, but the small beady eyes only stared back at me through a pair of glasses that were the only identifiable feature about his face. This type of arrogant egoism was a trait that was developed by many prisoners in the Maze; they rarely made eye contact, but rather, would walk past you as if they owned the place. He wore an oversized woolly pullover, jeans and boots. His beard, bushy hair and scruffy appearance made him the epitome of the trendy left. All that was missing was the Moses sandals, and I am sure they would have been worn if the climate conditions had pennitted. When the visit was over, we returned him to his compound and Herbie handed me the security book and said. "Leave that in the PO's office!" As I walked into the office, I opened the book and looked at the name. It was 'Gerry Adams'.

The next morning I reported to the training college to complete my course, and when we were all gathered in the classroom, we exchanged our experiences of the Maze. On completion of the course the PO asked us our preference of station for posting. He explained that he could not guarantee our particular choice, as it would depend on the staff requirement for each prison. As some of the men in the squad came from the north of the Province, they applied for Magilligan prison in County Londonderry. Others lived in Belfast so they preferred the Crum as the most convenient posting. I was undecided at first but I had enjoyed my visit to the Maze, so I finally decided on the Maze as my duty-station. There was a sense of adventure about the compounds. It was a place where anything that could happen usually did happen, and I looked forward to the challenge of serving in the thick of it.

On the 10th November 1975, I drove into the Maze prison. Of the squad of officers whom I had trained with, only five had been posted to the Maze. We all met at the training office, which was a red brick building with a slated roof. It was one of the dispersal huts that were used to house RAF crews during the war. When we were seated at our desks, the PO informed us we would be on the 'white sheet' for a week. This basically meant we were on a week's probation, during which time we would be under the control of the training department. He continued by giving us a lecture on the history of Long Kesh and the Maze Prison. "When you hear of Long Kesh today, it strikes a chord based on today's terrorist unrest. But Long Kesh, situated about three miles west of Lisburn in County Antrim, has another history, which the present events have forced into the background. Its role then was as important to the security of the United Kingdom as it is today. The Royal Engineers constructed the airfield in 1941.

At the time there were 21 such aerodromes in Northern Ireland, and it was first used for squadrons to train in low-level close support during army exercises, and for the defence of Belfast." He continued to describe the evolution of Long Kesh up until the compound style prison it was in 1975:

"Constructed in six phases, phase one was initially built to accommodate the detainees who were transferred from the HMS Maidstone after she was decommissioned as a prison ship. Long Kesh was opened as a prison in September 1971, and had a total of 22 compounds, each of which held up to 120 prisoners." There were four Nissen huts in each compound, three of which were living accommodation and the fourth was divided in the centre with a stud wall, which provided a half-hut as a dining room, complete with hot plate and boiler. The other half of the hut was equipped with a workbench and tools and was used as a hobbies shop, where the prisoners made wooden harps, Celtic crosses and dolls' houses, which were sent out as gifts to their families. Each hut was centrally heated with a radiator in each cubicle, which made them warm and comfortable in the winter, and they were cool and airy in the summer. A twelve-foot sterile area surrounded the compounds on all sides, which acted as a buffer zone between the compounds and the perimeter fence. In 1972 a number of sentenced prisoners were committed to Long Kesh, and as a result it was renamed the 'Maze prison.'

When the classroom session was over, we were taken on a tour of the administration area of the camp, before entering the prison. It was obviously a place that was built in a hurry. It was a complex of portacabins and some more solid buildings, covering an area of about three square acres. There was a car park containing a number of touring caravans, that made the place look like a gypsy's camp, rather than the staff accommodation of a prison. Other prefabricated huts were constructed with aluminium sheeting, which shone in the sun, and were clearly visible for miles around. This area was nicknamed 'Silver City'. Near the Army camp, there was a helicopter pad that was busy with choppers taking off and coming in to land. Some helicopters were parked in one of the T2 Hangars, that were used to house Spitfires during the War. It was almost bizarre to see a pilot negotiate his craft into the hangar and set it down in a space between two other choppers, like a child with a toy.

Our tour of the prison started when we walked through the wall-gate into the tally lodge and proceeded along a narrow passageway to the Chief Officer's office. The PO told us to wait for a minute, as the Chief wanted to speak to us, and he disappeared into a wooden hut that bore a sign, 'The duty office'. A few minutes later the Chief Officer came out and stood on the step, with the PO by his side. The most senior uniformed officer in the prison service, he looked more like an admiral of the fleet than a prison officer, with the white braid on the peak of his hat, the Sam Browne cross-strap across his chest and the coloured ribbons that indicated the medals he had won in the War. He had served as a Company Sergeant Major in the Irish Guards and spoke with a clipped, military accent. He had a rough voice that sounded like gravel being flung from a shovel. "Men! I want to welcome you to the Maze prison," he said as he started his pep talk. "Now that you have finished your training and you have been posted here to work with us, I would encourage you to make a career of the prison service and do the job to the best of your ability. Keep yourselves clean and tidy and take pride in the uniform you wear. This is a very important job. It is vitally important, for the survival of the society in which we live, that we keep these people locked up in this prison." Although he was only of medium height, he was a Guardsman to the fingertips. He was about fifty years of age with thinning hair, but his bearing made him an imposing figure. He was impeccably dressed and had a no-nonsense manner, and as he spoke we sensed that what we were doing was deadly serious. "Men! As you carry out your duties in this prison, you will probably meet people you know, prisoners who might even come from your own neighbourhood. Have nothing to do with them. Above all we want your loyalty in the prison service." As he finished his lecture I realised the truth of his words, because we had been warned at the training college about fratemising with prisoners.

As the weeks and months passed, and I got to know the Chief a bit better, I have to say that apart from his bluster he was a much-liked character. He retained his austere military comportment, and walked with a Guards swing. As his Christian name was Mervyn, he had acquired the nickname from the staff, 'Merve the Swerve', although we were very careful he didn't hear us using the name. I kept my distance from him, as I did from most of the senior ranks in the service. We passed like ships in the night.

In the phases, twenty five-foot high walls segmented the prison to keep the factions apart, and to ensure that any outbreak of trouble could be isolated and dealt with more efficiently. The perimeter wall and fences of the prison encompassed not only a functional prison but also many other departments, and as I became more familiar with the place I met some of the civilian staff. There were schoolteachers, doctors, welfare workers and even men in the building trade whose task it was to maintain the buildings.

On entering the prison, the first buildings we came to, were Nissen huts that were part of the administration zone. The guardroom was situated beside the inner tally lodge, where the staff paraded for inspection, before going on duty. The Emergency Control Room (ECR) was in a sealed-off part of the guardroom hut. The ECR was the home base for all radio transmitters, and was in constant contact with every radio officer, and monitored the movement of all prisoners, vehicles and staff in and out of the jail. The trades department occupied a full-length Nissen hut, which accommodated the workshops. There were joiners, painters, bricklayers and electricians. These were the tradesmen who carried out the repairs and kept the place ticking over. The prison hospital effectively was two Nissen huts that were joined in the centre by a corridor. One hut was set out in rooms, one of which contained a doctor's surgery, an examination room and a waiting room. The second hut was a ward, complete with a row of tubular steel beds along each side, and a dispensary at one end where hospital officers dispensed drugs and medications. The hospital functioned more as an outpatients clinic where prisoners were treated for burns, scalds, or similar minor ailments, or convalescents. But any major medical problems, such as patients requiring surgery or more serious medical attention, were transferred to outside hospitals, either the Lagan Valley in Lisburn or the RVH in Belfast. The prison reception encompassed Nissen huts enclosed in a compound, surrounded with a high mesh fence and barbed wire. It was one of the first compounds constructed in the Long Kesh camp. All committals were documented and processed in the reception. Here they were photographed and fingerprinted, their sentences recorded and all their details taken. They were then allocated to a compound. When a prisoner was being discharged, he too had to be processed with his fingerprints taken and matched with those taken on committal, to make sure the right prisoner was being released.

As I met and got into conversation with members of the staff, I found that about half of them were 'detached staff,' men who were on temporary transfer from prisons on the mainland. It was interesting to hear the different dialects, and the stories about prisons in the other regions of the country. When the detached staff were talking about Northern Ireland, they would use the term 'out here', as if the Province were a far flung corner of the Empire, rather than a region of the UK only twelve miles from the mainland. But as I got to know them I enjoyed the banter and the comradeship. There was a Principal Officer from a London nick who was in charge of a loyalist compound in Phase six. He was a small, stout man with a bald head and baggy eyes and he had a permanently motionless expression on his face. He sat behind his desk, with his fingers locked in front of his stomach, which inevitably resulted in him acquiring the nickname 'The Buddha'. Another PO, who was on detachment from the Scottish service, was in charge of the prison visits and was a very likeable, fatherly figure in his late fifties. When he was on night guard, he would stroll about the phases with his walking stick, as though the Maze were his private, highland estate, so the staff gave him the nickname 'The Laird', which was appropriate and must have made him feel at home. The Ulster staff were mainly ex-servicemen. Every regiment in the army must have been represented, along with the RAF and the Royal Navy. All these men brought their own colour to the place.

One night I was reporting for night guard, and I parked my car at the side of the T.2.Hangar as usual. I started to walk towards the tally lodge, which took me past the staff social club and near a portacabin used as an assistant governor's office. As I approached, there seemed to be a bit of a ruction going on, with a great deal of grunting and shouting. Out of the darkness I could see three or four officers manhandling a large goat through the office door, that had been busted open. The animal belonged to a herd of wild goats that roamed the old aerodrome, and they used to forage around the army camp at night, looking for scraps of food. I put my head down and hurried on, hoping that no one saw me in case they would think that 1 was part of the escapade. As I walked in through the tally lodge, I wondered if there had ever been so many crazy people gathered together, other than in a loony-bin and that was only the staff!

Pet names were given to the different factions who occupied the separate phases. The loyalists were nicknamed 'The sally rods'. (The prods). The Official IRA were called, 'The stickies', apparently because, during the Easter Commemoration ceremonies they used paper Easter lilies which they stuck onto their jackets. The name Provisionals was abbreviated to 'Provies', evidently to show the immature mentality of the people who were members of that organisation.

When our week of training with the Principal Officer had come to an end, and we were taken off the 'white sheet', the five of us were detailed from the duty office, which meant we were split up and from then on we didn't see much of each other. I was assigned 'general duties', which meant that I was not detailed any particular duty but each day I was given a different post. My first day's duty was on an IRA compound and started at 7.30am, when the compound was unlocked and the regular compound staff went into the huts for a head count. When all the numbers in the prison were returned and found correct, the huts were left open and two officers walked around the inside of the compound to check the wire fences and make sure they were all secure. The two officers then patrolled around the inside of the compound for one hour, before coming out for a break. This one-hour patrolling stag continued through the day and only stopped when the prisoners were locked in their huts again that night.

It was my first opportunity to see the inside of the huts and the compounds. Each hut had an aisle running down the centre and each side was divided into stud-walled cubicles, with a hanging curtain as the door at the entrance. There was a TV and radio in each hut, with double doors at one end and a pedestrian door at the other which led into a small hall. During the day some of the prisoners would walk around the compound in bunches of five or six and occasionally they would jog at a leisurely pace as a form of exercise. The prisoners in each compound were allowed to use the football field twice a week, and in the long summer evenings each compound team was allowed one evening match per week. The first day I saw them playing in their full football kit-which the prison department supplied-it seemed so absurd that people who had committed some of the most horrendous crimes should be treated as though they were responsible for a minor traffic offence. Each compound contained a large ablutions hut with a felted roof. The inside was fitted out with wash-hand basins, toilets and showers. A large square weather-boarded study hut sat in each compound and was set out with tables and chairs. A blackboard covered most of the gable wall, and the other three walls were covered with portraits of Karl Marx, Vladimir Lenin, Fidel Castro, Che Guevara and some other distant patriots. Some of the study huts also displayed large posters of the armalite rifle broken down into its component parts, complete with instructions on how to assemble and maintain the weapon. It was a terrorist training academy, a prison that turned terrorists into more accomplished terrorists. When I saw the inside of the place, I thought how naive it would be to think that streetwise criminals suddenly became choirboys after they were sentenced to a term of imprisonment inside the Maze. It was a looking-glass world, where simple but unpalatable truths were wished away.

There was a watchtower in each phase, and an eight-foot high mesh fence surrounded each compound. The fence was nailed to wooden posts about six feet apart, with an electric light on the top of each fourth one. Symmetrical rows of electric lights on the walls and fences seemed to stretch for miles, and lit up the prison to such an extent that the orange glow resembled an inferno and could be seen from twenty miles away.

Lock-up in the detainee phase was at 10.00 P m, but for the sentenced prisoners it was 9.00 p m. About ten minutes before the given time, all the prisoners came out of the huts for a last stroll around the compound for the night. At this point the staff went into the compound, locked the pedestrian door in each hut, and waited at the back double doors to count the prisoners in before securing the hut. At precisely two minutes before nine o'clock, a prisoner screamed-out an order in Gaelic and immediately all the prisoners ran to a clear area of the compound and came to attention in military formation. Another order was shouted out in Gaelic and the parade was dismissed. They all ran to the huts, where two officers at each hut followed them in and counted them. They stood in two lines the length of the hut, and my colleague and I took a side each and walked briskly down to count them. There was a bunch of them standing just inside the door, and as I walked past they stared at me, in an obvious attempt to embarrass and make me feel uncomfortable. I didn't stare back, but just ran my eyes over them quickly, familiarising myself with their faces for future reference. They were the IRA's front line troops, the hard men, who were at the cutting edge of sectarian terrorism in Northern Ireland. We walked out of the hut and locked it and the numbers were returned to the P.O, who radioed them into the central control room. As the keys were attached to the keyboard, we all stood at the compound gate and waited patiently for all the numbers in the prison to be returned correct and for the magic words from Control: "All numbers returned correct, all day staff may stand down!" We all walked off vigorously towards the tally lodge and home.

There were five IRA compounds in Phase five, and six loyalist compounds in Phase six. The prisoners in each phase were organised in a similar command system, with a commanding officer (CO) of the phase and a CO in each compound, who detailed his men for their daily tasks; dining hall orderlies, who served the meals; yard orderlies, who swept the yards around the huts; and hut orderlies, whose job it was to sweep and polish the floor of each hut. And although it was the policy of the authorities not to recognise the command structure, and therefore the particular organisation, but to treat them all the same, as convicted criminals, it was done in an unofficial way, if only to achieve the smooth running of the prison. It was a system that clearly offered a great deal of autonomy to the particular paramilitary groupings, and could have been seen as veiled recognition by the authorities that they were not criminals but had been granted some sort of political standing.

In some of the loyalist compounds the prisoners were into keeping and breeding birds. Large aviary-type cages had been constructed at the back of the study hut, containing budgies, cockatoos and finches. They took a genuine interest in the birds and took very good care of them. It was not unusual to see a prisoner on his way to visits on a Saturday morning with a couple of birds in a cage. But there was one thing that the various paramilitary organisations in the jail had in common: they were constantly in an unending battle of wits with their keepers. One day in early December I was on evening duty. It was a dinnerguard assignment at a post called 'the wall gate' and I reported about twelve thirty, to relieve the static post officer for his lunch. When he returned at 2.00pm, I reported to visits, before returning at 5 OOpm. I would relieve him and remain there until lock-up. When I arrived to take up my post, the officer told me about an incident that happened early that morning. "Two cons cut a hole in the fence of compound ten. They were disguised as tradesmen, wearing overalls with prison officers' hats and carrying a ladder between them. They tried to walk out of the phase, but only got as far as the wall-gate when they were recaptured and taken to the cellblock." It was the first attempted escape from the Maze since I joined the service. As he handed me the radio transmitter (R T) and left, I gave a test call to the control room to make sure it was working, just in case. Another escape attempt took place a few weeks later, when some IRA prisoners were caught trying to climb over a fence. But their mistake was that the fence was around the visits area and their efforts were bringing them deeper into the prison complex rather than towards the perimeter wall.

Chapter 9

Christmas was approaching and it would be the first festive season for me in the prison service, and I did not cherish the idea of spending Christmas day walking around a compound in the Maze. So I applied for a rest day and was pleasantly surprised when the duty roster was posted and I had got the day off. I was detailed evening duty on Christmas Eve and a straight day (from 8.00 am to 5.30 pm) on Boxing Day, but I was happy enough that I had got one of the days off. We brought Delta's mother down to stop with us for a few days over the holiday, as she lived alone since her husband had died a short time earlier. She returned home to Bessbrook on Tuesday the 30th December and it was late in the evening when I drove into the village. It was then that we learnt of a shooting incident that had taken place about four hours earlier in the town-land of Tullywhinney, about a mile and a half outside the village.

It happened at the home of a man whom I had known since I was on the police in Bessbrook. He was Sam Rodgers and he was seriously wounded in the shooting, which happened as he and his wife were leaving the house to attend a Gospel Meeting at Mullaglass Free Presbyterian Church. They attended the church every Tuesday, and Sam had just opened the door of his car when the gunmen, who were concealed behind a hedge, opened fire with automatic weapons. Sam was shot in the leg and back, and his car and garden fence were riddled with bullets. Mrs Rodgers, who was not injured in the attack, courageously dashed forward, grabbed her husband and dragged him into the house, where she raised the alarm. I had become good friends with Sam and his family over the years, as I attended the Mullaglass Church every Sunday we were in Bessbrook.

The IRA always claimed to be socialist and non-sectarian in their ideology, but the mythological nature of their claims was vividly exposed by the brutal pogroms of ethnic cleansing against the Protestant people, particularly in the border areas. This was poignantly illustrated on Monday the 5th January 1976. I was detailed a long day on Compound 13, in Phase 5, which meant I was on duty from unlock at 7.30am until lock-up at 9.00pm. In the association period from 5.00pm until lock-up it was part of my task to relieve the officer on the segment wall gate for a tea break . I was on the post and it was approaching 9.00pm. The wall gate was situated between Compounds 11 and 12, and I could hear the sound of the television in Compound 12. I could hear the tune that introduced the 9.00 o'clock news, and suddenly there was an instant ecstatic cheer and applause from the prisoners. Although I could not hear the words of the newsreader, it was clear that a serious incident had taken place. A few minutes later an officer was walking past, and I asked him, "What was that on the news headlines?" As he continued walking, he turned his head and said, "The provies have shot-up a minibus in South Armagh, a lot of people have been killed!" As the numbers were returned, and the night guard took up duty and I started to walk towards the guardroom, the story about what had happened in South Armagh began to circulate. But it was when I arrived home that Delta told me the full story, as she had been listening to the TV news bulletins on the atrocity.

The IRA had stopped a minibus that conveyed mill workers from Compton's Spinning Mill in Glenanne, to the Bessbrook area, and the passengers were taken out and murdered. At the end of just another working day the bus had left Glenanne, on the 5-mile journey to Bessbrook. At a secluded part of the road in the town-land of Kingsmills the minibus was stopped by about a dozen armed and masked men, and the 12 occupants taken out onto the road. Of the twelve, one was a Roman Catholic and eleven were Protestants and when the gunmen had identified them, they ordered the Roman Catholic man to run up the road. They then lined the Protestants up against the minibus and opened fire. Ten of the men died instantly, but ironically one man survived. His name was Alan Black. When the police and security forces arrived at the scene, the victims were all removed to Newry's Daisyhill Hospital. As the days passed, the police were able to piece together the sequence of events that led up to the slaying, especially when the wounded man had regained consciousness.

As the minibus left Glenanne and the driver made his way along the dark, narrow, country roads, they approached the brow of a hill at Kingsmills crossroads. It was here that the driver saw a red light signal, about a hundred yards ahead, indicating him to stop, and as he slowed down he thought it was an army checkpoint. But he was mistaken. As the horrified passengers watched, the man with the flashlight was immediately joined by about a dozen others. They were all wearing army-style combat jackets. As they approached the headlights of the bus, the mill men were suddenly gripped with fear when they saw that the men were wearing masks. They realised then it wasn't the army. The back door opened and a coarse voice said, "Get out!" As they climbed out of the vehicle, each man was asked his religion, and it was then that the Roman Catholic man, Richard Hughes, was ordered to run away from the scene. The eleven Protestants were then ordered to line up against the side of the minibus, and seconds later there was a hail of automatic gunfire as bullets ripped through the bodies of the men. Alan Black was hit with the first salvo and as he collapsed onto the road, some of his work-mates fell on top of him. As he lay on the rain-soaked road unable to move with the pain, he remained conscious and could hear the same coarse voice shout out: "Make sure they're all dead!" Immediately there was a second salvo of concentrated fire and more bullets ripped into the pile of bodies.

Ten of the men died instantly but although 18 bullets had punctured Alan Black's body, miraculously, and against all odds, he still lived to tell the tale. In the days that followed, the heart-rending photographs in the newspapers of the bullet-riddled minibus, with its flat tyres, and the lunch boxes strewn on the blood-stained road, proved beyond doubt-if ever proof were needed-the myth of the IRA's claim that their armed struggle was on behalf of the working-class people of Ireland. Provisional Sinn Finn had a quick-fix logic, an all-embracing answer to every question. They even had the gall to claim they were following the Marxist philosophy. Meanwhile, police in the Republic found the vehicle that was believed to have been used by the IRA murder gang. Found south of Dundalk, it was a Ford Transit van and it had been hijacked a week earlier in the South.

It was still raining two days after the slayings when the coffins bearing the bodies of the murdered men were brought at hourly intervals to the Church of Ireland and the Presbyterian Church in Bessbrook. Onlookers stood in eerie silence, the only sound that of the mourners' steps on the road. The funerals took place the following day and it continued to rain as thousands of people attended the services. In the Presbyterian Church, where six of the victims were members, the front pews were removed to make room for the coffins. Both places of worship were filled to capacity, and crowds of people stood outside under umbrellas as the services were relayed through loudspeakers.

The small, close-knit community was paralysed with grief, and every time Delta and I visited the village, we were reminded of that day over a quarter of a century ago, by the simple, black granite memorial that stands close to the town hall in the centre of the village. A commemorative stone that could easily be missed by the casual visitor, yet the names it bears are engraved in the hearts and minds of those who live, or who have ever lived, in Bessbrook.

'The Kingsmills Massacre' represented a rapidly deteriorating security situation and one in which the Protestant people were losing faith in the government's will to protect them. The IRA death squads were going about their terrorist business like locusts that were immune to pesticide, and the loyalist people could only brace themselves for the next atrocity. A few years later I met one of the first policemen to arrive at the scene of the massacre at Kingsmills. He explained to me how it had been raining on that fateful night and how the blood ran down the side of the road. He told me, when he got home that night he had to wring the blood out of his trouser turn-ups onto the floor. However, in response to the murders in South Armagh, which was now being dubbed, 'Bandit Country', the Labour Government sent in extra troops and, for the first time in Northern Ireland, the Special Air Service was officially deployed. Bessbrook became the main operational base for the army in South Armagh and the village has, over the years, virtually become an armed garrison with the army headquarters in the now defunct linen mill.

As the New Year progressed, I was well into the routine of the Maze and my everyday duties were now becoming rather mundane. But my motivation was raised one day when I was detailed to the cellblock. The only solid brick building in the complex, the cellblock was designed to hold prisoners who were charged under the code of discipline. It was a prison within a prison, with specially reinforced concrete bars on the windows and the walls; the floor and roof were solid concrete too. Every conceivable security device that could be fitted was fitted. There were pairs of fail-safe entrance grilles that could only be unlocked one at a time, and the block was inside a miniature compound. The cellblock was totally self-contained, and when the prisoners were admitted, they were held there until they had completed the sentence awarded by the governor, under the code of discipline. That day's experience in the cellblock turned out to be valuable, as it was a precursor to many years in the H Blocks, which had a similar structure and environment.

One day I was detailed evening duty in Phase five and was patrolling along the front of the compounds, when the phase PO arrived. His name was Dessie Irvine, and he walked along with me as we talked about the events that happened over the years. Among the stories he related to me about the jail which remain in my mind and seemed at the time to be a warning of things to come, was a mass escape from the compounds which occurred just over a year before, in November 1974. Thirty-three IRA prisoners escaped through a tunnel, but were recaptured at the perimeter fence when they were challenged by an army patrol. When one refused to stop, he was shot dead by a squaddie. As we walked along together, he was like an acknowledged estate agent, pointing out the various compounds and describing some of their inhabitants and the crimes-which were their call to fame-that caused them to be locked up in the Maze. But he was also good with advice, in putting me wise to the possible pitfalls of the job.

But one escape that I will not forget took place about six months later. I was night guard in Phase six on Tuesday the 4th May 1976. The following morning, when the compound staff reported for duty and the headcounts were carried out in the phase, the numbers were returned correct and I got the order to stand down. I left the phase and was walking towards the guardroom when suddenly an urgent message came over the R. T: "All night guard staff to report to Compound five immediately!" Compound five was the most southerly compound in the prison and was backed by a sterile area and a twenty-foot high fence before the perimeter wall. Members of the Irish Republican Socialist Party (IRSP), a splinter group from the IRA, occupied the compound. When I was walking through one of the segment gates, I saw one of the men I had gone through training college with. He was the gate officer, and I asked him what was wrong. He told me there had been an escape from Compound five and about nine or ten cons had got away. I could not believe it, because I knew the compounds were searched regularly; in fact Compound five had been searched only a short time before. When I arrived at the compound, I joined about fifty other staff who were lined around the inside of the fence, facing towards the huts. One of the officers told me that nine prisoners had escaped after crawling along a tunnel. They had cut their way through the security fence and scaled the perimeter wall. He said, "The tunnel starts in that hut; go on in and have a look."

When I walked into the hut, I could not believe my eyes. There was a large mound of soil piled on the floor beside a trapdoor. The trapdoor had been made with a piece of plywood, two-foot square and had four plastic floor tiles stuck to it. The hole in the floor obviously had been there for some time, because it led into a forty-foot long tunnel. In order to identify the nine that got away, we started to move all the prisoners who were left into an empty hut, identifying each one with the photograph in his security book. At the same time the security PO ordered one of the physical training instructors to go down the tunnel and crawl along to the end, to find the line it had taken. I watched with amazement as the PTI jumped into the hole; his head disappeared below floor level and he vanished into the tunnel. When he got to the wall, he discovered a rope made from sheets and blankets tied together, and a hook at one end made from a tubular chair.

When the security department established the inquiry into the escape, it was the general consensus that the prisoners had been working at the tunnel for some time. They firstly had made the trapdoor and then dug through the concrete floor. As they would not have taken the risk of digging during the day, all the work would have taken place at night. The rubble that was dug out each night was placed back in the tunnel before daybreak and the hut brushed and cleaned, so that there was no evidence of anything untoward taking place in the hut. This laborious work was carried on for weeks until they had achieved their objective. A serious failure in security, which must have assisted in the escape, was that an old tunnel, that had been discovered a few years earlier, had been filled in with concrete beyond the compound fence. The new tunnel was dug in a line until it met the old tunnel at the end of the concrete, and from that point they used the remainder of the old tunnel, which took them to the wall. Immediately after the escape, police started a search for the jail-breakers and one man was recaptured, when he was found hiding in long grass near the Sprucefield roundabout close to the M 1. Motorway.

It was the last successful escape to take place from the compounds, although many other unsuccessful attempts were made. One was five years later, in 1981. It took place at the northern end of the prison at a segment wall gate, known as the north gate. It was the gate that divided Phase five from Phase six and acted as a buffer zone between the two factions. It was in the early hours of the morning when a dog-handler who was on night guard was on his way to relieve a colleague. As he went through the gate into an area of waste ground, he let the Alsatian off its lead and the dog dashed forward, then stopped, in a pointing pose, looking in the direction of some long grass. The handler walked slowly forward to investigate, and suddenly two men stood up, raised their hands in the air and said, "OK we give up!" The handler put in an 'urgent message' call on his radio to the ECR, and immediately the general alarm was sounded. Extra staff moved into the area and the would-be escapees were taken into custody and removed to the cellblock. The prisoners had got out of Compound ten and a party of officers was dispatched to search the compound.

They found that the two got out by cutting a hole in the fence at the back of the compound, which led into the football field. In all they had cut their way through seven fences, which only left them the interior and then the perimeter wall. When the search team went into the compound, they found all the prisoners were fully clothed. Some had their faces blackened with boot polish and they were all soaking wet. There was a raging storm with heavy rain at the time, which indicated they were all out of their huts and ready to follow their two leaders. Later when the security department began to piece all the evidence together, they came to the conclusion that the two men were the cutters and the advance party, and once they had cut their way out, the others would follow. The two had in their possession, ropes made from strips of blanket woven together and knotted about a foot apart. Home-made bolt cutters were found in the grass nearby; they were two pieces of metal, bolted together and shaped, making them very effective for cutting the wire fencing. They had several layers of clothing on them, some of which would apparently be used to cover the 'S' wire on top of the wall. Razor blades were sewn into the sleeves of their jackets to act as lances if guard dogs had attacked them. This final break for freedom ended with the perpetrators being charged with attempting to escape from lawful custody. After being sentenced they were moved to the blocks.

On the 7th February 1974 the Prime Minister, Mr Edward Heath, called a general election, to be held two weeks later on the 21 st. On the mainland the main election issues were the miners' strike, inflation and the rising cost of living. When the vote was counted, a minority Labour government was formed, and on the 5th March, Mr Merlyn Rees became the new Secretary of State for Northern Ireland. The new government was set on ending special category status in the Province and established a committee, chaired by Lord Gardiner, to report on the problem. In early 1975 the Gardiner report was published and recommended that internment without trial should be ended at the earliest practical opportunity. The report stressed that it should be made absolutely clear that there would be no amnesty for the internees.

On the 9th July, in the House of Commons, Mr Rees announced the gradual phasing out of internment. On the 4th November he announced that special category status, termed by the IRA as political status, would be ended and would not be accorded to anyone convicted of terrorist-related crimes committed after the 1 st March 1976. The announcement caused protests from both loyalists and republicans but, within a little over a month, on the 5th December the last detainees were released, which brought to an end detention without trial in Northern Ireland. From August 1971 when internment first started, 1,981 people were detained in Long Kesh; 107 of these were loyalists and the rest republicans.

Since I arrived in the Maze, I noticed that major building work was going on outside the perimeter wall of the prison, on the old airfield. It was something that did not attract much attention within the prison, but one day I asked an officer what they were building. "Two H. Blocks," he said. "Cellular-type prisons, for all the sentenced committals after the 1st March." Little did I imagine at the time, but before my career in the prison service would be over I would know all about the H Blocks.

The command structure in the Maze was a Number 1 governor, his deputy, and about eight assistant governors, who included a security governor, a personnel governor, phase governors and their relief. The governor grades were responsible for the administration, logistics and the day-to-day running of the prison. There were four other chief officers apart from the Number 1 Chief Officer, and they were responsible for the discipline of the prison staff. Principal Officers came next, and below them were the Senior Officers. The whole command structure seemed to be top heavy with managerial and supervisory ranks. To me, all the senior ranks were the same. I could have taken them or I could have left them alone. The sudden outbreak of trouble in Northern Ireland meant the instant advancement in rank of some men who only saw it as a greater opportunity to play to the gallery. Their own importance far outreached their capabilities. However, there was one exception-the No I Governor. He was a quiet, scholarly man who had gained the highest regard of everyone in the prison, prison officer and prisoner alike. He had a neat, methodical mind and the will to impose order even in the midst of chaos. I often thought he was unaware of the awe in which the staff held him. But he also had a remarkable gift for knocking people off balance. Sometimes when he was doing his rounds in the phases with the chief officer, he would suddenly stop, walk over and ask, "How many prisoners have you in there, officer?" At which I would have to do a quick bit of mental arithmetic.

The one duty in the Maze that I found difficult to cope with at times was night guard. The winter of 1975-76 was particularly cold, with hard frosts that caused dense fog to engulf the compounds during the night. It was often said that there were so many steel gates and fences in the jail, that the temperature was a few degrees colder than anywhere else in the country. However, whatever caused it, the cold was almost unbearable at times. The lack of exercise, or the fact that the body's resistance is at its lowest in the early hours, may also have had something to do with it. Sometimes when I got home after a night guard, I would tell Delta that I was going to pack the job in, because of the cold. This would immediately cause a squabble that would calm down after a warm breakfast. Her gentle but perceptive nature had learned to appreciate my soft interior, as she would sometimes show when we were having a difference of opinion about some family matter, by exclaiming: "Look! You're not in the Maze now, you know!" A melting smile would indicate my total submission to her authoritative status in our house.

Sometimes the loneliness and monotony on night guard was as hard to stick as the cold, especially if I was on static post and there was no one to talk to. One night I was on such a post at the republican compounds in Phase five. It was in the early hours and I was feeling rather tired, when suddenly I heard the wall gate being opened. As I started to walk towards the gate, a tall figure in uniform, wreathed in a halo of swirling fog stepped out, and started to walk towards me. As he got closer, I recognised him. It was the night guard Senior Officer and it was the first time I had met him, although I had seen him in the guardroom earlier that evening when I was coming on duty. His name was Pat

Kerr and he was about six-foot tall, well-built and immaculately dressed even in his greatcoat. "Goodnight," he said. "Goodnight Sir," I replied, coming to attention as a mark of respect for his rank. "All quiet?" He asked with a slight smile. "As quiet as a teddybear's picnic," I replied as he gave a slight laugh and said, "That's good." We walked along the phase, at the front of the five compounds, and talked quietly in general conversation. We turned at Compound nine and walked back to the wall gate, where he wished me "Good night," and let himself through the gate back into the admin again. It did not seem much at the time, but it was the beginning of a long friendship. I was left on my own again with nothing but the swirling fog as company until the arrival of the welcome daybreak, when the roar of a helicopter only broke the nightlong silence in the early morning.

The chopper with photo-reconnaissance cameras on board, fitted with infra-red heat-seeking equipment, would streak the prison in an attempt to pick up body heat to identify prisoners digging tunnels. The efforts of the army helicopter crews were not always successful, as the digging of tunnels seemed to be a covert pastime for the prisoners in the compounds. One day the prisoners in Compound eight had been moved to another compound, to allow renovation work to be carried out. A digger was brought in by the contractors to lift some heavy equipment. As it was being driven along the side of the compound, suddenly the ground subsided and the digger rolled over onto its side. On investigation it was discovered that the vehicle had driven over a disused tunnel that had been abandoned when the prisoners were suddenly forced to vacate the compound. It was a long-standing joke among the staff in the Maze that there were so many tunnels in the jail that someday there would be a loud rumble and the whole prison would drop about three feet into a hole.

The duty of pre-night guard was from 8 am until 12 noon, which allowed the staff to go home and get some rest before taking up their duty that night. Each morning the pre-night guard staff was formed into a search team, who would converge on a compound and carry out a search without the prisoners being aware that anything was going to take place. When the search team would enter a compound, the prisoners would stare at us with taut expressions. The conveyed message was clear-we were not wanted and their dislike towards us was obvious. But I have to say the sentiment was mutual.

The search was for any kind of contraband articles, or anything that could be used in an escape attempt. But the main find was generally illicit alcohol, or 'hooch'. The boiling and fermentation of fruit and some other ingredients, along with yeast and sugar, brewed this. After the concoction had fermented for a given time, it was poured into disused milk cartons and hidden in the huts. Sometimes a sheet of corrugated iron was removed from the inside wall of the hut and the cartons of hooch stacked into the wall-cavity and then the sheet replaced. The only problem, from their point of view, was the offensive smell. There were times when we searched a compound and as soon as we walked into a hut; the stink of over-seasoned hooch would have lifted the cap off your head. So it was only a matter of following the smell to its strongest. Their spirits were kept high on the manufacture and drinking of the stuff, but the excitement of trying to outwit the 'screws' probably gave them a buzz as well.

When a find of the illicit cocktail was made, the cartons were stacked onto a trolley, taken out of the phase and emptied down the nearest drain. When the trolley was being pulled out of the compound, we would come under a barrage of hostile shouts.

"Hi, mister, don't drink all that at once, it'll make you go blind!"
"Them screws are stealing our hooch!"
"We know ya!"

The insulting comments were endless. Sometimes the remarks were menacing, when there would be a shout:-

"Ask that screw why his neighbours are flitting!"

These comments would come out of a crowd and it would be impossible to identify the culprit. More sinister finds, like wooden gun replicas, were made from time to time. Automatic pistols, revolvers and rifles, and even army battledress uniforms made from overalls, dyed in green and brown blotches to give a camouflage effect, were also found. Occasionally cameras were found and when the film was removed and developed, to the surprise of some of the compound staff they had been covertly photographed.

One day I was detailed discipline officer to the prison cookhouse, which was an enlightening experience as it was the first time I saw the working of this important part of the prison. All the food for the prisoners in the jail was prepared and cooked in the cookhouse and, considering the numbers involved, it was no small operation. I reported to the cookhouse at 7.30 am and was told to go and collect the work party from Compound 15. The compound contained young prisoners (YPs), who were between 16 and 21 years of age and were sentenced for stealing cars, joyriding, assault, aggravated burglary and crimes of that nature. When the compound staff took up duty at 7.30 and unlocked the huts, the inmates attended to their ablutions, washed and dressed themselves in their grey denim uniforms, before tidying up their dormitories. After breakfast they got ready to go out to work and at 8.15 they paraded in the exercise yard, to be inspected by the compound P.O. before being permitted to leave the compound. When the inspection was over, the class officer took the security books and called each prisoner out by his name. As he did so, he handed me the security book for that inmate, and I checked the photograph with each one as they fell into pairs ready to walk to the cookhouse. There were 14 prisoners and when all was ready, I called out "OK" to the gate officer, who opened the gate, and the seven pairs filed out, with me at the back, carrying an armful of security books. The gate officer radioed the compound numbers change to the ECR, and we walked the four hundred yards to the cookhouse.

On arrival every prisoner knew his task and made his way to his workplace. I filled in the details in the security books and left them in the PO's office, before walking out to what would be my duty post for the rest of the day. As discipline (Uniformed) officer, it was my job to supervise the YPs at their work and generally observe their behaviour in the kitchen. It was a modern kitchen, recently built to replace the cookhouse, which had been burned down in the riots a year and-a-half earlier. Three large, stainless-steel boilers were used to boil potatoes and vegetables. A row of ovens and deep-fat fryers ensured that all meat portions were cooked to a very high standard. At one end of the kitchen there was a long bench, used to prepare all the vegetables, after they had gone through a mechanical rotating wash. The produce was then sliced and chopped, before it was put into the boilers. When the contents began to simmer, a YP would stir the ingredients with a long, wooden ladle with a flat end that made it look like an oar. At the other end of the cookhouse a steam-cleaning machine was used to scald the aluminium containers and trays. The box-like containers, into which the trays of food were placed, were known as 'Dixies', or sometimes nicknamed 'hayboxes'; they were made with a double-skinned vacuum to hold the heat and used to convey the meals to the compounds.

When the food was cooked, it was placed in the trays and slid into the Dixies, which had been pre-heated, and then the door was closed and sealed. Round, doubled-skinned tubs of the same vacuum principle were used to convey the mashed potatoes and vegetables, and when all was ready, the meals were loaded onto a Bedford truck, and delivered to the compounds in each phase. The lunch meal had scarcely left the kitchen when the whole process started again, in preparation for the evening meal. With it went a container of dry rations, cornflakes, bread, butter, tea and sugar, for each compound. This was for the inmates, who prepared their own breakfast in the mornings. The PO and staff who ran the kitchen were all chefs. They were ex-servicemen, who had learned their trade in the forces. The YPs carried out the more menial tasks in the kitchen, cleaning the floors, containers and equipment. All the produce and supplies for the kitchen were delivered to a loading bay, which was situated outside the prison, near the army camp. All deliveries had to be searched before they were loaded onto a prison van and brought into the cookhouse.

When the tea meal was delivered to the compounds, the lorry driver and his mate, who were both prison officers, collected the empty lunch containers and returned them to the kitchen. The final task of the day for the YPs was to place the empty containers on a conveyor belt that brought them through the steam cleaner. Then they were set out to dry in preparation for the following morning, when the whole series of operations would start again. As I marched the work party back to Compound 15 that evening, I was content that I had served another interesting day in the Maze, although I was glad to see my first day's duty in the prison cookhouse over.

I was back in Compound 15 a couple of weeks later. It was on the 31st July, and I was detailed a long day in the compound. It was a Saturday, and as I made my way in for 7.30 start, I was looking forward to working with the young prisoners again. The daily shortfall of compound staff, because of men being on leave or rest days, resulted in two general duty officers being detailed to the compound each day. When the compound was unlocked, the prisoners were counted and the numbers returned. When we got the 'Unlock', the huts were opened and the daily routine started, the ablutions, breakfast and parade for the PO's inspection of all work parties before they left the compound. There was the normal dozen or so who went to the prison kitchen, as well as cleaning parties that consisted of only two or three YPs whose task it was to sweep around the phases and gather up all loose papers and rubbish. The afternoon was much the same, and when the inmates left the compound to go to their various places of work, we sat down in the office for a short break. One of the staff switched on a transistor radio to listen to the football results, when suddenly the programme was interrupted with a 'news flash!' A policeman had been shot dead in Lurgan, where he had been manning a security barrier leading into the town centre. As the news flash ended, I was anxious to hear the name of the policeman, as I knew I would probably have known the man.

I was devastated later that evening when I heard who the murdered policeman was. He was Tommy Cush, my old friend whom I had first met when I joined the B Men, 20 years ago, and was so kind and helpful to me with advice. Tommy was on duty at a permanent checkpoint in Church Place about 12.50pm, when a single shot was fired from a high-powered rifle and he was struck in the chest by a bullet. He fell bleeding to the ground, where colleagues administered first aid to him. The area was crowded with shoppers, and Tommy and his policewoman colleague had been on duty at the checkpoint for some time when the killer struck. The woman constable was badly shaken, but escaped injury in the attack. Immediately after the shooting, soldiers and police cordoned off the area and began a search for the gunman.

Tommy, who was rushed to Craigavon Area Hospital, was found to be dead on arrival. The IRA sniper had fired from the remains of a derelict public house about 80 yards away from the scene. Two men were seen running away from the area shortly after the shooting. A married man with two of a family, Tommy was also an uncle of the famous Northern Ireland International footballer, Wilbur Cush. He was the ninth full-time policeman to be murdered by the IRA in Northern Ireland in 1976, and the tenth policeman to be assassinated in the Lurgan area since the troubles began. At the time, the murder rate among members of the RUC in Lurgan was the highest than in any other town in the Province, and only four years earlier, Lurgan police station had been totally destroyed in a bomb attack. Once again the single shot assassin had delivered a shattering blow to the peace of the town.

The major riot and burning of the compounds that took place in October 1974 had overwhelmed the prison staff in the Maze, and resulted in army riot squads being deployed to regain control of the prison. This resulted in IRA claims that army interference in the prison illustrated that the IRA prisoners were not criminals, but a military force, held in a prisoner-of-war camp. As a result the Prison Department took the decision that any future disorder in the Maze would be dealt with by the prison service, with the army as back-up, only to be used in the event of an emergency, even if this meant reinforcements of prison staff being brought in from other prisons in the Province.

In early September 1976, a minor event occurred in Phase 6, which developed into a major incident. The problem started when one compound was searched and a number of potential weapons found. The security department then took the decision that a major search should be mounted in all three compounds, numbers 16, 17 and 20. The prisoners refused to allow the search teams into the compounds and then armed themselves with everything and anything that would resemble a weapon, and a stand-off situation ensued. Reinforcements of prison staff were brought in from the Crum, Hydebank Wood Young Offenders Centre, Armagh Prison and some were flown in by helicopter from Magilligan. It was Friday the 10th September and I was detailed evening duty on the H Block gates. I reported for duty about 12.15pm as usual and expected it to be a normal dinner-guard duty, but when I arrived at the inner tally lodge, I was told to report to the trades hut beside segment gate one.

As I walked around the hut, I was amazed to see what appeared to be hundreds of prison officers, standing in riot gear. A PO I had never seen before asked me my name, marked it off a sheet and said, "Go to that hut and get yourself togged up in riot gear, then report to the PO in charge of that far group." I did what he said and walked down to the third group. All the men were lined up in three sections and I took my place in one of the lines. We waited until all the evening duty staff were present, but we still didn't know what was going on. It was not until the whole parade started to walk forward that I realised the three different groups were splitting up and heading for three different segment gates that led into Phase six. The section I was in walked in a straight line, one behind the other, to a segment gate behind the republican compounds in Phase five. As we did so, the IRA prisoners came out of their huts and watched with amazement the large numbers of prison officers who were walking past their compounds. When each section was assembled at their pre-arranged point, a radio signal was given from the ECR, the three segment gates opened at the same time and the staff walked into the phase, one group being assigned to each of the three compounds which was systematically searched. It was the first such operation I was ever in since I had joined the service, and the last major incident to occur in the compound Maze. It rained throughout the afternoon, which made it all the more depressing. The IRA complained later that the large numbers of prison staff were soldiers dressed up in prison officers' uniforms - an absurd suggestion, the stupidity of which was proven within the following few years, as the H Block phases were built and occupied with greater numbers of staff.

The H Block gates were in the perimeter wall on the southern side of Phase one, which linked the compound prison to the two H Blocks, and each time a new H Block phase was constructed, the perimeter wall was extended to encompass the new buildings. External watchtowers were erected on each section of the wall and manned by soldiers of the Maze guard force, who monitored the security in that particular area. The soldiers were nicknamed 'Squaddies' by the prison officers, most of whom had been in the army, prior to joining the service. In fact some soldiers who were married and living in Northern Ireland when their military service ended simply transferred into the prison service. The H Block link gates were manned to allow staff accessibility to the two Blocks.

The exchange of duties between staff was not usually permitted, but one swap that was allowed was the association part. That was the period from 5.30 pm until lock-up, and allowed an officer to have an evening off, provided his colleague would stand in for him. It was an acceptable practice, and only required the two officers to verify the swap by signing an association exchange book. One day a friend asked me to work his association for him because he wanted to go home. I agreed, and after we had signed the association book, I checked the detail and discovered that the duty was in H Block 2, which was rather surprising as there were no prisoners in that block. But I knew some staff were detailed each day as a fireguard precaution. I arrived in the block about a quarter past five, and was posted to 'C' and 'D' grille, which were on the right hand side of the central (circle) area. It was an airlock grille system between 'c' wing and 'D' wing, and at the entrance to each wing, there was an inner grille also manned by a prison officer. As the grille officer, it was my duty to monitor all movement of prisoners in and out of the wings, as well as being the contact officer between the wings staff and the PO in the circle.

It was the first time I had ever been in an H Block and it certainly was a new experience. The H Block staff were nicknamed 'Super Screws' by the compound staff, and I thought I must be privileged to be joining them, even if it was only for one association. The whole place smelt of fresh paint, the black asphalt floor was shining as if it had been recently polished, and the wings had the sterility of a hospital ward. I was not long on post when the association staff came in from the circle and four officers went down 'C' wing and the same number went down 'D' wing. One of the officers in 'D' wing came to the grille and told me that the YPs from Compound 15 were being moved into the Block and being admitted to 'D' wing. About a half an hour later the Young Prisoners started to arrive in the Block. They were transferred in a minibus ten at a time, and all their personal belongings were conveyed to the Block on the kitchen lorry, which had been commandeered for the purpose.

As the PO checked each inmate's identity against his security book, he was passed through the circle grille to me and I directed him into the wing. The process continued until all the YPs were in the wing, where they were counted and the numbers were returned to the circle. The wing class officer appointed two of the boys as dining hall orderlies, who were responsible for making the tea, and soon they were all seated in the dining hall, watching television and taking their supper of tea and scones. An observation window in the wall allowed me to see into the dining hall.

It was a long, rectangular room, lined with tables, with four chairs at each. At one end there was a stainless-steel sink unit against the wall, and to the side there was a stainless-steel hotplate with sliding doors, behind which the two orderlies served the tea and scones. A boiler sat on a stand in the corner, supplying the hot water for the tea. Each inmate was issued with a plastic knife, fork and spoon and a plastic mug and plate. At about 8.45pm the night guard staff came on duty, and at 9 o'clock the PO called, "Lock Up!" All the prisoners were locked in their cells, and when counted by the night guard staff, the numbers were returned to the circle, where the PO phoned them to the ECR. When all the numbers in the prison were returned and found to be correct, we got the word, "Day staff stand down!" As we all walked towards the tally lodge, I couldn't help thinking that I had just finished my first stint of duty in one of the famous H Blocks, and had seen the first prisoners admitted to the new cellular prison Maze.

A few weeks later H Block One was opened and made ready for prisoner occupation. The PO, who had previously been the security Principal Officer in the compounds, was assigned to be in charge of the new Block and he set about selecting his team. As more and more prisoners were admitted to H 2, and then HI, so too did the staff numbers increase in the blocks. It was policy from the start that the new prison would be run by the Northern Ireland staff and the detached staff would only be deployed in the compounds. The obvious intention being, that as numbers would decrease, so too would the numbers of detached staff and eventually the prison would be in the charge of Ulster staff only. However, many of the mainland staff transferred to the Ulster service and have settled here. They were fondly called nationalised Ulstermen by the local staff, and were integrated into all ranks in the service.

The 15th September saw the first prisoner committed to the Maze convicted of a terrorist crime after the 1 st March deadline, and not accorded special category status. His name was Kieran Nugent, and when he arrived in reception, he was documented and handed a suit of the grey, denim uniform, worn by convicted prisoners of all classes and creeds, who were convicted of all types of crimes. (Often referred to as 'Ordinary Decent Criminals' or 'ODCs,' to distinguish them from those convicted of terrorist crimes. He refused to wear the prison clothes by claiming he was a political prisoner and would only wear his own clothes. He was committed to HI, and when the prison van arrived at reception to take him to the Block, he wrapped the bath towel he had just been issued with around him to cover his nakedness. He was allocated a cell in 'C' wing, and one day when he was unlocked for his ablutions, he had discarded the towel and was wearing one of his cell blankets. This was the beginning of what became known as the 'blanket protest'.

A couple of days later I was on duty at the reception gate, when some block staff walked past on their way to H 1. The PO in charge of the Block was among them, and when he came level with me, he turned and walked over. "Mr McKane?" He asked. "Yes, Sir," I replied as I brought my feet together as a mark of respect. He looked me in the eye and said, "I'm picking men for the Block and I would like you to join us." I said, "Yes Sir," wondering what exactly I had agreed to. As he turned to walk away, he said, "I'll speak to the duty office about it, so you can watch the detail and I'll talk to you later!" He walked away at a quick pace to join the rest of his men. I was surprised with the encounter, because although I had seen him from time to time, we had scarcely spoken before, and I wondered why he had picked me to serve in the Block. But at the same time I looked forward to the prospect of joining the 'Super Screw brigade' in H 1. The two Blocks had now been designated a separate prison from the compounds and were called 'The Maze Cellular'.

Chapter 10

The duty roster always appeared a few days in advance of the day on which the duty was to be performed, and I watched with anticipation for my name on the H Block 1 list. Finally the duty went up, and 1 was detailed 8 am start in H I on the 19th October. I arrived at the Block gate a few minutes before 8 o'clock, and waited while the gate officer, who was sitting in a small wooden hut inside the airlock, opened the pedestrian gate and let me in. As he opened the gate, I stepped into the airlock and he asked, "What's your name, officer?" His tone was abrupt and probably designed to make me feel that I had just trod on hallowed ground. He made me think all the banter about 'Super Screw' had gone to his head. Certainly he moved in a higher orbit than the rest of us. As he locked the gate behind me, I told him my name; we walked across the airlock, he opened the inner gate, and I walked through without another word.

I walked the length of the front courtyard, with a wing of cells on each side, to the front door and opened it. An officer stood in the hall, and as he opened the grille, I stepped in and he locked it behind me. 1 was between two grilles and had to wait for a few minutes for the circle officer, who was busy opening another grille. I glanced across the circle and could see the PO at his office desk, on the opposite side. As the grille opened, 1 stepped into the oblong-shaped central area, or 'circle' as the staff called it. There was a grille on each of the four sides, and seven doors with nameplates that displayed their function. On the wall beside the grille to my left, were the letters 'A' and 'B', and beside the grille to my right were 'C' and' D', and a grille on the opposite side of the circle, gave access to the Block stores. The door signs showed 'Ladies,' 'Gents,' 'Medical room,' 'POs office,' 'Welfare room,' 'The Governor's office' and the 'Communications room.'

The PO walked briskly out of his office and smiled as he met me. He was in shirtsleeve order, as were all the staff in the Block. The place was centrally heated, which was a pleasant change from the cold, autumn morning outside. He told me I would be on general duties in the Block for a few days until I got into the 'swing' of the place. He introduced me to an officer called John, who said he would take me around the Block and explain the layout and the routine. As we left the Block and walked down the courtyard, I thought my first encounter with the PO had gone rather well. He was a loud man who didn't encourage small talk, but I knew I was going to get on well with him. I followed John as he walked up to a large side gate and stopped. Taking a bunch of keys from the key-pocket in his trousers, he started to explain the function of the different keys and what he was going to do with them. He opened a gate that led into a sterile airlock, then another gate that brought us into 'D' wing exercise yard. As we walked the length of the exercise yard, he opened another two gates which led into another sterile airlock and then another exercise yard. As we walked along, he explained the day-to-day operation of the Block, in what seemed to me a very clear and rehearsed patter, like an enthusiastic salesman who was carried away with his new surroundings.

"The H Block is so called because it is built in the shape of an H, with four wings forming the two uprights. Each wing holds 25 cells and each cell is intended to house one inmate only, but two can be accommodated without great discomfort, thus some wings have 30 prisoners. Each wing has its own dining room, exercise yard and hobbies room where the inmates can engage in hobbies, like making children's toys, woodwork or other similar pastime occupations. The central bar of the H contains a communications room, staff offices, medical treatment room and stores." The incessant patter continued.

"Prison officers control steel grilles which regulate movement into and around the Block and the central administrative area, or 'circle' as we call it, has a communications room known as the Block control room. The control room provides constant contact with the Emergency Control Room (ECR). The Block gate is manned by an officer who remains between the gates, inside the airlock."

As we proceeded, we tested the Block's alarm system. This was a procedure that was done every morning and was almost a ritual. A number of alarm buttons were placed at strategic observation points in the sterile areas of the exercise yards, close to where an officer would be standing. Every single alarm button was pulled, which caused it to be registered on a panel in the Block control room, as well as in the ECR. Simultaneously the same process was being carried out by the wing staff, the object being that all the alarms in the Block were tested to ensure that they were all in working order before the prisoners were allowed out into the exercise yards.

Before I knew it, we were back in the courtyard at the front of the Block and John's tour of instruction had brought us back to where we started. It was all very interesting, but I already knew most of what he told me, and I have to say I was very impressed with the place, particularly with the security. The blocks were state-of-the-art as far as security was concerned.

Rumours had it, that when the two Blocks were built and the Governor was inspecting them before he received them on behalf of the Prison Department, he viewed the security precautions that had been adopted, and said, "There will never be an escape out of this prison!" Given the enterprising quality of the prison population in the Maze, I for one would never have made such a statement.

For the first few days I was detailed 'standby'. This effectively meant relieving officers inside the block for tea breaks and generally I was on call if needed. I served my first night guard on the Sunday night and I have to admit, it was a much more agreeable duty than I had previously experienced in the compounds. When the bitter cold was enough to try the patience of Job and on nights when the fog was so dense, the watchtowers were stood down and the tower officers were ordered to take up ground patrol duties instead, as it was impossible to see the bottom of the tower.

Five officers made up the block night guard team, and after lock-up when the day staff were stood down, the block became quiet and peaceful. The night duties rotated so that we were detailed a night guard stag once a week, which meant I became good friends with my four night guard colleagues. Each member of the group would take it in turn to cook a meal in the early part of the night. We called the supply of the ingredients for the meal the 'syndicate,' or 'syndie' for short, and the light-hearted banter that accompanied the cooking of the meal was almost a ritual and was probably designed more to relieve the boredom than to satisfy the hunger.

But when on night duty in the Maze, like any other prison the most important part of the task was the observation and monitoring of all prisoners in one's charge. This was done by head-counts that were carried out at irregular intervals.

I was on evening duty on the Tuesday and was dinner guard on 'A' and 'B' grille. The two wings were now occupied by conforming prisoners, who eventually made up the large majority of the prison population in the Maze. These inmates wore the denim uniform and complied with the prison rules. They were from all backgrounds, and just wanted to get on with their lives, do their time and get out. The protesting blanket prisoners were in 'C' wing, and 'D' wing was also a conforming wing. The block was always quiet after lunchtime, when all the prisoners were locked in their cells. I heard the jingle of keys and looked up to see the circle officer opening the 'C' and 'D' grille. One of the protesting prisoners walked out into the circle and went into the medical room. Although I had heard about them, it was the first time I had seen one of the dissidents. He was stark naked from head to foot, except for the blanket he had wrapped round his waist. As he disappeared into the medical room, I asked the circle officer,

"Hi Dennis, who's the con in the blanket?"
That's a streaker!"
"What do you mean, a streaker?"
"He's one of those provies who are on protest."

It was the first time I had heard the word 'streaker' mentioned in the context of the Maze. Streaking was much in the headlines at the time. It was a craze, which had originated in the States, particularly among students on University campuses. They would cast off all their clothes and run a gauntlet between two rows of screaming fellow students, in a humorous and defiant gesture. I thought it was comical to draw a comparison between the students and the protesting IRA men.

The construction of the H Blocks continued with the opening of Phase 2, which included H Blocks 6, H7 and H8. A few months later another segment gate was opened permanently, giving access to Phase 3, which included H Blocks 3, H4 and H5. There were now 8 H Blocks in the Maze complex, all of which were built with maximum security as an imperative and each block effectively a prison within a prison, surrounded by a 16 foot high mesh wire fence with corrugated iron sheeting half way up. Each block cost £ 1 million to construct. But in addition there was a whole new administrative area, a modern kitchen and hospital, education block, trades department and everything that went to make up a modern, well-equipped prison. In other parts of the complex there were two outside, all-weather football pitches that had a solid, underlying foundation and were covered with stone-dust.

The largest building in the prison complex was a vast indoor sports hall and gymnasium that was equipped with the latest sports equipment and was under the charge of a Principal Officer, a Senior Officer and four members of staff, all of whom were fully qualified physical training instructors.

The prison hospital was constructed in the design of half an H Block, with a wing on either side of the circle area. The wing to the left of the circle was the South wing and had nine wards, eight of which were single rooms which were self-contained with toilets, wash-basins etc. The ninth room was a domlitory with six beds. All the rooms had wooden doors, that were kept open during the day and were only locked during the night hours. There was a large dining room with a TV, a snooker table and other games, and at the end of the wing there was a bathroom, toilet and a sluice. The wing to the right of the circle was the North wing, an administrative wing that contained a fully equipped x-ray unit, a doctor's surgery and treatment room, and a grilled-off pharmacy where all the medicines and drugs were kept. The wing also contained offices and a patients' waiting room. At the bottom of each wing there was a yard grille, that gave access to the two exercise yards. The hospital was in the charge of a senior doctor who was known as 'The Senior Medical Officer', and The wards were staffed by prison officers who were qualified hospital officers and were under the control of a Hospital Chief Officer, a Principal Officer and a Senior Officer. A Hospital Officer was also in charge of the medical room in each of the H Blocks.

The education department was under the control of a full-time education officer, and a number of full-time teachers took study classes in the blocks, for YP's and the other conforming inmates. Some part-time teachers came into the prison to conduct evening classes and study lessons. Many of the prisoners availed themselves of the free, top-class further education prospectus that was available to them.

In Phase 3 a series of workshops were built, constructed in Nissen-type huts and segmented by high fences. These were much larger than the Nissen huts in the compounds and comprised of shops for motor maintenance, bricklaying, painting, plastering and joinery. There was also a prefabrication shop, where sectional sheds and huts were manufactured. There was even a concrete works, which made garden ornaments. It was intended that many prisoners would learn trades in the workshops and leave prison with a better prospect of providing for themselves and their families.

At the main gate a complete new tally lodge and movements control was constructed, and the perimeter wall around the whole prison was over two miles long. There were now 14 watchtowers on the outside, manned by the army, and 12 on the inside manned by prison officers. Outside the wall, a road ran around the entire prison complex and was patrolled by an army vehicle 24 hours a day. The eastern gate was set into the outer fence at the eastern side of the prison and led onto a public road, the Halftown Road, which runs from Lisburn to Hillsborough along the eastern boundary of the Maze. At night the orange glow from the long rows of dotted, geometrical lines of lights could be seen twenty miles away. And from the air, the symmetrical shapes resembled a giant dot-to-dot puzzle on the black landscape.

When the new prison was completed and functional, the Governor and the army Guard-Force Commander were having one of their frequent meetings to discuss security matters. The Governor happened to say he thought the Maze was now impregnable, and the army officer, seemingly taking the remark as a challenge, said that he would speak to his superior about the suggestion. A week later the soldier met the Governor again and asked him to observe an isolated section of the perimeter wall, through the closed-circuit TV monitors in the ECR, at a certain time one evening.

The Governor went to the ECR at the time stated, and observed the area of the wall as instructed. At precisely the synchronised time, an army truck appeared on the road and came to a stop at the pre-arranged spot. As the Governor watched with total disbelief a unit of soldiers jumped out of the truck, scaled the unscaleable wall and dropped into the sterile area between the wall and the inertia fence, re-scaled the wall, baled into the truck and took off at high speed. The whole operation took less than two minutes, and probably left the Governor wondering if he had just seen a mirage. This incident was recorded in the 'Reader's Digest,' December 1981 under the title, "Into action with The Special Air Service."

Over the following months more and more prisoners were committed to the Blocks, and it seemed as if an endless, clanking conveyor belt of society's misfits were passing through the place, most of whom had the prevailing spirit of indifference towards the prison staff and authority. Many of them were people who had progressed through Care Homes and Borstal, until they had finally attained the ultimate, the Maze Prison. Armed robbery was, to some of them, simply the evidence of their macho image. All the protesting republican prisoners were committed to the streaker wing, and the conforming inmates who included both loyalists and republicans - were placed in the other wings, which became known as the conforming wings.

The four wings in HI were now almost filled to capacity and another protest wing was opened in Phase 3. I worked mainly in the three conforming wings, and generally the prisoners who occupied them were not too difficult to get on with, or perhaps it would be more circumspect to say there was an air of mutual co-existence between them and the staff. However, there were some particularly young married men-who had received long sentences, and as the months and years passed them by, they became unstable.

There were a few who would suffer from deep depression and they would sit or lie in their cells, with the light on, for hours at a time. During these periods the staff would leave them alone and stay away until the mood had passed. Some of these same characters, at other times, were quite polite and well-mannered and, on being told to do something, would obey without a word of dissent. If you didn't know who some of them were, you would have thought they were well-bred men with impeccable decorum. They would speak to me with intense sincerity. But knowing who they were and the vicious crimes they had been found guilty of, filled me with foreboding.

It would have been very easy for an inexperienced officer to take their over-politeness as a sign of sincerity, or weakness. This would have been a very dangerous mistake. This type of inmate had to be approached with extreme caution and a great deal of forethought. A rude, inadvertent remark could spark a sudden and unexpected response, with the prisoner losing total control and lashing out with both fists in all directions, and having no thought for the consequences.

One morning I was on duty on 'A' and 'B' grille when one such incident occurred in 'B' wing. An officer unlocked the cell door of an inmate who had been suffering from deep paranoia. As soon as the door was opened, the prisoner charged out in a mad psychotic rage, grabbed the officer and sank his teeth into his forehead. It all happened so quickly that I didn't see anything until the officer, screaming with pain, struggled to free himself from the con's grasp. I immediately pulled the alarm button, as the officer staggered up the wing with his face covered in blood from the head wound.

We overpowered the prisoner, cuffed him and took him to the cellblock whilst at the same time the officer was rushed to the Lagan Valley Hospital. The attack was totally unjustified, as not a single word had passed between them, and the officer was a quiet, lightly built lad who caused no offence to anyone. From this early point in my career I decided to take things easy, when dealing with long-term prisoners and try not to get into confrontation with them. In all my service I didn't charge more than six inmates under the Code of Discipline. However, the Maze was a warrior society, where kindness was often seen as weakness, and my lack of zest was not always appreciated.

When I was on duty in the wings, I used to observe the behaviour of the prisoners. It was a practice that gave me a whole new perspective on life. I often thought how amazing it was that the mind tended to accept as normal, bizarre occurrences and events that became commonplace. But if the bizarre is commonplace, is it then normal? No! I should think not!

In each of the four dining halls in the block, a colour television sat on a shelf in the corner and, as it was rarely switched off, produced an unremitting din from the incessant range of the day's programmes. To some of the inmates the TV was their whole life. From unlock to lock-up they would watch everything and anything, all the trivial nonsense of a day's viewing, until year after year their passive entertainment would finally result in their total intellectual demise. Some of them, particularly the older ones, were given up as brain-dead.

Comparatively speaking, the average age of the inmates in the Maze was younger than in other prisons on the mainland, their crimes ranging from joyriding and burglary to murder, and the sentences ranged from three calendar months to life. But, by and large, the prison contained people found guilty of terrorist crimes, the large majority of whom were republicans who wanted nothing to do with the blanket protest and conformed to prison rules and regulations.

As one would expect of a large group of young men who were locked up together in a penal institution, there was not a great deal of respect for their keepers. Many considered themselves prisoners of war and saw themselves honour-bound to try to escape. They also felt it was incumbent upon them to exploit every opportunity to the full and make the establishment, as represented by the prison officer, to look as foolish as possible. This could be achieved in many ways and in many guises. But one exploit that was obviously enjoyed by the cons was 'phantom calling.' It was a practice engaged in by the prisoners, mainly at night after lock-up when the night guard was on duty. As an officer would be doing his hourly headcount, a prisoner from the far end of the wing would-using an assumed voice-shout some remark, so that its source could not be detected. I have to say that, after practice, some of the cons became artists at the performance. At times their shouts seemed to be a comical, but scornful expression of contempt for the plight they found themselves in, as the mystery voice would call out, "Hi mister, the joke's over, I want to go home!" During the night the head-counts were carried out by looking through the observation window in the cell door, and at the same time switching on the cell light. Sometimes when I was night guard and moving quietly from cell to cell counting the prisoners, the echo would reverberate down the wing, "Hi mister, are you an honorary member of the Nosey Parker's Club?" At times, just as I would get to the end of the wing, the mystery caller would suddenly cry out, "Hi mister, my mamm'll be looking for me. I want to go home!" It was a type of banter that was endless and the best way to deal with it was to ignore it because if they saw that an officer was allowing it to annoy him, they would immediately up-the-ante.

One joker discovered he could make a sharp trumpet sound by blowing down the leg of his tubular cell chair. This was achieved by removing the plastic tips from the end of two of the legs and blowing down one leg, in a single blast. After some practice he found it was put to best effect by placing the opposite chair leg to the crack at the side of the door. One single, long blast from the instrument would absolutely petrify you. Even the cons in the other cells were paralysed with fear. Some nights when I was night guard on the grille, the fanfare would start and in the quiet of the night it was terrifying. There would be one long blast, followed by two or three shorter and then total silence. As I would make a dash down the wing in an effort to catch the culprit, I lifted the flap covering the observation window and put on the light in each of about ten cells, at the bottom of the wing. I realised I was wasting my time because every con was comfortably in his bed and apparently sound asleep.

The elusive horn-blower became a topic of conversation among the staff in the block, as officers on the other night guard teams also became the target, of his prank. The reason he always seemed to elude capture was that he would only get up to his tricks on irregular nights and at different times on those occasions. One night when I was night guard with my four mates. When the day staff had left and the block was sealed, we sat down to a cup of tea and the conversation came round to the secret musician. After some discussion we decided to try to catch the prankster at his work. We switched off the landing lights in 'B' wing, which left the wing in total darkness, and one of the boys took off his boots, walked down the wing in his socks and stood quietly against the wall at the bottom. We all waited for some time in the silence that was only broken by the continuous sound of music from an inmate's radio in a cell at the top of the wing, near the grille. Someone had nodded off to sleep and left his transistor on.

Suddenly, there was a deafening shriek from the horn, and before he had the chance to blow a second blast, the officer was at the cell, lifted the flap, hit the light switch and shouted, "We've got you!" He was caught red-handed, with the leg of the chair up at his lips ready to give it a second blow. It was the end of that particular ruse. The officer prepared his report, and the following morning the prisoner was charged under the Code of Discipline with disturbing the peace of the prison and removed to the cell block. The episode resulted in an appreciable lowering of the tension in the wing, but such pranks were commonplace in the block. There was a constant supply of tales and mischievous tricks, that were used in a variety of situations as weapons against the staff and their authority. Perhaps it was all a countermeasure to distract the cons from the reality of their plight.

It was Christmas again and I was detailed night guard on the night before, which suited me well because it gave me an after guard on Christmas Day. When I got home in the morning, I had a few hours sleep that left me refreshed for the rest of the day. The year 1976 was at an end and there was little prospect of 1977 being any more peaceful.

In early January the prison service staff were issued with new uniforms.

They were navy with white shirts, that replaced the drab, black uniforms and blue shirts that had been the prison service apparel for over a hundred years. The supply of new uniforms inspired some unworthy comments from some senior members of staff, particularly about the white shirts that were handed out. They thought the white shirts made the basic grade officers look too superior for their work. It was all a bit adolescent for me. One of the individuals who made the remark was a man renowned for his powers of self-promotion. He treated his staff with arrogant disdain.

It was late on Saturday night the 5th February when I got the news of the murder of my good friend and former colleague, Bob Harrison, in an IRA ambush in Gilford. Another part-time Reserve Constable, whom I also knew very well, was seriously injured in the attack. The incident happened when the two Reservists were out on mobile patrol duty, in and around the town. At about 7.30 pm they received a radio call from the station that an anonymous telephone call had been received, claiming that incendiary devices had been planted in a drapery shop in the main street.

The two constables made contact with the key-holder of the shop and asked him to open the premises to allow them to search for the bombs. After searching the shop for about three quarters of an hour, the two men returned to the police car, where they radioed the station to report that nothing had been found and it must have been a hoax call. Suddenly, a car came up the street, travelling at speed. As it approached the police car, it slowed down and there was a burst of automatic rifle fire from the two passenger windows, on the near side of the vehicle. Bob Harrison died instantly, and although his fellow constable was shot in the left wrist and blown into the street with the impact, he courageously gathered himself, dashed to the car radio and put in an 'urgent' call for assistance. He was later rushed to Craigavon Area Hospital, where his left hand was amputated. The constable, like many other members of the Ulster security forces, is disabled for the rest of his life.

Bob was employed in the caring profession as a nurse in Banvale Special Care Hospital, and his assassination came as a heavy blow to the patients as well as the people in the town and district. Apart from this savagery, which had always been a marked feature of the IRA's tactics, there is little doubt but that their crimes were always a deliberate attempt to exasperate the security forces. In the hope of providing material for their propaganda campaign, which portrayed the perpetrators of some of the most sadistic murders as heroes and their crimes as honourable, patriotic actions.

Bob Harrison was one of nature's gentlemen. His murder was the second IRA atrocity in just over a year to plunge the small town into a state of despair. The murders of three local people took place only fourteen months earlier at a New Year's Eve bombing in a public house on the main street of the town.

The Central Bar was a well-known, licensed premises and a place I knew well when I was on the police in Gilford. The bombing - the most serious incident in the Province over the New Year 1975/76 - came shortly after 9.00 pm as the ground floor public bar and the upstairs lounge were crowded with customers celebrating the New Year. A customer in the public bar spotted a duffel bag in the hallway, but it exploded as he shouted a warning.

The blast tore through the building, killing two men and leaving twentyeight other customers injured, some of them seriously. A fleet of seven ambulances ferried the injured to Craigavon Area Hospital, six miles away.

Police were later checking reports that a car stolen in Banbridge, may have been used by the murderers. It was found abandoned in the town shortly after the blast. The two men who died at the scene were Mr William Scott and Mr Richard Beattie. The third victim was 30-year-old Mrs Sylvia McCullough, who died in hospital ten hours after the bombing. Mrs McCullough was the first terrorist victim of 1976.

The final act of the sectarian killings was enacted two days later when the funerals of the three victims took place and they were interred in Tullylish Parish Churchyard.

On Thursday the 24th February I was detailed circle officer, which was a 7.30 am start. It was a long day post, although the circle duty ended at 4.30pm when an evening duty officer took over the post. After a one-hour meal break I started association duty in one of the wings and was assistant class officer.

As circle officer I was literally on my feet and continually on the move all day, except when I was given a few minutes for a tea break. I had a long key, known as a 'Home Office Key', that opened the four grilles in the circle area, and I had to control all movement of staff and prisoners through the circle. Each morning the class officers in the wings took requests from the prisoners. That is, they took a list of names of those who wanted to see the Governor, doctor, or the welfare officer. No requests were taken to see the prison chaplains, as clergymen of the four main denominations had open passes, which authorised them to enter the prison at any time to see members of their congregations. So they visited the prison almost every day and had free access to the wings, where they could congregate with the inmates.

When the doctor arrived in the Block, sick parade was called and the inmates were allowed out to the circle, one at a time, to see the doctor in the medical room. The same process was put into practice when the Governor and the welfare officer arrived, and the prisoners were allowed access, one at a time, to the respective offices. These were the only times the prisoners were allowed out into the circle, except when they were going on visits. In that case, the procedure was the same as in the compounds and an escorting officer would arrive at the block to take the con on his visit. Before leaving the wing, the prisoner was given a rubdown search, and as he arrived at the circle grille, the escorting officer identified him before I opened the grille and let him into the circle. After letting the prisoner and his escort through the front grille, I changed the block numbers on the numbers board.

When the midday meal arrived at the block, the system was the same as it was in the compounds, the only difference being, instead of two officers on the truck, the driver had an orderly to help him with the food deliveries. The aluminum containers (Dixies and Hayboxes) were delivered from the prison kitchen in a Bedford two tonne truck. it was about 11.30 am each morning when the now familiar crashes and bangs of the metal meal containers being offloaded from the meals lorry could be heard throughout the block. No matter where you were, even the thick walls and doors couldn't do more than muffle the noise that reverberated around the block. However, the rumbling barrage was always accompanied by the appetizing smells of well cooked and obviously delicious, hot food.

The containers for 'A' and 'B' wings were stacked onto a four-wheeled barrow and pushed down the wings to the left; and the containers for 'C' and 'D' wings were put on a barrow and pushed down the wings to the right. The dining hall orderlies then carried the containers into the wings, and placed the trays onto the hot plate, where they remained for a few minutes before being served.

After lunchtime I heard some of the staff talking about a shooting incident that had taken place earlier in Lurgan. They said a policeman had been shot dead and some others were seriously injured, at the traffic control barrier in Church Place. But it was not until I got home that I heard who the policeman was. He was Harold Cobb, the policeman who I knew and looked up to, all those years ago. Harold had recently been promoted to Inspector and was on duty at the security barrier with two Reserve Constables.

They had opened the security barrier shortly after 8.30 am, to allow traffic into the town centre, and a number of vehicles had already entered before the gunmen struck. The IRA murder gang had lay in wait in a derelict cafe which was just 15 yards away from the barrier. From there, they ran up to the four policemen manning the checkpoint and opened fire with two, high-powered rifles. Harold and his two colleagues were caught by surprise in a hail of more than 30, high velocity bullets fired at close range. The Inspector died almost instantly and the two constables fell wounded in the stomach. The fourth constable escaped injury, but he was later taken to hospital suffering from shock. After the attack the gunmen made off on foot, through the derelict building to a car park at the back and presumably to the waiting getaway car.

Reinforcements were quickly on the scene and an ambulance rushed the wounded men to Craigavon Area Hospital, where they underwent emergency surgery. In a follow-up search of the Church Place area, the security forces found 'dozens of empty shells' and later forensic experts moved in to investigate further the murder scene. Harold was married with three children and he lived near Hillsborough in County Down. He was the eighth member of the RUC in Lurgan to be murdered on duty. The scene of the murder had also been the setting for previous assassinations. Only seven months earlier, my other good friend Tommy Cush had been killed while on duty at the very same spot and probably by the same death squad.

When Joanne became school age, she enrolled in Dickson Primary School in the Mourneview housing estate, which was the nearest school to where we lived. Delta walked her to and from school every day, which was a pleasant stroll for them as it took them over the elevated Monbrief playing fields that gave a panoramic view of the western side of the town. Delta told me that night how they were walking through the playing fields as normal, when they heard the burst of rifle fire from the direction of the town: "The sound was so clear in the winter air, but we didn't know what had happened until we heard Inspector Cobb had been murdered."

As the H Blocks in the Maze continued to fill up with prisoners who had been convicted of all kinds of crimes and came from all classes of society, one of the first things I learnt was not to judge them by their looks. Some of them, particularly those who had received long sentences, decided to adopt a fantasy persona, apparently to boost their own ego and increase their standing with their fellow prisoners. There was one inmate who had allowed his sentence to get the better of him and at first he was gripped with despair, but after a few weeks he started to come round. The other cons had nicknamed him 'Big Bat,' because he had a large bat tattooed on each forearm and smaller bats covered most of his body.

Tattooing in the Maze, like most other prisons, had become an acclaimed art by some of the inmates, who had acquired tiny bottles of Indian ink, smuggled into the jail. The instrument used for the operation was a pin that had been sterilized over a lighted match. The operation required the subject to sit still on a chair, whilst the tattooist dipped the pin in the ink and made a series of punctures on the skin, along the lines of a design that had been drawn with a biro pen. The amateurish result was known among the prison staff as a 'jail tattoo,' and only attained the letters 'HATE' on the fingers of one hand and the letters 'LOVE' on the fingers of the other hand. Sometimes the words 'Long Kesh 1977' underscored with a piece of barbed wire appeared on the upper arms of some of the cons. The name of the prison and the date he served in it was printed on his arm, apparently as a token of boastful pride that he had served time in the now famous jail. And when they got out of prison the tattoo was a status symbol in their own communities. Every time I see such an unprofessional tattoo, it is a dead give-away to the fact that the bearer is an ex-con, who has served a sentence in prison.

'Big Bat' liked the title because it made him feel important. He even tried to look like a bat, to the point of swaggering about with his chest sticking out and his arms akimbo. He would say, Big Bat wants this, or Big Bat says that. It was all probably designed to frighten the listener and thereby increase his jail status. He often used the doorframe crossbar of the toilet cubicles to do chinups and would have continued the exercises until he was exhausted. The rest of the prisoners continued with their own business and didn't pay a blind bit of notice to him.

The peculiarities had to be tolerated. There were various forms of fantasy that were enacted every day. But what we always had to be aware of was the dangerous, underlying personality. I often wondered what went through some of their heads, particularly those who had been charged under the Code of Discipline and had received a term of confinement in the cellblock. I talked to one man who had completed a stretch of isolation and he told me, "solitary confinement under the best circumstances can only be described as a most distressing experience. You can lose yourself in the fantasy world of a book, but after a few hours of reading, you have to set it aside. When you receive a letter, your spirit is lifted for a few minutes. When you send a letter out to your family, it reaffirms your contact with the outside world. The twice-a-day exercise periods free you from the claustrophobic confines of your concrete tomb!"

He continued in a most forthright and sincere tone. "Your weekly visit alleviates your emotional psyche and gives you precious contact with your loved ones. The visit redefines your personality, because without contact with your family there is nothing left. Time passes so slowly when you're 'on the boards' (slang for solitary confinement). You count the days left until you get out. You try to forget about them and still they stretch out in front of you. You think to yourself, can it be that I have only done five days, and another twenty-five stretch out in front of you like a distant, hypothetical prism."

Whenever a prisoner was returned to the wings after serving a stretch in the cellblock, he would remain in a passive melancholy state for a few days. But sometimes an inmate would take a grudge against the establishment, or against the prison officer who represented it, and he would sit in his cell like a silent, smouldering fuse. At times I felt in grave danger as 1 walked past them.

The staff in the Maze had to attend periodic refresher courses at the training college, to keep abreast with all the new prison rules, orders, standing orders and regulations. I was detailed to attend a course of instruction in the college for five days, commencing on Monday the 3rd October and ending the following Friday.

When I arrived in the college at 10 o'clock on the Monday morning, I discovered a few changes had taken place since I was last there two years before. The Governor had retired and was replaced by a younger man, and all the training staff had been replaced by older men. It seemed the Prison Officers Training College was a pre-retirement school for Principal Officers, in all likelihood to prepare them for that day in the future, when they would step down from the Olympian heights of power to mix once again with the troops on the ground. I knew the P 0 who took the class, because I had worked with him in the compounds before he was transferred to the college. He had a high opinion of his own abilities, but he was an immensely popular man and was an extremely competent officer to work with. As he gathered the men around him to speak to them, there was something of the manner of a trade union shop steward about him.

I was surprised to see an ordinary, basic-grade officer as a lecturer in the college. His name was Paddy Mackin and he had worked all his service in the Crum, where I met him whenever I first joined the service. Paddy was also approaching retirement and had joined the service after the war, when he first came to Northern Ireland from his native city of Liverpool. He was not much of a lecturer, but he was a good storyteller and I enjoyed listening to him relate tales about the early days of his career in the Crumlin Road prison. He told us how post-war Belfast was a comparatively peaceful city, like many other U.K.

cities of the time. There were the normal Saturday night disturbances and the normal Monday morning appearances in Court, of those who had been remanded in custody over the weekend.

Legal aid was not in vogue at the time, and as the prison officers filed into the Court room with their charges, a gaggle of solicitors were hovering around in the well of the Court like vultures and they would ask, "What's he in for?" And when they were told, the next question would be, "Has he any money?" If the prisoner had no money, he was passed over and the same questions were asked about the next inmate. If, on the other hand, he had some money in his possession, the excited reply would be whispered in the officer's ear, "Tell him I'll represent him!"

Clearly Paddy had a thing about solicitors. He would often say, when speaking about Court duties, "Remember this, the bent solicitor is the lowest form of criminal you will have the misfortune to meet. He's the type of character who would help an old lady across the street, only to make off with her handbag." I have to say it was not until 1 had retired from the service that I realised the wisdom of his words.

On the Thursday morning we heard the news that the leader, and founder member, of the Irish Republican Socialist Party (IRSP), Seamus Costello, had been murdered in Dublin. Both the Provisional and the Official IRA denied any part in the killing. It was the first time the leader of a political party was murdered in the Irish Republic.

I enjoyed the week at the college. The tutorials were held in a much more relaxed atmosphere than when I first joined the service. We sat around in easy chairs and listened to the crack. At lunchtime each day, 1 went for a walk along the seafront and breathed in the sea air. The clouds scudded across the flat landscape and the wind filled my lungs, relieving me for a short time of all the turmoil of the Maze prison.

The refresher course ended on the Friday evening, and as I drove out of Millisle, I switched the car radio on to hear the news. I was stunned when the news reader said, "The Chainnan of the Northenl Ireland Prison Officers' Association has been shot dead in Belfast." 1 knew immediately who it was. It was Dessie Irvine, whom I met when I first came to the Maze. He was the Phase Principal Officer in the Republican compounds, and 1 knew him well and had a great deal of respect for him. Dessie had been attending a union meeting at the Northern Ireland Public Service Alliance offices in Wellington Park, and as he left the building and drove out of the car park, the IRA murder gang struck! The two gunmen had been lying in wait in a Ford Transit van a short distance away. The car was riddled with bullets and Dessie was hit in the head and died minutes later on the way to the hospital. The weapons used were a high-velocity, armalite rifle and an automatic pistol and, shortly after the shooting, police scenes-of-crime officers found thirteen spent cartridges on the ground near the PO's car.

Chapter 11

When I reported for duty in the Maze the following morning, the main topic of conversation was the murder of Dessie Irvine, and the fact that he was the POA Representative in the Maze made the merciless slaying all the more lamentable. A married man who lived in Belfast, PO Irvine had only two weeks earlier appeared on a Thames Television programme about the Maze prison. The half-hour 'This Week' programme, called, 'Life Behind the Wire', was shown on Thursday, September the 22nd 1977, and Dessie had appeared in several lengthy sequences, facing the camera, whilst being interviewed by the reporter Peter Taylor.

Meanwhile IRA threats against prison staff throughout the Province continued and three officers from Magilligan prison and two from the Crum were also murdered. A number of bomb attacks and shooting incidents had occurred at the homes of prison officers, and the wives of three officers and a postman were injured by exploding parcel bombs in Lisburn and Belfast. The staff in the Maze lived and worked in danger continuously-not only under the pressure of work in the blocks, but also given the security situation on the streets-ever dependent on the help and courage of their comrades in the other security forces.

The Republican blanket protest had escalated when they smashed the windows of their cells, broke up the cell furniture, including the cell table, chairs and even the tin lockers, and threw them out through the windows. A few days later the protest got worse in what became known as the 'Dirty Protest,' when the prisoners smeared their unwanted food, mingled with body waste, onto the walls and ceilings of their cells. They now refused to leave their cells except when going on a visit, which was the only time they wore the prison-issue denim uniform, and they remained locked up 24 hours a day. Eventually the protesting prisoners destroyed everything in their cells and were left with nothing but a blanket and a mattress each. Because of the ever increasing numbers on the protest, each cell now housed two prisoners. There was always one empty wing in the protest blocks, to allow a wing of prisoners to be moved from a dirty wing into a clean wing each week. Some officers were specially trained in industrial cleaning techniques and were supplied with the latest equipment-steam power hoses that not only removed the excrement but took the very paint off the walls and large industrial vacuum cleaners that sucked up the urine and faeces from the floors. The cleaning squads became experts in cleaning the obnoxious mess from the cell walls and ceilings so that they were made habitable once again.

Inevitably the protest boiled over onto the streets, particularly in Republican areas, where their leaders claimed the Govenmlent was depriving the prisoners of their basic human rights. But it was well known that any deprivation the inmates were suffering was self-inflicted. It has to be said that, throughout the Dirty Protest, the prison staff in the Maze always tried to encourage the prisoners to use the facilitate allotted to them. In particular they tried to persuade them at least to wash themselves or use the showers and baths. The ablution facilitates were always ready for use.

In HI we still had only one protesting wing and three conforming wings.

But when the Dirty Protest started, it was decided to move all the prisoners from HI to H6 and make 'C' and 'D' streaker wings. The main reason for this move was to isolate the conforming inmates in case of an outbreak of disease in the dirty wings. It was Sunday morning the 14th May 1978, when the transfer was set to take place. The buses that were used during the week to convey visitors from the car park to the visits area were driven into the courtyard of HI, and the prisoners were transported, a bus-full at a time. I was detailed 'A' wing and 1 went with the first detachment. The shuttle of buses continued between the two blocks until lunchtime. H Block 6 was exactly the same as the block we had left. All the blocks were identical and when you were standing in one, there was nothing to indicate which one it was.

Occasionally I was detailed to work in the protest wings, but generally I worked in the conforming wings. Usually the littering of the catwalks and sterile areas outside the cell windows was not done deliberately, but rather through laziness on the part of some of the cons. When locked in their cells, sometimes unwanted items, were just thrown out of the windows as if into some imaginary rubbish dump. In some cases when the inmate needed to go to the toilet in the middle of the night, rather than use the plastic chamber pot, he would relieve himself on a sheet of newspaper and throw it out the window. The block orderlies called these finds 'mystery parcels'. It was a filthy habit, and sometimes I wondered what sort of mentality or upbringing some of them had, because, as everyone knew, it was the yard orderlies who had it to clean. It was almost impossible to find out who was responsible, as they could hold the parcel out of the window and swing it from side to side before letting it go, so that it would drop outside someone else's cell window.

When a discovery was made, we would question the prisoners who occupied the cells nearest the spot. We knew they would never inform on their mates, but at least the phantom, mystery, parcel-thrower must have felt some shame, as the others would have had a good idea who he was. In most of the old Victorian prisons, like the Crum, the problem with mystery parcels often reached epidemic proportions, as a result of the type of clientele confined in the old jails-large numbers of dossers and similar low-standard people, whose squalid behaviour and general standards of cleanliness were abysmal.

Some of the confornling wings in the Maze were now occupied by an assortment of inmates who represented all the paramilitary organisations in Northern Ireland. There were many provies, who did not join the protest. And there were equal numbers of UVF and UDA prisoners, all in the same wings. This inevitably created a problem when they were all unlocked in the moming for their ablutions, for, given half a chance, they would have fought like cats and dogs. The factions were placed in alternate cells in the wing, apparently in the forlorn hope that in time the two would mix together. But I always thought it was a bit naive to think the two sides would mix together in prison, when the two communities were segregated throughout the country. In the blocks the Loyalists and Republicans were both sensitive to any encroachments on their respective empires. The problem was made worse on a Sunday, when all the prisoners had to have their breakfast and ablutions in time for their respective religious services, which started at 10.00 o' clock.

The best of two worlds was achieved by allowing one faction to have breakfast, whilst the other group washed themselves and cleaned out their cells. Then when it was time for the two factions to change places, all the prisoners had to be locked in their cells, and one group was then unlocked and put in the dining hall, where the grille was locked behind them. Then the second group could be unlocked for their ablutions, without the danger of a clash. It was a system that worked amicably, provided all the inmates participated without objections.

I was assistant class officer in 'B' wing one Sunday morning when the Republicans were in the dining hall and the Loyalists in the ablutions. The wing ablutions area was a large room about 30 feet square and set in a recess to the left hand side of the wing. The area consisted of three toilets and a urinal on one side, a bench in the centre with seven wash hand basins and a slops sink at the end. On the opposite side there were three showers and a bath cubicle. It was time for all the inmates to be locked in their cells and the Loyalists were ordered to 'lock-up!' One prisoner who had arrived in the ablutions late, and was just starting to wash himself, refused to go to his cell. The class officer again ordered him to lock-up, and again he refused. The class officer cautioned him and told him he was putting him on report, when the prisoner suddenly charged out of the ablutions, grabbed the officer and punched him a number of times in the face. It was a virtuoso perfonnance of zero self-control.

I dashed forward, grabbed the con by the waist and slung him round backwards into the ablutions. Instantly some of his mates rushed out of the ablutions towards me. But they stopped as I shouted, 'Get back!' They all stood there, looking at me aggressively. I walked up to the first man and shouted into his face, 'Get back now!' I knew there were six or seven of them, but psychology was all-important now. If I had backed off, it might have been taken as a sign of fear. That could well have encouraged them to come at me. As it was they were not intimidated by me in the slightest, but my walking towards them had made them uneasy and they started to move backwards into the ablutions. Battle lines were drawn. The prisoners knew what they were entitled to and they knew it was a waste of time to ask for anything more.

Any serious breach of the Code of Discipline, like an assault on an officer, could have been dealt with by the prison Governor, but he could also delegate the Board of Visitors to adjudicate in the case. The prison Board of Visitors was a tribunal of three to five people, who were drawn from the community. They were appointed by the Secretary of State to hold office, under

Section ten of the Prisons Act, and could inquire into any offence against prison discipline. The chairman of the Board of Visitors and his committee had wide ranging powers within the prison establishment and had free access at any time to all parts of the prison. They were also permitted to visit any prisoners at any time and to interview any prisoner, out of sight and hearing of prison staff. In short, the Board of Visitors was, and still is, a public watchdog committee, set up by the Government to scrutinize the treatment of prisoners and to ensure they are managed and taken care of to very high standards in UK prisons.

The adjudication was held in the Governor's office and I was called to give my evidence about the assault on the officer. A few days earlier I had heard that a new Chief Officer had taken charge of the jail and he had taken up residence in the admin building. Although I had not seen him, I was told he had served all his service in the Crumlin Road and had been promoted to Chief only recently.

The Governor's office was set up like a courtroom, with three members of the Board of Visitors sitting at a long desk along one side of the office. The prisoner was brought in and we were all ready to give our evidence. The door into the circle was still open and the Chief Officer walked in. He addressed the gathering and began to explain the circumstances surrounding the assault. It was the first time I had ever seen the man. He was a small man, clearly not overly endowed with intellectual skills. His whole discourse was exaggerated and went far beyond his station in life. I thought it was all probably designed as a substitute reinforcement for his slight figure. I took an instant dislike to the man.

After a lengthy sitting, in which we gave our evidence and at times the inmate questioned us on some points, the chairman passed judgement and the con was awarded a period of confinement in the cell block and the adjudication concluded.

A couple of weeks later I was on night duty in 'B' wing. I entered the wing and started to do my head count, which was an every-night occurrence when the night guard took over the wing. I had hardly reached the bottom of one side of the wing when a voice from a cell somewhere further along shouted out, "Hi boys, who's that screw on night guard?" There was silence for a few moments, whilst I continued with the door-to-door procedure, ignoring the phantom caller. Suddenly from a cell somewhere on the opposite side of the wing came the awaited reply, "It's Killer Kane!" There was a muffled sound of laughter from the cons in the other cells. I suddenly realised I had been christened. Like everyone else in the jail, staff and inmates alike, everyone was known by whatever label was put on him.

'Killer Kane' was the name of a character from a science fiction fantasy that was screened on children's television at the time. The nickname was a comical slight at me. It certainly could not have been seen as being in any way aggressive. At least they hadn't taken my actions too seriously during the punch-up a couple of Sundays earlier. 'Killer' was a nickname that would hang over me like a trophy of war for the rest of my service. Some officers whom I worked with for many years only knew me as 'Killer,' and were very surprised when they heard my first name. Even yet in my retirement, when I meet colleagues who served with me over the years, they still call me 'Killer'.

As the numbers in the Maze continued to increase, so too did the numbers of committals with medical problems of various kinds. The prisoners in the two streaker wings in H6 were moved into one of the blocks in the streaker phase, which left us in H6 with two empty wings. So it was decided to open a wing solely for inmates suffering from medical ailments. The prisoners in 'B' wing were transferred to one of the former streaker wings, and 'B' wing was set -up as a medical wing for the treatment of inmates who were suffering from all kinds of disorders.

All the cons in the wing were on medication of some kind or other. Those who were on the heavy stuff were not allowed out of the wing, because they posed a danger to themselves as well as everyone else. Some of them suffered from epilepsy, but mostly it was a mild form of the disorder. There were two or three who suffered from the violent form and when they took ill, went into severe convulsions before total loss of consciousness. Some were aware of the symptoms, and knew for some time before that they were about to suffer an attack.

The wing was not long in operation when the inevitable happened and it was nicknamed 'The Rubber Wing'. Certainly the behaviour of some of its residents inspired such a title. One inmate was on heavy medication and he walked about in a total daze from morning to night, as if he were continuously under the influence of strong drink. Those who were willing and able to work were taken each morning to the workshops. There was a recurring ritual every weekday morning when about fifteen or twenty cons would form up, usually two abreast, in the wing. Before leaving the wing, they had to be searched, and as they walked past the dining hall grille and the cons who were remaining in the wing, they would raise their fists and shout, 'Yo-ho! Yo-ho!' which would cause a barrage of banter between the two groups.

One morning as I gave them a rubdown search when they were leaving the wing, one elderly inmate had a small tin box in the inside pocket of his jacket. As he stopped in front of me, the contents of the tin gave a rattling sound. "What's that?" I asked. And as he took the tin from his pocket and opened it, 1 could see eight or nine small white tablets. "What's these for?" I asked, and as he looked me straight in the eye, he said, "They're for putting under my tongue when I get the pain; you see I have a bad apple tart (heart), Mister!" "That's OK, put them back in your pocket," I said, as he closed the tin and walked on to join the rest.

A ragged column would then leave the block with an officer at each end, and walk through the segment gates to the workshops in Phase 2 of the compound Maze. The Nissen huts in Phase 2 that housed the IRA detainees only a few years earlier, had now been refurbished and made into workshops for the prisoners in the blocks.

Because of the vaguely military style of the marching column of inmates from the 'rubber wing,' the other cons in the block had nicknamed them 'Dad's Army!' It was comical to watch the bizarre group wind their way to and from work each day. Although the other inmates joked about the work party, it was done in a covert way, because there were too many disturbed individuals among them who might not have seen the joke!

Some of them were driven by their own aggressive nature that would not allow them to get involved in any kind of camaraderie. A few were united in their hatred for the legal system that put them in jail and for the prison system that held them there. It was a hostility that, if their equilibrium were disturbed, would cause them to crack up with a vengeance, even towards each other. I never met one inhabitant of the 'rubber wing' who wasn't erratic in one way or other.

I was assistant in the wing one day and I was walking past the open cells when I came to one that was occupied. I looked at the name on the cell-card. It read 'Frank Lyttle,' and he was doing a four-year stay with us. He was an elderly man, at least in comparison to the rest of the inmates in the wing. He was about fifty, with thinning hair that was combed straight over his head, the few strands barely covering his pate. He had that anaemic, washed-out look that can come from long years spent in jails. He didn't notice me at the cell door as he paused at the window. He reached forward and picked up a pair of spectacles from the window ledge, held them up to the light from the window and looked through them. Wiping the lenses on his shirt cuff, he put them on and sat down on the chair at the cell table. He finally noticed me at the door and a little white face peered up at me, with all the wonder of someone who had just spent his first day on planet Earth. Who did he look like? What did he look like? I couldn't tell. I knew nothing about him. But I could tell by his appearance and his demeanour that he was an old con, with plenty of experience of jail life. For better or worse, intuition always has a part to play in the art of jail craft.

I spoke quietly to him. "How are you?" There was silence for a few moments as I looked at the cell table. A partially built model-house sat on one side and a pile of matchsticks with a tube of glue on the other. He was obviously into the manufacture of matchstick houses. The reply finally came. "I'm keeping rightly mister, as long as I'm left alone." It was clear he was a loner, the type of con who didn't mix, even with the other cons. I decided to try and make some further conversation.

"What do you think of this wee jail?" I asked, in an attempt to draw some information out of him. "This is the best wee jail ever I was in," came the sudden reply and I immediately had to ask the inescapable question, "How many jails have you been in, then?" "This is the seventeenth jail I've done bird in. All over the UK-England, Scotland, Wales, Northern Ireland. I've even done time in the South!"

As I continued to chat with him, I could see that Frank was a character who could not cope with life on the outside. He was a recidivist who had become institutionalised in a haven of security. He was like the model policeman - he didn't talk much about himself but he asked plenty of questions. He was a connoisseur of prison regimes, a jail veteran who had seen escapes, riots and solitary, but he, was having none of it now. The old prison adage 'You done the crime, now do your time' meant what it said and Frank had decided, a long time ago, to do his bird the easy way. Then I heard an officer's voice shouting, "Exercise yards!" The other inmates in the wing were being let out to the yards for their one-hour's exercise, and I turned to Frank and said, "It's exercise time. Do you want to go out for a breath of fresh air?" "Air, I think I will, a bit of fresh air would do me the world of good. A stretch in the Maze plays havoc with the school-boy complexion!"

I was night guard in the block on Friday the 16th June, which left me after guard on Saturday and free to take Delta to Bessbrook on our weekly visit to see her mother and the rest of the family. I had a few hours sleep in the morning, and after lunchtime we headed off. When we arrived in the Brook, Delta's mother told us she had just heard there was a shooting near Camlough Lake and Hughie McConnell and another policeman had been killed.

I had served with Hughie's father on the police in Bessbrook, as a mobilized B man in the late 1950's and early 1960's, and 1 kept in touch with the family over the years. Hughie lived with his parents, two brothers and a sister in College Square in the village, until he got married and he and his wife Ann went to live in Derramore Crescent. He had joined the police in 1974 and was glad to be stationed in his home village. Later that evening as the news came in, we heard the sequence of events surrounding the double murder.

What was to be Hughie's final tour of duty in the RUC, began at 2 pm when he and his colleague, Constable William Turbitt, left Bessbrook police station on a routine mobile patrol. They were travelling in an unmarked police car, on the main Newry to Crossmaglen Road. About three quarters of an hour after they had left the station, the police at Bessbrook received a 999 call saying that a police car had crashed on the road at Sturgeon Brae, and that a policeman was lying on the road behind the vehicle. Police immediately rushed to the scene and found Hughie, who had been the driver of the car, lying dead on the road. But Constable Turbitt, who was the observer in the patrol, was missing. The car was riddled with bullets and the police recovered more than forty spent shells lying around, what was clearly the ambush position. After the first salvo was fired into the police car, the gunmen then approached the crashed vehicle and fired several more shots. It was believed Constable Turbitt was taken from the car bleeding badly, and dragged to a waiting vehicle a short distance on the Crossmaglen side of the murder scene.

The ambush and killings must have taken several minutes, and it was believed a number of vehicles passed along the road at the time. Camlough Lake is still a popular tourist attraction in the South Armagh area, and a spot that was very familiar to Delta and me when I was on the police in the Brook. Later that day and in the following days, police conducted a massive search around Camlough and the South Armagh area. Checkpoints were set up in many parts of the border region, as the hunt for the missing policeman continued.

Grief-stricken Bessbrook, which had suffered so much at the hands of the IRA, was in mourning once again on Tuesday 20th June 1978, when the final tributes were paid to my friend Constable Hughie McConnell. As Delta's brother Morton and I attended the funeral from the McConnell home at Derramore Crescent, the silence only broken by the sombre music from the RUC Band. Hundreds of mourners, from all walks of life, blocked the road in the immense cortege, which included senior police, army and UDR officers. It was another day of grief for the model village and the Church of Ireland, which was filled to overflowing. Hughie was survived by his wife Army and their two children, Sharon and Clifford.

He was a popular member of the community and a keen sportsman. Before joining the police, Hughie was a drummer in the local Crimson Arrow Pipe Band, and when he was murdered, another Bessbrook man and band member, Tom Robinson, composed a march for pipe band music. The march was in memory of his friend and fellow band member Hughie. The composition, 'The Constable Hugh McConnell March', was presented to the RUC Pipe Band and is included in a book of music for the Highland Bagpipes, 'The Ulster Scots Collection'. The Crimson Arrow Band came second in grade two in the Pipe Band World Championships 1986.

Security forces on both sides of the border continued their search for Constable Turbitt. It was only after his wife Margaret made a heart-rending appeal to the IRA, in which she said, 'Please disclose the whereabouts of my husband's body so that a Christian burial can take place', that the IRA announced they had murdered the constable.

William Turbitt, a native of Monaghan, joined the police in 1958 and served most of his service in South Armagh. Before being transferred to Bessbrook, he was based in Forkhill. He lived in Richhill with his wife Margaret and four sons, aged between 6 and 14 years.

It was 24 days after the ambush, on the 10th July, when police finally recovered the body of William Turbitt. It was hidden in a farm outbuilding at Drumlougher, near Cullyhanna. A few weeks later when the post-mortom report by the Deputy State Pathologist was read to jurors at the double inquest in Armagh, it was disclosed that Constable Turbitt's body had been hidden in a bog or swamp for a considerable time, and only later removed to the derelict house where it was found. The IRA had claimed they were able to interrogate the policeman before they murdered him, but the pathologist's report showed that the head wound received by the 47-year-old constable was likely to have caused instant death. The report stressed that it was inconsistent that the constable could have survived after being hit on the head by the high-velocity bullet.

Open verdicts were returned on the two constables, and the coroner described the murders as foul and cowardly. The treatment of Constable Turbitt's body was particularly revolting and showed the utter depravity of the IRA murder gang. Evidence was also given, that as the gunmen lay in wait to ambush the police car, they ate sandwiches and drank from a bottle. Police recovered the evidence - three discarded sandwiches in a package and an empty bottle - close to the terrorists' firing position, which was on a corner and to the rear of the policemen's car.

Jurors were told twenty bullets struck the rear of the police car before the gunmen approached the vehicle, firing more shots into the two constables. After the murders the killers stole all the weapons the officers were carrying, but an M I carbine magazine - the type of weapon favoured by the IRA - was found lying near the car. The terrorists had dragged the dying policeman out of the vehicle and a trail of blood led for 300 to 400 yards along the road towards Crossmaglen.

The cold-blooded murders showed the professionalism of the IRA death squads. They were confident that the vast majority of people in nationalist areas were too frightened to report them to the police and would certainly not give evidence in open court. In these areas people were so fearful of the IRA that most of them were coerced into sheltering gunmen and supplying information about the security forces, for fear of reprisals that they knew the Provies were ruthless enough to enforce.

In 1978 the IRA developed a new strategy of organisation based on a cellular structure, in which small units of men, about three to four strong, were formed. Secrecy was the keyword, and the units were established on a need-to know-basis. Anything they did not need to know, they were not told, and each group was segregated to prevent infiltration by the security forces. The system was developed by the IRA after suffering a number of setbacks in the previous two years.

My work in the Maze continued and the periodic release of prisoners from the block, having served their sentences, meant that from time to time there were a few empty cells in a wing. I was detailed night guard on Tuesday 2nd July, and when I was carrying out the headcount, I saw there was a few vacancies in the wing. When the numbers were returned, the day staff left the block and the place was locked. I went into the mess and started to prepare the meal (syndicate) for myself and my four night guard colleagues. During the cook-up my four companions covered for me, by doing the headcounts and the pegging. The 'mutual cover' was reciprocated when it was the turn of one of the other squad members to cook the syndic on the next, night guard stag.

The pegging system was a procedure designed to monitor the night guard staff rather than the prisoners. A series of press-button meters was installed at various key locations throughout the inside and outside of the block in the circle, at the bottom of the wings and at numerous places around the exercise yards. When each button was pressed, it registered the time and location on a clockregister that was situated in the Chief Officer's office and indicated that the staff were at their posts.

When the meal was prepared and dished up, I called my mates and we all sat down to the banquet. The light-hearted banter started as they began ribbing me about my cuisine and the culinary delights that I had prepared. The wisecracks continued, and by the time the meal was over and we were clearing the dishes, they finally cracked. All four of them grabbed me as one of them shouted, 'Right, Killer, we'll harden you!' They partly carried and partly dragged me down the wing, slung me into an empty cell and slammed the door. I listened in the silence as their laughter and the clatter of their boots on the asphalt floor faded into the distance. All was quiet now. The empty cell had an eerie, oppressive atmosphere.

Being locked-up, I felt a rising tide of apprehension. It must have been a familiar feeling to many cons when they were locked in a cell for the first time. What if I couldn't get out? I knew they were only acting the wag, but what if they forgot about me? A hot surge of almost panic gripped me. The unyielding silence of total solitude became persistent, I tried to look through the small window in the door, but I could only squint through a tiny pinhole at the side, as the outside flap was closed. To distract attention from my temporary plight, I focused on my surroundings.

A window about four feet square was set in the outside wall opposite the cell door. The steel framework held one large pane of glass the full length of the window and on top, two small windows could be opened out for ventilation purposes. Just inside the window four, thick concrete bars about six inches by four inches ran vertically from the bottom sill to the top lintel and with the sides, the whole frame had been shaped in a single concrete mould. In consequence, it was a window that fulfilled the requirements of the cell. The two side walls were bare and featureless. The inner wall bore the heavy, steel-clad cell door and frame that sat in a slight recess. The door was attached to the frame by a bearing that allowed it to swivel when being opened or closed. The heavy glass in the small observation window sat in the door about eye level, and was shielded on the outside by a metal cover that could be lifted to allow the officer to look in.

To the right of the cell door at about waist-high, an emergency bell-push was set in a panel along with a light switch that allowed the lights to be dulled or put out. Over the door a small air-vent allowed fresh air to flow from the two, small windows on the opposite wall. The ceiling was flat, made with solid concrete and painted a dull white. In the centre of the ceiling there was a light, its metal housing and thick glass cover allowing an adequate amount of brightness to illuminate the cell. The lights were also controlled from the outside of the cell, and 'lights out' was at II pm. The floor, like the rest of the floors in the block, was black asphalt, its cold surface gleaming in the light. On the wall below the back window, two three-inch heating pipes went through the cell walls and ran from cell to cell the full length of the wing.

If the cell decoration was minimal, the furnishings were decidedly sparse. A heavy, metal bed with a mesh spring lay tilted against the corner wall. It had a foam mattress inside a red cover. Two white sheets, two blankets and a pillow were placed at the head of the bed, all in a neat bed-pack ready for the next occupant. The bed stood about eighteen inches high so that the inmate could place his shoes and some of his belongings underneath. Against the back wall stood a small, wooden table with flimsy legs, and next to it was the steel tubular chair, of slightly stronger construction. Attached to the wall, over the table, there was a small bookshelf. In the corner at the bottom of the bed, near the cell door, stood a tall metal locker with a shelf and on the floor beside the locker was the now familiar, plastic chamber pot with its lid. A water gallon and a Bible sat on the small table.

As I perused the inside of the cell, my mind slowly drifted back to the present. I could hear the distant sound of footsteps on the asphalt, the excited babble of voices and the clang of a grille as it shut behind them. It was not much consolation, but at least I wasn't completely alone. As the footsteps came closer to the cell door, the patronising banter started again:

"What about you, Killer?"

"Do you want out?"

"Say please!"

"OK! Let me out. Even the cons will be talking about you, you bunch of idiots," I said as I heard the cell key being inserted into the lock. Then the tumblers were lifted by the key, and the door slowly opened. They were all standing there, screaming with hysterical laughter. As I walked out, I smiled at them to show I wasn't too annoyed. But it was no joke!

By now there were about 350 IRA prisoners on the dirty protest in the Maze, and it was plain to see their foul protest was having no effect, so they increased their attacks on the prison staff in an attempt to put pressure on the Government to capitulate to their demands for the return of Special Category Status. On Sunday 26th November the Deputy Governor of the Maze, Mr Albert Miles, was shot dead by the IRA at his home in north Belfast. Albert had joined the prison service 20 years before, and I met him when I first came to the Maze in 1975. He was an Assistant Governor and I came to know him well, since the blocks opened in 1976.

Albert was the seventh prison officer to be murdered by the IRA since the start of the terrorist campaign. He had been recently promoted to Deputy Governor of the Maze Cellular and was well liked by the staff. On the Sunday evening he was at home with his wife and son, when there was a knock on the front door. Normally, as Mrs Miles said later, she would go to the front bay window and look out to see who was there. But this time she went straight to the door and opened it. Two gunmen burst in through the open door. One grabbed Mrs Miles and held his hand over her mouth to stop her from shouting a warning to her husband, whilst the other one dashed on down the hallway. As Albert ran out of the kitchen, the gunman opened fire and his victim collapsed to the floor and died instantly. The two gunmen were about 25 or 30 years of age and they were not wearing masks. Mrs Miles was treated for shock at the scene, and later she said she didn't know how many shots were fired as there were just flashes and bangs. Some time later an IRA man was sentenced to life imprisonment for the murder of Governor Miles.

I was detailed 'C' and 'D' grille on evening duty, which was a very quiet spell of duty because all the prisoners were locked in their cells over the dinner guard period. It was on duties like these that you learnt to recognise the small sounds of the jail: the slow drip of water from an ablutions tap, the click of a cell light-switch far down the wing, the faint whisper of a con as he recites his Rosary. After being in the quiet of the wings for a while, you got to know every sound, even the smallest of sounds that only register subliminally. Even the 'rubber wing' was quiet over lunchtime every day.

I was assistant class officer in the 'rubber wing' the following Saturday, and as the workshops were closed at the weekends, all the prisoners remained in the wing and had the choice of either playing football in the exercise yard or watching the sport on television. I would carefully observe the behaviour of the inmates, as they would go about the wing. There was one con who would walk along the wing, and at every step he would take, he thumped the side of his fist off the wall, in an aggressive gesture. He had his head shaved and he carried his spectacles around his neck, the frames tied with a piece of string. He was all menace and macho, but with a gaping hole where his front teeth used to be. His adopted persona was that of a professional boxer or a martial arts expert-at least he wanted to come across as a hard man, in an effort to achieve a high-status position in the establishment. But, without making eye contact with him, I quietly put him in the picture. I had met these toughs before-thoroughly nasty pieces of work who would enjoy dominating someone weaker.

When a newly sentenced prisoner, particularly a first timer, arrived in the wing, it seemed his first quest was to find the 'Big Shot' in the wing. He would ask, "Who's the lifer?" And when he would find him, he would shake hands with him and greet him like a celebrated personality. As the lifer would tell 'war stories' about his past bird, the newcomer would stare in amazement like an indulgent father at the performance of a favourite son. This was the philosophy of prison life: the heroes were the hard men, the cons who could beat the system. In fact they were all-time losers, the social failures.

I was at the dining hall grille, and a snooker game was in progress inside. I glanced round and there was a prisoner walking towards me I had never seen before. He had only been committed to the wing the day before. As he approached, I opened the grille and he walked into the dining hall without speaking a word. I got a sideways glance at his face as he passed. He was the walking epitome of prison life.

After serving for some years on the police and the prison service, I had met some dangerous looking people. But this was something new. A short figure, broad at the shoulders, his body seemed to taper down to his feet, which gave him a resemblance to a charging buffalo. He had a crew-cut, of grey hair that joined a furrowed brow at the front, and a pair of black eyes peered out of dark sockets.

As he got into conversation with the other inmates, his mouth twisted to one side in an effort to emphasise particular points, and as he talked, his hands moved in short, jerky gestures to underline his distaste for the people and events he was discussing. Experience told me that a clear sign of neurotic illness is an individual's inability to control his own performance. As I watched the newcomer, I formed the opinion that he was a character who would not have been out of place in a psychiatric institution. But then, a percentage of the inmates in the 'rubber wing' would probably have felt at home in such an establishment.

There was no let-up in the attacks on prison officers' homes by the IRA, and in some cases Loyalist paramilitaries were involved. Shots were fired at some of their houses, petrol bombs and paint bombs were thrown at their homes, and in some areas the cars belonging to prison officers were set on fire. The families of prison officers were intimidated, and even at school their children were coerced and threatened to such an extent that some families had to leave their homes and move to areas where they were not known. The sacrifices made by the prison staff and their contribution to the security of the state have never been adequately acknowledged.

But it was the dreadful murders of a retired prison officer and his wife that demonstrated the dangers and sacrifices of the prison staff. It was Saturday night, 3rd February 1979, when the IRA death squad struck! It was at the home of my old friend Paddy Mackin, whom I had last spoken to less than a year-and-a-half earlier, when I was on a refresher course at the college. Paddy had retired from the service in November, after serving as an instructor in the training college at Millisle.

He was with his 58-year-old wife Violet, in their north Belfast home, when the two IRA gunmen burst in through the back door. They dashed to the lounge, where they opened fire and Paddy was shot dead as he sat in a fireside chair. The distraught Violet lunged forward at the gunmen, in an attempt to protect her husband, but the assassin turned the gun on her and shot her dead.

The gruesome discovery was made the following morning by their son, who was with his wife and children on their regular, Sunday morning visit. Neighbours reported hearing 'bangs' from the home around nine o'clock on Saturday night, but no one went to investigate. Less than two years before, Paddy was awarded the Queen's Jubilee Medal, presented to him by the Queen herself as she was on a visit to the Province.

Police later recovered the car that was used by the gunmen in Ardoyne, only a short distance from the Mackin's home. The following Tuesday, after a brief family service at their home, the funeral of Paddy and Violet took place. Hundreds of prison officers lined the road outside the house, and there was a large turnout of staff from the prison officers' training college. A few days later the IRA made a statement to the effect that Mrs Mackin was not their target. And after such a sadistic, double murder, they actually had the gall to state that they also wished to inform prison officers that if they resigned from the prison service and made their resignation known to the IRA, then they would consider removing their names from their murder list.

On the 14th April 1980, a 22-year-old Ardoyne man appeared at Belfast Crown Court charged with the double murder of Paddy and Violet Mackin. At the end of the trial, on the 9th May 1980, the man was jailed for life, for his part in the double murder.

There was two exercise periods each day for the prisoners in the block, one in the morning and one in the afternoon. Two officers were detailed to each wing to escort the prisoners to the exercise yard but, before entering the wing, they would draw the keys for the exercise yard from the control room. Access to the yard was gained through the exercise grille at the bottom of the wing, but before the prisoners were allowed out, the security of the yard had to be checked. When the officers went into the yard, their first task was to walk around and check the yard fences, to make sure they were all secure. The security gates between the sterile areas were also checked to make sure they were locked. Then when they were satisfied all was correct, one remained at the yard fence gate whilst his colleague opened the yard grille and the class officer in the wing unlocked the cells. As each cell was opened and the two inmates walked to the grille, they were given a rubdown search before they proceeded into the yard. The process continued until all the prisoners were in the exercise yard.

When the yard numbers were verified with the class officer, the fence gate and the yard grille were locked, and one officer remained in the sterile area whilst his comrade was locked in the catwalk, where he patrolled along the back of the wing. There was an alarm button attached to the wall at the far end of the catwalk, which could be used to call reinforcements in an emergency. As they entered the yards, some of the cons would start jogging and a few would run at a leisurely pace with short strides. But others would sprint at full speed for a number of laps and then slow down to a more manageable pace. Others would simply walk around the yard in bunches of two or three, and sometimes in larger groups when they would be engaged in deep conversation.

Sometimes they played football, when they would pick two teams and play half an hour each way. Pullovers or similar garments would be placed at each end of the yard to represent goal posts, and they would play as if it were an international match at Wembley, the game only being interrupted when the ball was kicked over the fence. In that event, we would hear, "Hi mister, can we have our ball back?" When the exercise period was over, the procedure was the same for the prisoners returning to the wing, as it had been for them going to the exercise yard, and they each got a rubdown search. When the yard was cleared, the fences and gates were checked again, the officers returned to the block and left the keys back in the control room. The exercise periods were, in retrospect, a welcome break for both officer and con. The fresh air and the open space seemed to emphasise the claustrophobic confinement of the block.

Chapter 12

Although we had a touring caravan and spent an odd weekend along the Ulster coastline or in the Fermanagh Lakeland, Delta and I had not had a proper holiday since we were married twelve years earlier. So as I had two weeks leave to take in April, we decided to have a short break and get away for a while as a family. At the time I worked with an officer in the Maze who had friends in the Republic, and they owned a guesthouse in Bray, County Wicklow. It was the Easter weekend and I made reservations for four days, from Saturday 14th to Tuesday 17th. We left home on the Saturday morning, and drove to Bessbrook to visit Delta's mother and Morton and his wife Adrienne, before leaving for Bray. We left the Brook in the late morning and drove along the Millvale Road and then on to Newly, where we joined the Dublin Road.

The holiday was most enjoyable, as we used our guesthouse as a base and toured the south eastern counties of Wexford, Carlow and Kildare. The only problem during our short vacation was, there was a strike by telephone workers in the Republic, and we could not contact our families at home during our stay in the south. However, Tuesday morning arrived and we said goodbye to our landlady and headed back through Dublin and then on towards the border.

We drove through Newly, onto the Camlough Road, but when we approached the junction with the Millvale Road, the army had a checkpoint at the comer and they were diverting traffic along the main road. As we drove further along the Camlough Road, to where the land slopes down towards the Millvale Road, we could see a scene of utter devastation, with the police and army sifting through wreckage. There had clearly been a horrendous explosion, and when we arrived in Bessbrook, we heard the full horror of what had happened. Four policemen had been killed in a huge bombing outrage.

The four died when the Land Rover they were travelling in was blown to pieces on the Millvale Road, a short distance outside the village. They were based at Bessbrook Police Station, and were on a routine patrol when the massive half-ton bomb exploded. Up to that time it was the largest bomb the IRA had ever triggered in the Province. The policemen left the station earlier to patrol the area and were accompanied by an unmarked, private car with a sergeant and another policeman in it, as they approached a suspicious-looking van that was parked at the side of the road, and as they drew alongside the vehicle, the bomb, which was packed inside, was detonated by remote control perhaps from as far away as a half-a-mile. The van disintegrated and left a 5 feet-deep crater in the road. The two policemen who were following the Land Rover in the other car were also injured, as the force of the explosion blew the windscreen in around them. A wheel from the police vehicle was thrown 70 yards and crashed into another car. The driver and his two daughters had to be taken to hospital suffering from shock. The van bomb had been parked only 400 yards from a housing estate and an old people's home, and many families living in the area had amazing escapes. Altogether there were 13 people who had to be taken to Daisyhill Hospital in Newry.

I was deeply saddened when I heard who the four dead policemen were.

They were 25-year-old Paul Gray, who came from Belfast; 30-year-old Noel Webb, from Lurgan; 28-year-old Richard Baird, from Scarva, and 44-year-old Robert Lockhart, who came from Mountnorris. Constables Gray and Webb were both single, although Constable Gray was engaged to be married the following June. Constable Baird was married with two children aged 7 and 3 and Reserve Constable Lockhart was survived by his wife and three children aged 9, 13 and 19.

I was shocked when I learnt that Constable Baird was the same Richard Baird who I had worked with in the Courtaulds Factory in Lurgan. I had known him when I was on the police Reserves in Gilford, and he was on the Reserves in Banbridge at the time. But when I joined the prison service, I lost contact with him. Richard had joined the full time RUC in November 1976 and, after passing out from the RUC Depot at Enniskillen in February 1977, he was posted to Bessbrook. I knew Noel Webb, too. Noel came from the Gilford Road in Lurgan, where he lived with his parents, six brothers and three sisters. I knew the family very well, as they only lived about a half-a-mile from my home.

The van that was used to carry the deadly bomb cargo was hijacked at Cullaville, near Crossmaglen, almost three hours before the remote-controlled blast. The vehicle had been on its way from Dundalk to Castleblaney in the Republic, when it was stopped by three armed and masked men. The driver was taken out, an anorak placed over his head and he was taken to an unoccupied building nearby. Police later traced the exact route of the van from where it left Crossmaglen, to its arrival at its target area. It was hijacked at 8.45 that morning, and left at the Millvale Road almost two hours later. The light-blue coloured Transit was owned by a firm in Dunleer, County Louth. The driver was held until after the explosion had occurred and was then released near Castleblaney, more than 12 miles away. Police were not sure how many terrorists were involved, but they did discover that the van was accompanied all the way by a scout car. A transmitter was used to detonate the bomb, and owners of shops on both sides of the border where the device could be bought were questioned.

The highest level of co-operation between the RUC and the Garda took place in the investigation. The IRA had used radio-controlled bombs before, but the device used on the Millvale Road, was thought to have been made even more deadly by using parts from model aircraft equipment. The blast was heard for miles around. In terms of casualties it was the worst attack - up to that time on the RUC since the present IRA terror campaign had started.

Since I retired from the Prison Service, I have had time to reflect on some incidents in the Maze that were probably designed by the cons for all intents and purposes to embarrass, rather than to actually injure, anyone. I have one abiding memory of an occasion when they made me feel a bit stupid. It was during the association time in the wing and some of the prisoners were in the hobbies room. They were using various types of material for their hobbies and someone had made a pair of spurs out of cardboard and balsawood. I was patrolling the wing when a prisoner stopped to speak to me. With the benefit of hindsight, I should have realised everything was not correct, because he approached me like a felon mounting the gallows, and when he spoke to me, he was like Oliver with his proverbial bowl asking for more!

As I was engaged in the conversation, another inmate came up behind me and stuck the spurs onto the heels of my boots. I knew nothing till I saw the prisoners pour out of the hobbies room. They were all laughing and looking down the wing in my direction. I could not understand what all the amusement was about, and looked round to see what they were laughing at. By this time they were all shouting, "Yippee!" "Get-up!" "Ya-ho!" I suddenly realised they were laughing at me, and as 1 glanced down and saw the spurs, I turned and started to walk towards the class office. At this point the laughter had reached a crescendo, with everybody joining in, even the prisoners in the dining hall on the opposite side of the wing. The whole dining room erupted, cons jumping to their feet, howling, and others pounding their tables with their fists in a frenzy of excitement.

It was like a scene straight out of 'High Noon'. I walked down the wing to the class office before removing the spurs, because I didn't want to give them the satisfaction of seeing me stooping down and taking them off. Even the other officers in the wing saw the funny side of the prank and were laughing uncontrollably.

It was a painful lesson for me, which showed a singular lack of 'jail craft' on my part, a failing that I would set out to remedy in the future. When I examined the spurs, complete with their cardboard bootstraps and revolving toothed wheel, one had to accept the thought and ingenuity that went into their manufacture, all to get a laugh at a 'silly old screw!'

When the pandemonium died down, I ventured back out onto the wing and was instantly met by one of the orderlies, who couldn't wait to tell me how much he enjoyed the stunt: "Hi Killer, the last time I laughed like that was in the Crown Court. The judge gave me 15 years, as if he were giving away toffee apples!" I looked at him as he walked away, still laughing. On his feet were a pair of brownish slippers that were so badly worn that the lack of any rigid sole made him drag his feet to cushion the impact of every step. But with every step the back of the slipper struck the heel, which caused a flip-flop sound. Thus he had attained the nickname 'Flipper' from the other cons. He was a man more fool than rogue.

In June 1979 a Senior Officer arrived in the Maze on promotion from Armagh prison. His name was Ken McGee, and the word soon got around on the grapevine that he was a Christian and didn't stand for any nonsense. He was detailed to H Block 7, to replace a Senior Officer whose wife was shot in the face when she answered a knock at the front door of their home in Belfast. Her husband was transferred to the Crum after the murder attempt, so that he could be close to his wife and children. H7 was a conforming block with a mixture of Loyalists, Republicans and ordinary prisoners, and therefore it was a melting pot of tension. So the task of running and keeping order in the block for the new Senior Officer was even more fraught with danger for both him and his staff. However, the new man settled in quickly to his posting and, like any evangelist drawn to the Bible, he began to proselytize the Gospel among the inhabitants of the block, both officer and inmate alike.

One evening I was on association duty in H6 when the PO asked me to take something down to H7. As I walked into the PO's office in H7, the new Senior Officer was on duty. It was the first time I had ever spoken to him, and 1 asked him how he was keeping. He said, "I'm keeping fine; I was just listening to a tape of Gospel songs by the Reverend William McCrea last night and it was mighty Gospel singing." 1 asked him what church he belonged to and he told me he was a member of a Free Presbyterian congregation, and he had been saved earlier in the year. I told him I also was a member of the Free Presbyterian Church and we continued in conversation about the church and spiritual matters, before I left him and returned to H6.

In the days and weeks that followed I met him occasionally, usually at lunchtime when he was sitting in his car in the car park reading his Bible, and I would have spoken to him there. Normally I would have spent my lunch break walking around the 2-mile perimeter wall for a bit of exercise. I hadn't seen Ken for a while and someone told me he had opened a disused office near the transport depot at the main gate, where he and some other Christians met each lunchtime for Bible reading and a time of prayer.

On Friday morning, the 2nd July, I heard the shattering news that my former colleague and friend, Jim Wright, had been killed in a booby-trap bomb explosion near his home in Portadown. I had known Jim since I was on the police Reserves, when we were on duty at the local Petty Sessions in Portadown. Jim was a member of the Salvation Army and he played in the band. He was known locally as the 'singing policeman', as he had released some LP's of Gospel songs.

Jim died when his car exploded as he tried to start it, outside his Corcrain Drive home, and his daughter Ann, who was with him in the car, was critically injured. The name of his daughter was the last word Jim ever spoke when the three-pound bomb exploded under the car. It was 8.50 on Friday morning when they left home and got into the car. Ann was in the passenger seat beside him and as he was about to ask her something, he turned the ignition key and the car blew up.

The vibrations of the engine caused the magnetic bomb to detonate, only a few inches under his body, and he was dead within seconds. Although twenty-one-year old Ann was badly injured, she remained calm and told neighbours to notify her mother. Within minutes the police and ambulances were on the scene, and both victims were rushed to the hospital, where Ann received emergency surgery. Jim had left the police Reserves in 1977 and had moved to live in the Isle of Man, but he wasn't allowed to stay after being refused a work permit.

The Irish National Liberation Army (INLA) claimed responsibility for the murder. The mercury-type bombing was a carbon copy of the one that killed Mr Airey Neave four months earlier. Mr Neave was the Conservative Spokesman for Northern Ireland and he died after a bomb exploded under his car as he drove out of the underground car park at the House of Commons. Mr Neave had advocated a strong security policy to combat terrorism in Northern Ireland and would almost certainly have become Secretary of State after the May election. The Conservative manifesto for the general election stated, that in the absence of devolved Government in the Province a Conservative Government would establish one or more elected regional councils, with a wide range of powers over local services. But with the death of the manifesto's author the proposals never came to fruition. During the Second World War, Airey Neave was a prisoner in Colditz Castle. He was one of the few who successfully escaped from his German captors.

For some time my father had been in declining health, suffering a number of slight strokes that had weakened him and restricted his movements around the house. On Friday morning, 21st September 1979, I was on duty in the Block when Delta rang me to say my father had taken another stroke. I immediately explained the situation to the PO, and he told me to go on home.

When I arrived home, I changed out of uniform and went straight over to my parents' house, which was a cottage on my brother's farm. My mother was in a very distressed state and the doctor was still with my father. My mother told me how he had been fine earlier that morning until he had taken the seizure. Later I spoke to the doctor, and his prognosis of the condition was very gloomy. He told me straight he thought my father had been so weakened by the stroke that a recovery was very unlikely. I stayed with my parents the rest of the day and my father remained in bed; but although he was very weak, he was aware of my presence and conscious of the family around him.

When I look back at that period of my life, I am glad I had the opportunity to stay with him and talk to him, because in the late afternoon he finally succumbed to the illness and passed away. This was undoubtedly the most unhappy time of my life. The death of my father was a bitter blow to me. Thankfully I still possess happy thoughts and the fondest memories of a truly wonderful man.

In the days that followed my father's death, I felt despondent as I returned to the Maze and my duties in the block. Every time I met Ken, he tried to comfort me by quoting portions of scripture and telling me the fellowship were praying for me.

The staff in the Maze were detailed one weekend off in each fortnight, but if we were required for duty we could still be detailed to work on that weekend. However, it was routine practice that we would not be detailed night guard on our weekend off, so I was taken aback when I was detailed night guard on Sunday 18th November, because it was my weekend off. Nevertheless, the duty suited me and I didn't complain, but decided to do the night guard. I reported at the normal time, was assigned 'C' and 'D' grille and I took up my post. When the prisoners were locked in their cells and counted, the numbers were returned as nonnal and the day staff went off duty. I remained at the grille, and a short time afterwards the circle officer told me that the control officer in H7 had rung to say the night guard Senior Officer was on his rounds and would be calling to inspect the block.

A Principal Officer or Senior Officer was always in charge of all the night guard staff in each phase, and it was his duty to count the prisoners in each block and inspect the staff in his phase. He also had to patrol the area and check that all was secure throughout the night. He would then base himself in one of the blocks, where the ECR and the phase staff could contact him in the event of an unexpected occurrence.

I had just carried out a head count and returned to the grille when I heard the circle officer returning the block numbers to the SO. As he walked into the circle, I was surprised to see it was Ken, because I didn't expect him to be night guard. When he saw me he was also surprised that I was night guard, because he knew it was my weekend off.

When the security checks were completed, the SO decided to stay in H6, and when he took charge of the PO's office, I called in to speak to him. Soon the conversation got round to religion, and as he opened his Bible and read some passages of scripture, I have to say 1 was taking it all much more seriously than I had ever done before. He told me the testimony of his conversion to Christ and how his life was restored after the experience. After a lengthy conversation on the subject he closed the Bible and began to pray. It was during that prayer that I made a decision for the Lord, and in the unlikely surroundings of the Maze prison I put my faith in God and accepted Christ as my own and personal Saviour.

I am convinced that at that moment, through faith, I passed through a religious experience and was saved. Much has been written and said about the religious experience-its nature, validity and extent. But it has involved for me a commitment to the Christian faith that has given me a deep sense of purpose and determination to try and succeed in living the Christian life, as my parents had done before me.

When I arrived home from work that Monday moming, Delta was the first person to be told of my conversion, and later that day I called with my mother and told her that I was saved. She was delighted, and explained to me how she and my father had prayed for years for such a change in my life. I could appreciate their concern for my spiritual wellbeing and I could under-stand their religious principles, as opposed to the material and temporal values of the world. The news quickly spread around my colleagues in the Maze and I became a member of the Christian Prison Officers' Fellowship, to which I

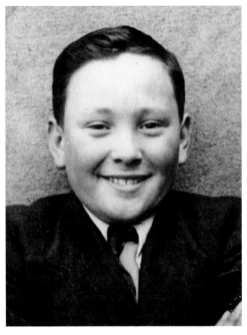

This school photograph of me was taken in 1949 when I was 10 years of age.

This photograpgh of me with my old friend Jackie Stewart, (wearing the RUC blazer badge), was taken in 1958.

*As a mobilised
Special Constable,
this picture of me
was taken
in 1962.*

*Delta and myself signing the
register after our marriage on
7th September 1966. Also in the
picture is the Reverend H.S.
Carser who officiated at our
wedding.*

As a Lance Corporal in the Royal Irish Rangers, this photograph of me was taken at Summer training camp near Thetford Norfolk in 1973.

Northern Ireland
Prison Service College

An old postcard of the Prison Service Collage at Millisle Co. Down.

The construction of phase one of the Long Kesh Internment Centre in 1971, on the site of a Second World War airfield. The runways are still visable along with the black hanger on the top right of the picture.

An aerial photograpgh of Maze Cellular, taken shortly after it opened.

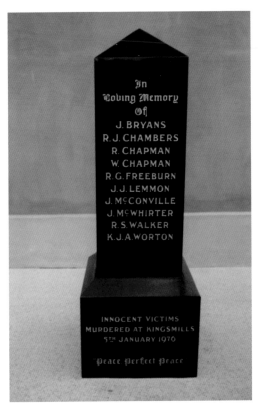

The memorial to the ten protestant mill workers who were murdered by the Provisional IRA on the 5th January 1976. The monument was unveiled in January 1986 by Alan Black, the sole survivor of the Kingsmills Massacre.

In
Loving Memory
Of
J. BRYANS
R. J. CHAMBERS
R. CHAPMAN
W. CHAPMAN
R. G. FREEBURN
J. J. LEMMON
J. McCONVILLE
J. McWHIRTER
R. S. WALKER
K. J. A. WORTON

INNOCENT VICTIMS
MURDERED AT KINGSMILLS
5TH JANUARY 1976

Peace Perfect Peace

The plaque in Tullyvallen Orange Hall in memory of the Lodge members who were murdered by the IRA sectarian death squads.

TO THE GLORY OF GOD AND IN MEMORY OF
MEMBERS OF L.O.L. 630 KILLED BY TERRORISTS IN THIS HALL
ON 1ST SEPTEMBER 1975
BRO. JAMES McKEE J. P. W.M.
BRO. W. R. (RONNIE) McKEE
BRO. JOHN JOHNSTON, CHAP.
BRO. NEVIN T. McCONNELL, SEC.
BRO. WILLIAM G. HERRON
ALSO
BRO. WILLIAM MEAKLIM
TORTURED AND KILLED BY TERRORISTS ON 15TH AUGUST 1975
AND
BRO. JOSEPH A. McCULLOUGH, CHAP.
KILLED BY TERRORISTS ON 5TH FEBRUARY 1976
VENGENCE IS MINE, I WILL REPAY SAITH THE LORD.

Joanne with myself on her wedding day the 20th July 1993.

In 1998 I graduated with a Bachelor of Science (Honours) Degree in Social Science from the Open University.

Northern Ireland Prison Service

Commendation

I hereby commend

Officer W.A. McKane

who on 25 September 1983 at HM Prison Maze Cellular acted with

conspicuous bravery in attempting to foil an escape by armed and

dangerous prisoners.

I have great pride and pleasure in recording my appreciation of

this conduct which was worthy of the highest traditions of the

Prison Service.

Michael Scott.

Parliamentary Under Secretary of State
Northern Ireland Office

The commendation for bravery that was awarded
to me after the escape from the Maze in 1983.

remained a faithful and committed member until my retirement from the Service in 1999.

After so many IRA attacks on the homes of prison staff and their families, extra security precautions were introduced to protect them. But on Saturday morning, the 24th November 1979, we were greeted in the Maze with the depressing news that another officer had been murdered. He was Gerry Malville and he served with me in the compounds when I first joined the Prison Service. Gerry was murdered because he was a soft target. He lived alone, in a quiet part of Glengonnley, on the outskirts of Belfast. Gerry had been shot twice through the head, and his body was found in the living room of his detached bungalow on the Hightown Road. His body was discovered by police who burst into the house about midnight the night before, after colleagues in the Maze raised the alarm when he failed to report for night guard duty at 9p m.

Police were of the opinion that because the front door of the house had not been forced and there was no sign of a struggle, that Gerry had unwittingly let the killers into the house after speaking to them on a security intercom fitted to the front door. A keen Hawaiian guitar player, Gerry enjoyed the company of people from the musical fraternity, and it was believed the murder gang had tricked their way into the house by claiming they were guitar musicians.

Around the same time as the murder was discovered, an anonymous phone call was received by a news agency in Belfast, claiming the attack was carried out by an IRA murder squad. Gerry was last seen alive on the Friday afternoon, by his next-door neighbour who had known him for over 30 years, when the family first moved to the area after his father retired from the RUC. He was the youngest in the family and stayed at home to look after his elderly mother after his father died some years earlier.

He joined the Prison Service after serving his apprenticeship as a motor mechanic, and continued to live in the home place after he was married. Gerry's three brothers emigrated to America and he had a sister who I lived in Scotland. He was a real gentleman. It was a privilege to have known him. He lived alone after the death of his mother in 1977, and I think it was his intention to stay in the Prison Service until he would retire and then emigrate to America, to be near his brothers.

Security around the homes of Prison Officers had been tightened after a spate of similar murders and gun attacks, especially in the Belfast area. In a statement admitting the murder, the IRA said, "So much for the extra protection promised by the British Government for the mercenary service of screws!" And they added a warning that Prison Officers would be killed, whenever and wherever possible.

In the conforming wings of the block at meal times a long queue would form, snaking its way from the hotplate in the dining hall and through the grille and along the side wall of the wing. Men of all shapes and sizes shuffled forwards, towards the counter where the two orderlies served the food from the containers. As he was served, each con would go to his table and sit with his three mates. Each table was the private domain of the four cons who sat at it, and at no time would an inmate sit at another table without being invited. After they had eaten, they would huddle around the table in conversation or sometimes a game of cards would be played, to help the meal go down. At the end of the meal period the mugs, plates and cutlery were cleared from the tables and washed. Each prisoner was responsible for his own gear and would set it out neatly on his cell table. The prisoners were locked for one hour before the association period would commence.

Sometimes I was detailed the dining hall grille for the association. This duty consisted of the controlled movement of all prisoners entering and leaving the dining hall. The snooker table was the main pastime and soon a game would be in progress between two opponents, with a crowd of other prisoners standing around waiting their turn for the table, amidst the continuous banter of excited voices. Underneath all the cheerfulness was an underlying tension of nervousness. Tempers were sometimes short. It was like the strained calm before a battle. All the pressures that had built up through the day were going to be discharged in one game of snooker.

It was an education in psychology just to watch the escapades some of the cons got up to. There was one inmate whose voice had a high-pitched tone, so his associates nicknamed him 'Squeak'.

The normal crowd was at the snooker table and there was a hubbub of many voices, some raised in an attempt to be heard over the din. I watched as total silence descended over the gathering and Squeak picked up his cue and walked slowly to the table. His eyes were almost closed as he scrutinized the position of the balls. Then suddenly, with hunched shoulders, he would charge along the side of the table, only to stop and then retreat backwards to his original position. He carried the cue at the 'slope', like a Zulu warrior going into the attack, and his gaze was fixed on the cue-ball like that of a hunter on a small animal. Sometimes, with quick short steps, he would scurry backwards into the crowd, which would open up as everyone would move out of his way so as not to annoy him. Meanwhile his opponent would stand motionless to the side as though he was too frightened to move. And so the antics would continue until his adversary would take to the table. The place was full of the most unbelievable absurdities.

It was Christmas 1979. 1 was set to spend my fourth Christmas in the Prison Service and I was detailed to work over the holiday period. But as I had a rest day on Saturday the 15th December, Delta, Joanne and I decided to go to Belfast to do some Christmas shopping. Like many other UK cities, Belfast is a very busy place on a Saturday afternoon, and because it was so near Christmas, the streets were thronged with people, making it a tiring experience. However, we visited most of the big stores and bought a selection of presents. And at the end, we marked a most enjoyable day in Belfast by having a meal in the same Chinese Restaurant in Royal Avenue, where we had a meal on the day Delta and I were engaged in 1964.

I was detailed the control room on Christmas Day, which wasn't too bad an assignment, as duty in the block on a Christmas Day was, what they called, 'Sunday routine procedure'. This effectively meant that because the workshops and visits were closed, there was very little movement out of the block. Another acceptable point about the duty was, we worked a split-shift system on Christmas Day. I reported for duty at 7.30 in the morning, and relieved the night guard, took over the control room and remained there until 2 pm. Then 1 was relieved by another member of staff and allowed to go home. So at least I had the afternoon and evening at home with my family.

In the following months, the Maze became the scene of a fateful battle of wills between the Northern Ireland Office and the IRA, a controversy that would ultimately result in ten IRA men starving themselves to death. The prisoners were determined to gain political status and therefore be recognised as prisoners of war, not criminals. Special Category Status would allow them to wear their own clothes, but it would also give them other privileges not enjoyed by ordinary prisoners, the freedom to associate and to organise their own activities, which would include the right not to work. The Northern Ireland Office, and the large majority of people in the Province, held the view that the situation in Northern Ireland was a sectarian, terrorist campaign and in no sense a war, and as a result the IRA prisoners should be treated as common criminals.

The leaders of the IRA claimed that the Government's position was a denial of its principle that it was engaged in a war of liberation, and that its convicted comrades were prisoners of war. It was the IRA's view that they had been sentenced in Diplock, no-jury Courts because of the political nature of their offences, which alone was an acknowledgement that they were political pnsoners.

In fact the Diplock Court system was introduced into Province as the result of an inquiry into the legal system. On the 20th December 1972 a report into the legal proceedings required to deal with terrorist-related cases was published. The report of a committee headed by Lord Diplock dealt with the problem of intimidation by terrorist organisations of witnesses and jurors in terrorist-type cases. In fact the practice of bullying and coercion among terrorist suspects had become so blatant that in some cases the defendant would sit in the dock, look at the jury and raise his right index finger to the side of his head in a 'clicking gesture'. The threat was so intimidating that some of the witnesses refused to give evidence in the court, and some individuals refused to do jury service. The Diplock Report recommended that trials of scheduled offences should be heard by a Judge of the High Court, or a County Court Judge, sitting alone without a jury, but with the normal rights of appeal. The recommendations for the controversial 'Diplock Courts' were later included in the 1973 Emergency Powers Act.

What influenced the Republicans to maintain their position was the fact that they had achieved Special Category Status once before. In 1972 a number of IRA prisoners convened a hunger strike at the Crumlin Road prison, demanding political status. The Secretary of State at the time, Mr William Whitelaw, capitulated to their demands after 37 days of the strike, and before any of them died, they were given Special Category Status.

Before being eligible to sit the Senior Officers' promotion examination in the Prison Service, an officer had to complete four years service. I had completed the required four years on October 1979, and at the beginning of February 1980 a notice was posted to the effect that a promotion examination would be held on the 3rd March. I decided to put my name forward to sit the exam, and a few days later I received notification that it would be held at the training college. The first paper would be from I I 00 hrs to 13 00 hrs and the second paper from 13 45 hrs to 15 15 hrs. I started to brush-up on the vast array of Governor's orders, Chief Officer's orders, Standing orders and rules and regulations and the various Laws and Acts of Parliament regarding the detention of prisoners. On the day of the exam I headed off for the college with a packed lunch and a flask of tea, as the instructions I had received from the Prisons Department had explained that there were no food facilities at the college. I had to make-do with a cup of tea in the car at lunchtime. The appointed venue for the examination was the gymnasium which was fitted out with rows of small class-tables, and when the exam started, a couple of teachers walked slowly up and down between the rows, like village constables on the beat.

When the examination was over, 1 talked to some of the officers who were from the Maze. Others were from the Crum, the Young Offenders' Centre at Hydebank Wood, and there were some staff from Magilligan. As I drove home that evening, I had a good idea that I was not going to be successful with the promotion exam, because I thought I hadn't done enough to achieve the required marks. My fears were realised a couple of weeks later when the results were posted and I had failed.

Since the beginning of 1980, the Governor decided to rotate the staff duties in the Maze to allow all the prison officers to acquire experience of work in the 'H' Blocks. From that time onwards I was detailed posts outside the block, and most of the time I was assigned duty in the visitor's car park. The visitors' car park was situated about 500 yards from the prison main gate and about 100 yards from the extern gate. This was the reception area for all visitors to the prison, where they were documented, searched and then transported up through the main gate into the prison. Access to the visitors' car park was from the Bog Road, which ran along the northern side of the prison, parallel with the outer fence. At the entrance, which was surrounded by a twelve-foot high corrugated iron fence, there was a large notice board that listed the prisoners' entitlements as regards food parcels and hobby equipment that were pernlitted into the prison. The notice board also listed prohibited articles, and warned that any attempt to smuggle such contraband into the prison would be deemed as illegal trafficking, which was prohibited under the law.

The parcel censors were situated in a large prefabricated building alongside the car park offices. Here all food parcels and hobby equipment sent into the prisoners was searched and examined. As each parcel was accepted over the counter at the front office, it was placed on a conveyer belt that carried it through an x-ray machine, which would detect metal or any foreign body and show the contents on a monitor screen. Each parcel was then opened and every item recorded, along with the name and number of the prisoner for whom the parcel had been left. The number of his block was also recorded and when it was processed, the parcel was left aside to be delivered that evening. The contents of an average food parcel were tobacco, cigarette papers, cigarettes, soap, razor blades, radio batteries and fruit. Sometimes magazines and books were also allowed into the prison.

The Personnel Governor sent for me one morning and asked me if I would like a spell of duty in the tally lodge. I told him I would appreciate the experience of a change of duty and would like to give it a try. So on the 10th March I reported to the tally lodge and went to see the Principal Officer in charge. It was Pat Kerr, whom I had worked with in the compounds. He was a Senior Officer then, but since that time he had been promoted to PO and was now in charge of the tally lodge. He welcomed me and introduced me to the rest of the men in the squad, about twelve in all. They were divided up into separate units to cover the evening duty, association duty and night guard. From now on, all my night guard duty would be carried out in the precincts of the tally lodge. On the day shift there were two book men who recorded the times of all staff in and out of the prison, and there was a search team who gave everyone entering or leaving the prison a rubdown search.

The tally lodge was run on the same pass-change system as was operated in the compounds, with a gate-lodge and a series of gates manned by officers. But at the side of the gate-lodge there was an airlock, about 20 yards long by about 8 yards wide, extending from the main gate to the inner fence gate. This area was known as movements-control, where all vehicles entering and leaving the prison were searched and the details of all passengers recorded.

A small, reinforced-concrete building to the side of the tally lodge was the prison armoury, where all firearms had to be lodged, as weapons of any kind were not permitted inside the prison. This regulation was brought into force after an incident in Armagh prison in the early 1970's, when a policeman was overpowered by IRA prisoners and his gun taken from him. The siege later ended without bloodshed, when the prisoners gave themselves up. Every morning was a 7 0' clock start in the tally lodge and the association duty didn't finish until 9.30 at night, when all the staff had left the prison.

On the 3rd May 1979, the Conservatives, led by Mrs Margaret Thatcher, won the General Election. Meanwhile, the protest in the prison and on the streets in some nationalist areas continued, but the Northern Ireland Office was even more determined not to give in to the Republican pressure. By now there were 1,365 prisoners in the Maze; 837 were Republicans, 341 of whom were on the dirty protest. The Maze had now attained the status of the largest prison in Western Europe. But perhaps it should be remembered that before the IRA campaign started in 1968, Ulster had proportionally the lowest prison population in Western Europe. But within a few years it had the highest; a sudden increase that was purely the result of the troubles. Moreover, the campaign, both in the Maze and on the streets, for the restoration of special category status, by now was running out of steam, and as far as the IRA leadership in the prison were concerned, there was only one more card to play: 'Hunger-strike'.

When the IRA in the Maze put the suggestion to the leadership of the Republican movement on the outside, they were against the idea because they knew that if it failed, it would strengthen the N.I.O.'s prison policy and probably break the morale of the prisoners inside the jail. But as there were more IRA men inside the Maze than there were active terrorists outside, the conviction of the prisoners could not be ignored. The leadership on the outside finally agreed and on the 2nd October 1980, seven prisoners refused breakfast and began a hunger-strike.

At that time the Prison Department realised that a proper hospital wing would have to be prepared for the hunger-strikers, and all the prisoners in 'A' wing of H Block 3 were dispersed to the other two streaker wings in the block, as well as to the other streaker blocks. 'A' wing was then cleaned, painted and made ready as a serviceable hospital wing, and the seven hunger-strikers were moved to their new sterile surroundings. The wing was manned 24 hours a day by medical staff who carried out observations and recorded any abnormalities that arose in the patients.

When the hunger-strikers - who were led by Brendan (Darkie) Hughes were on the fast for 30 days, they were moved to the prison hospital for closer medical supervision. As the hunger-strike continued, seven women from the women's prison in Armagh joined the protest on the 1 st December, and within a few more days the total number of protesters on the fast in the Maze had risen to 30. As far as the public were concerned, the Government were resolute that they would not talk to the hunger-strikers, but behind-the-scenes negotiations were taking place between the IRA and Government representatives.

Protests on the streets of Belfast had spread to Londonderry and some other towns in the Province, as well as Dublin and some towns in the South and on the fifty-third day of the hunger-strike one of the prisoners, who was nearing death, was transferred to the Royal Victoria Hospital in Belfast.

Meanwhile, the negotiations had produced a possible solution to the hunger-strike, and a courier was sent from the Foreign Office in London to the Maze with a plan that could be a resolution of the problem. When Brendan Hughes heard about this development, and believing the prisoner in the Royal Victoria Hospital was nearing death, he called off the hunger-strike. But when the Foreign Office Official arrived in the Maze, it became clear that the document he was carrying did not meet the IRA's demands, and by now the strike had been called off and Hughes had no bargaining power. As a result the IRA perceived that they had been out-manoeuvred by the British Government, and there was a serious disagreement between Brendan Hughes and the rest of the IRA leadership in the Maze.

It was after lock-up when the go-between from the Government arrived at the prison hospital. I was speaking to one of the night guard officers the following morning as he was going off duty. He told me about a meeting that had taken place in the hospital in the middle of the night. He said a minibus was sent round the IRA blocks to collect some of the leaders, including Bobby Sands, and they were taken to the prison hospital, obviously to discuss the correspondence that had arrived from the Government.

The very idea of top IRA men being unlocked from their cells in the early hours, and a minibus driving around the prison to collect them and take them to the hospital, was a contradiction of the most basic rules of prison security. It was a breach of security that was talked about in staff circles for years.

Bobby Sands, who had taken over as the IRA's spokesman in the Maze, was determined that a second hunger-strike would get results, and therefore set about persuading the IRA leadership that a new strike would be successful. Sands had studied the lessons they had learnt by the October strike, and he told the leadershIp that its main weakness had been that too many prisoners refused food at the same time. He argued that a new hunger-strike should be organised on a rolling basis, with one prisoner going on the fast each week. This, on average, would lead to a death each week, which would put increasing pressure on the Government to concede to their demands. The IRA prisoners in the Maze agreed with his theory and he convinced the outside leadership of the merits of his plan. They also agreed with him and he immediately stood down as the so called commanding officer in the Maze, in anticipation of the second hungerstrike.

The movements control area of the prison front gate came under the supervision of the tally lodge PO, which meant from time to time I was detailed as vehicle search officer on the post. I was 8 o'clock start on movements control on Monday 29th December 1980 and, before I left home, I watched the early morning TV news. The main point of the news was about the murder of a 42-year-old Warrant Officer in the T.A.V.R. in Armagh. Then to my horror his name was revealed. It was Hugh McGinn, my friend and colleague whom 1 had known in the Royal Irish Rangers, and served with many times on the headquarters guard force at the Battalion Headquarters in Armagh. Hugh was now a Colour Sergeant Major in the Battalion, and was the first T.A.V.R. officer to be murdered since the terror campaign began.

The murder happened at about 11 o'clock on Sunday night, when Hugh answered a knock at the front door of his home at Ungola Villas. When he went into the hallway and asked the identification of the caller, he was given the name of a person he knew, and as he opened the door, he was shot by a burst of machine-gun fire.

He was an easy target, and his murder worried security chiefs that other members of the low profile army force could also be systematically picked out as further easy targets by the murder gangs. Security chiefs were concerned at the new twist in the Republican murder campaign, because the T.A.V.R. was under N.A.T.O. control and therefore had never been on active security service in Northern Ireland.

Hugh had served in the Regiment for over 25 years, and in his day-to-day job he worked for a washing machine firm. Only four hours before his murder he had left his wife and six children in their home, while he travelled to the other end of town to visit his mother. Then he returned home, and had just settled down to watch TV when the deadly knock came to the door. Shortly after the murder a telephone call was made to the BBC in Belfast, and a man claiming responsibility for the killing gave a code word used by the Irish National Liberation Army (INLA). Police later received infornmtion about a car that sped off towards the KilIylea Road, and they were working on the theory that it was the getaway car. Hugh had escaped injury in an attempt on his life a few years earlier.

The Archbishop of Armagh at the time, Cardinal Thomas O'Fiaich, said that the murder was rendered all the more horrifying by the circumstances in which it took place, at Mr McGinn's home in the middle of the season of peace and goodwill. He said it had also taken place 'only a few hours' after the religious leaders of the country had gathered in Armagh to inaugurate a week of prayer for Ireland and he pleaded to all to ensure that the peace of Christmas would not be shattered by further violence.

Three days later, on New Year's Eve morning, a lone piper played a graveside lament as the Battalion's final tribute to Sergeant Major McGinn, who was buried from his home. The funeral was to St Patrick's Cathedral, with the burial afterwards in the adjoining cemetery. The lone piper, playing solemn music, preceded the coffin bearing the dead Sergeant's caubeen and belt, as it was carried by comrades through the Cathedral grounds on the start of its halfmile journey to the cemetery. About 300 mourners walked behind the cortege, taking the 'long way' to pass along the Mall West, on the opposite side of the roadway to the T.A. Centre where the dead man had served.

As the procession reached the cemetery, the hearse came to a stop as a contingent of Hugh's superior officers and comrades, along with civilians including the chairman of the District Council Mr William Henning, joined the funeral. Cardinal Thomas O'Fiaich, who had condemned the murder as 'horrifying', was unable to take part in the ceremony because of a prior engagement in Dublin. However, he did visit the family home earlier, to express his sympathy personally. During the Mass, sympathy was expressed on behalf of the parochial clergy to the widow and family. The day following the murder the DUP leader Dr Paisley visited the family and expressed condolences and Mr Harold McCusker, who was MP for Armagh at the time, also visited the home.

Chapter 13

The situation in the Province remained volatile with the brutal murder of Sir Norman Strong, the 86-year-old former Speaker of the Stormont Parliament, and his son James, who were murdered by the IRA at their home, Tynan Abbey, near the border. An IRA statement was issued later admitting to the killings.

On the 5th February the Republican prisoners in the Maze issued a threat that there would be fresh hunger-strikes, if they were not treated as prisoners of war, and on the 1st March Bobby Sands refused breakfast and told prison officers he was going on a hunger-strike.

The 1st March was, by coincidence, the fifth anniversary of the day on which the Government had started to phase out special category status in 1976. Sands was serving 14 years for firearms offences, and when the news broke, the Roman Catholic Bishop of Derry, Dr Edward Daly, criticised the action by saying it was not morally justified in the present circumstances. With the hunger-strike tactic upping the stakes in their campaign for political status, the Republican prisoners called off their dirty protest the following day to focus all attention on the hunger-strike.

Five days later, on the 5th March 1981, Mr Frank Maguire, the MP for Fermanagh - South Tyrone died, and in the ensuing days there was considerable debate in the nationalist camp over whether there could be an agreed candidate to contest the by-election. Provisional Sinn Fein were slow at first to see the opportunity that the election provided, and at first they were happy to see Maguire's brother, Noel, stand. Bernadette McAliskey undermined this arrangement by declaring her own interest in the seat. But after the Roman Catholic Bishop of Clogher spoke in favour of Maguire's candidacy, McAliskey made it clear that she would only stand down in favour of an H Block prisoners' candidate. The idea was quickly picked up by the Provisional Sinn Fein leadership, who were at first concerned about the political repercussions of losing the by-election, but finally agreed to put forward a candidate, Francis Hughes, who was serving a life sentence for murder. Bernadette McAliskey, formally Bernadette Devlin, held a seat before. It was in April 1969, in a byelection caused by the death of Mr. George Forrest the Unionist MP for Mid-Ulster. Devlin, standing as a Unity candidate, was elected to Westminister by defeating the former MP's widow. The turnout for the election was 92%. At the age of 21, Devlin was the youngest woman ever elected to Westminister and the youngest MP for half a century.

On the 15th March a second IRA prisoner joined the hunger-strike and on the 22nd March, Sands and Hughes were joined by Raymond McCreesh, another IRA prisoner, and Patsy O'Hara, leader of the Irish National Liberation Army (INLA) prisoners in the Maze.

On the 26th March Bobby Sands was nominated for the Fermanagh South Tyrone by-election, as what provisional Sinn Fein called an 'H Block

Prisoners' Candidate'. On the 29th March the Social Democratic and Labour Party (SOLP) withdrew the nomination of Austin Currie from the by-election, leaving two nationalist candidates, Bobby Sands and Noel Maguire. But a short time later the brother of the former MP Maguire 'yielded to moral pressure', and withdrew from the election, which became a straight fight between an Ulster Unionist and an IRA prisoner.

The emotions that the hunger-strike had created ensured a high turnout of the electorate in nationalist areas, and on the 9th April, when the by-election was held for the Westminister seat of Fermanagh - South Tyrone, amid worldwide media attention, the election had resolved into a straight contest between the leader of the hunger-strikers in the Maze, Bobby Sands (who was now 40 days on hunger-strike and becoming very frail), and the Ulster Unionist candidate Mr Harry West.

Mr West had held the seat between the two general elections of 1974. With the failure of the SOLP to put forward a candidate, nationalists in the constituency had the choice of abstaining, voting for the Unionist candidate, or the IRA man. On a turnout of 86.9 per cent, Bobby Sands received 30,492 votes to Harry West's 29,046 votes. Ironically, there were 3280 spoiled votes, which gave a major boost to the hunger-strike campaign, causing dissension within the SDLP and increasing the bittemess between Unionists and Nationalists throughout Northem Ireland. When the result was finally declared on the 11th April, there were parades celebrating the IRA victory in many areas, but the demonstrations deteriorated into riots in Belfast, Londonderry, Cookstown and Lurgan. As soon as the result was announced, the Government made it clear that the result would not make an iota of difference to prison policy on refusing special category status to the prisoners in the Maze. In fact, on the 2nd June, as a result of the IRA victory the Govemment published an amendment to the Representation of the People Act, prohibiting prisoners from standing in elections for Parliament.

It was well known at the time, and provisional Sinn Fein made it clear, that they were only 'borrowing the seat' in order to save Bobby Sand's life. In retrospect, it could be said that most of the people who voted for Sands did so because they wanted to save his life, rather than for any great support for the IRA. But at the same time as the count was taking place in Fermanagh - South Tyrone, Bobby Sands and his fellow hunger-striker Francis Hughes had already been moved out of their blocks to the prison hospital. Unlike the previous hunger-strike, when the prisoners remained in 'A' wing of H Block 3, they were now moved directly to the prison hospital from their own blocks. Eight days after his election to the House of Commons, Sands received the last rights of the Roman Catholic Church and an emissary from the Pope gave him a golden crucifix.

As a succession of intermediaries could do nothing to persuade him, or his fellow hunger-strikers, to give up the fast, the Governor of the Maze became concerned about the security of the prison in the event of Sand's death.

The Security Department saw the association interval as the most dangerous period, as all the prisoners were unlocked at that time; and since the strikers had given up their protest, there were large numbers of ardent terrorists with free access to the wings. It was decided to form a riot squad and about 30 men, under the control of a PO and an SO, volunteered each evening. A portacabin in the Trades Department, which had been used to store timber, was cleared out and chairs placed along the sides. The men were kitted out in riot gear, and two minibuses were ordered on standby each evening to rush the team to any block in the jail where there was trouble. As it turned out, they were not needed, because as each hunger-striker died, a solemn atmosphere descended on the Republican wings, similar, I suspect, to that which would have happened in the Crum after a hanging. But in the rest of the wings, the razzmatazz went on just the same. Meanwhile the Government was coming under increasing pressure to resolve the hunger-strike issue, and in the USA, Irish-American politicians tried to influence the US Government into doing all in its power to intervene in the situation in the Maze.

The Government in London was unnerved by the election results, but its hard-line approach to the hunger-strike was beginning to change. In public it seemed to be doing as much as possible to resolve the stalemate, but at the same time it was intent on not meeting the prisoners' demands. The Prime Minister made clear her resolve in interviews to the media, when she said, "Crime is crime! Is crime! It is not political, it is crime and there can be no question of granting political status to criminals." Nevertheless, the story that was circulating around the staff grapevine in the Maze was that the Government was weakening but the story was that a number of senior civil servants in the Northern Ireland Office who were acting as intermediaries between the prisoners and the Government had threatened to resign if the Government capitulated. And it was these threats that made the Government stand fast.

Bobby Sands lapsed into a coma on Sunday the 3rd May and died two days later, in the early hours of Tuesday the 5th May 1981, after 66 days on hunger-strike. The Northern Ireland Office in a statement to the media said he had taken his own life after refusing food and medical intervention for 66 days.

He was serving 14 years for possession of firearms when he was arrested after a bombing incident at Dunmurry in South Belfast. Although it was a very wet day, almost 100,000 people attended Sand's funeral which amounted to almost one fifth of the nationalist population of Northern Ireland. The coffin was draped with a tricolour, on top of which sat the usual black beret and gloves, the usual array denoting a fallen IRA volunteer. A similar display adorned the coffins of the remaining hungerstrikers who died, along with the masked guard of honour in their combat jackets, and headed by a lone piper. At the Republican plot in Milltown Cemetery where Bobby Sands was buried, a grandstand had been erected by the Republican movement to allow the army of photographers to have an uninterrupted view of the proceedings.

The NIO was surprised at the depth of feelings the death had caused. Sands had been elevated to the status of international hero, and some Governments, including the United States, expressed sympathy at the death. The event sparked major riots in nationalist's areas throughout the Province. The day after the funeral, Sands was replaced on hunger-strike by another IRA prisoner, and at 5.30 pm on Tuesday the 12th May the second hunger-striker Francis Hughes died, after 59 days on the fast. It was alleged that Hughes had been a Republican activist since the age of 16 and had been involved in more than 30 murders. He was serving a life sentence for murder, 14 years for attempted murder and two terms of 20 years for other offences. The news of Hughe's death increased the wave of rioting in nationalist areas of Belfast and Londonderry, which had persisted since the death of Bobby Sands. On the 14th May another IRA prisoner, Brendan McLaughlin, replaced Hughes on the hunger-strike.

It seemed that their strategy of a death a week was going to plan, and as they had forecast, and as the fast continued, the numbers of 'medics' in the hospital was increased. The hospital was always seen as neutral territory for all the prisoners in the Maze. No matter to which organisation or group a prisoner belonged, he extended to the hospital the respect it deserved and the hospital officers were held with similar regard. In fact as the hunger-strike progressed, some of the prisoners became on first-name terms with the hospital officers, as they realised they were doing all in their power to help them and to make life as comfortable as possible for them. This was recognised by the Maze Governor, realising that as the body's resistance to infection decreased in each inmate, there was a danger that the slightest impurity in ordinary tap water could cause death. He therefore ordered cases of Scottish Highland Spring Water, in an effort to keep the prisoners alive as long as possible. As each hunger-striker was admitted to the hospital, all visiting restrictions were lifted by the Governor and the families were allowed to visit at any time of the day. As the strikers' health worsened, a room was made available in the hospital for the families so that they could stay overnight if they wanted.

The NIO was convinced that support for the hunger-strike would diminish as time went on, and that eventually the strikers would give up when they realised their efforts had failed. On the 21 st May, Raymond McCreesh and Patsy 0' Hara died after 61 days on hunger-strike. McCreesh was serving 14 years for attempted murder, and O'Hara was serving eight years for the possession of a grenade. News of their deaths caused the now usual wave of rioting in Republican areas. Raymond McCreesh was buried near Camlough in South Armagh and Patsy O'Hara's funeral took place in Londonderry.

The first four hunger-strikers were now dead and the NIO were as unwilling as ever to make concessions to their demands. On the 28th May, an IRA man by the name of Martin Husson joined the hunger-strike, and on the same day the Prime Minister, Mrs Thatcher, was paying a visit to the Province. During her stay she claimed the hunger-strike was the IRA's last card, and rejected claims that the Government was intransigent and inflexible. On the 8th June another IRA man joined the hunger-strike; his name was Tom McElwee. On the l5th June he was joined by another IRA man, called Paddy Quinn, and another hunger-striker was approaching death.

At the same time, a number of approaches were being made to the NIO by groups who were working behind the scenes, trying to resolve the situation. One group stated that the hunger-strikers had decided they would be happy to see any changes in prison conditions applying to all prisoners in the Maze. This was an apparent easing of their intransigent position, thus opening an avenue for the Government to compromise. So the NI0 decided to start talks with representatives of the IRA on the outside, and a statement was delivered to the external leadership of the I RA which set out agreed concessions, except freedom of association, provided there was an immediate end to the hunger-strike.

Meanwhile in the Irish Republic there was a general election which resulted in two of the hunger-strikers winning seats in the Eire Parliament. On the 22nd June, Michael Devine of the INLA joined the hunger-strike, and seven days later, on the 29th June, he was joined by Lawrence McKeown of the IRA. The fifth prisoner to die on hunger-strike passed away on the 8th July after 61 days on the fast. Joe McDonald was serving a 14 year sentence for firebombing a Belfast furniture shop. After McDonald's funeral on the 10th July, rioting broke out when an army unit overpowered an IRA firing party at the graveside. The weapons were seized and a number of arrests made.

In the midst of all the trouble in Northern Ireland and the hunger-strike deaths at the time, a murder took place on the 2nd July that was as horrendous as any killing that ever happened in the Province. It was the kind of crime that would make your flesh cry out. It was the murder of a five-year-old Antrim girl called Julie Ann Cole.

Julie disappeared after leaving her home to return a friend's coat to a house only a few doors from her own home, on that Thursday evening. A search operation started after the alarm was raised by Julie's mother, only a half an hour after she had left home. As there was still no sign of her the following day, scores of police and army personnel using tracker dogs were backed up by civilian volunteers in a massive hunt for the missing girl. The searchers were out from dawn, combing the countryside and examining derelict buildings in the area. Police hurriedly issued information leaflets bearing Julie's photograph and description.

Fourteen hours after her disappearance, Julie's body was found in the attic of a house only a few yards from her own home. An unemployed Antrim man, Terence Graham, was arrested and charged with her murder. At the end of his trial he received a life sentence and arrived in one of the conforming blocks in the Maze.

One evening, a few weeks later I was on association duty in 'B' wing of H Block 6. The 'rubber wing' was where all the activity took place, a substantial part of which was in the mind. I was leaving the wing on my way out to the circle, and as the wing officer opened the inner grille, I stepped into the airlock and he locked the grille behind me: a tall con in his early twenties was already standing in the airlock. I glanced at him and, although our eyes did not make contact, I suddenly recognised him.

It was Graham. His eyes jerked constantly from side to side; he was like a trapped animal looking for the slightest opportunity to make a break. I could sense aggression, and it was near the surface. In prison a fleeting glance carries a thousand words, and as our eyes briefly met, my message to him was; if you make an aggressive move towards me, I will annihilate you. The non-verbal message was transmitted. He knew where he stood. We both knew the score. It was the only time in my career that I was in danger of losing control. Like all prisoners who were convicted of sex crimes, he was deeply unhappy. Perhaps he was now getting to know the nature of his own personality. He viewed those around him with intense fear and suspicion, and he carried with him a distinct aura of evil. I hastily put the memory behind me. The grille opened and he slithered across the airlock into the opposite wing. He was a clammy, unhealthy worm-like creature, which had no place in the bright sunlight that shone in through the block windows.

The talks between the NIO representatives and the IRA, by now, had come to an end and the situation was totally deadlocked. On the 13th July the sixth hunger-striker died. He was Martin Husson and he was serving a 20-year sentence for conspiracy to murder, possession of firearms and membership of the IRA. He had been on hunger-strike for 45 days. He was replaced on the fast the following day by an IRA prisoner called Matt Devlin.

As the hunger-strike continued and the health of each prisoner deteriorated and he was close to death, the atmosphere in the prison became highly charged. Sometimes we were told that a prisoner was not expected to live until the following morning, and we were instructed to prepare for any eventuality. The riot squad that had been formed before the death of Bobby Sands remained on standby each evening throughout the entire hunger-strike. But they were not needed. After each death the mood in the Republican blocks became sombre and mournful, but in the Loyalist blocks, life continued as usual.

In Dublin on the 18th July, a demonstration in support of the Maze hunger-strikers ended in violence, as the marchers were stopped from making their way past the British Embassy. A vicious riot developed in which 80 protesters and 120 garda were injured. The following day the hunger-strikers rejected attempts by the Swiss Red Cross to mediate in the hunger-strike. Neither the prisoners nor the NIO were willing to compromise on the question of special category status.

On the morning of the 1st August 1981, the seventh hunger-striker died. He was Kevin Lynch of the INLA, serving four years for firearms offences. He had been on hunger-strike for 71 days. I was detailed movements control that morning, which was a Saturday. I reported for duty at 8 o'clock and took up my post. It was a quiet Saturday morning as usual, and the conversation amongst the staff in the main gate area was about the death of the hunger-striker. A short time later a tally lodge window opened and the PO leaned out and said, "Hi, Killer, there's a hearse on its way up from the extern gate; it's going to the prison hospital. Let me know when it goes through." "OK, Sir," I replied as I started to walk down the airlock towards the main gate. A few seconds later I looked out through the observation slot in the gate, as the Volvo Estate car came to a stop outside. I opened the gate and there was a row of police Land Rovers parked on the opposite side of the road, all facing towards the extern gate. As the car stopped in the airlock, the two undertakers left the vehicle and went into the tally lodge to change their passes.

I gave the car a very quick check-over, and as the men returned, I opened the inner fence gate and the hearse drove into the phase towards the hospital. A few minutes later I heard permission being given on the RT for the vehicle to leave the hospital, and as it returned, I opened the inner fence gate and, without stopping, the vehicle drove slowly into the airlock. As it passed me, I looked through the side windows and saw the body bag in the back. Although he was a dead IRA man, a respectful and dignified silence descended throughout the gate lodge complex. Republican politicians had tried to make some propaganda milage out of the idea of 'a line of coffins coming out of the Maze prison', but not a single coffin came into, or went out of, the Maze. As the two men went into the tally lodge, changed their passes and returned, I opened the main gate and the hearse drove out and was met by its police escort. The whole cortege moved slowly off towards the extern gate.

The prisoners' resolve was to be finally fractured by a source much closer to home. It was in the form of a Dungannon priest, Father Dennis Faul, who had contacted the families of all the prisoners still on hunger-strike. The prisoners knew from the start that the greatest threat to their protest was from their own families, who, although they had shown total support for the hunger-strike, were facing a short private dilemma, because the law states that once a prisoner has lost consciousness, his life is in the hands of his next of kin.

Dennis Faul had been in close contact with the families from the start of the hunger-strike, and he believed the families did not want their kinsfolk to die in an effort to boost the political standing of Provisional Sinn Fein. It seemed that the IRA's weapon of protest through hunger-strike was changing from fasting, to big public funerals, which were being used as a propaganda stunt. So on the 28th July 1981, Fr Faul met the families in a hotel in Toomebridge. He told them that it was his opinion that the NI0 were not going to make any concessions, regarding the hunger-strike, and that nothing would be gained by more deaths.

A lengthy discussion took place, and when the meeting ended, it was the decision of everyone that the hunger-strike should be stopped. They decided to go there and then, to see the IRA leadership in Belfast. They arrived at Sinn Fein office on the Falls Road in the early hours, where a noisy debate took place after which the IRA leaders told the families that the organisation could not order the men off the fast. However. the following morning Dennis Faul received a phone call from the IRA leadership, stating that they were prepared to talk to the hunger-strikers, and if they decided to end the strike, then that could only be welcomed. The IRA also stated that the NIO were offering partial concessions to their demands, but despite this, the hunger-strikers were intent on continuing with the fast.

On the 3 lst July what the hunger -strikers feared most happened. At the request of his family, hunger-striker Paddy Quinn received medical treatment to save his life after 47 days on hunger-strike. Two days later, on the 2nd August, Kieran Doherty was the eighth hunger-striker to die, after 73 days on the fast. Doherty was serving 22 years for firearms and explosives offences. He was one of the republican prisoners elected to the Dail in June. He was followed on the 8th August by Tom McElwee who was serving 22 years, for the manslaughter of a woman during a series of firebomb attacks. He was the ninth hunger-striker to die. He had been on hunger-strike for 62 days. On the 20th August Michael Devine was the tenth hunger-striker to die. He was in the INLA and was serving 12 years for firearms offences. He had been on hunger-strike for 60 days. An NIO spokesman said he had taken his own life by refusing food and medical intervention for 60 days.

Against the backdrop of the continuing hunger-strike, the second byelection in the year, was held in Fermanagh-South Tyrone, as a result of the death of Bobby Sands. Owen Carron stood as an 'Anti H Block Proxy Political Prisoner', representing Provisional Sinn Fein. His main competition was from the Ulster Unionist and former UDR Major, Ken Maginnis. Other candidates represented Alliance, Workers Party/Republican Clubs, 'General Amnesty and Peace'. The SDLP again refused to contest the election.

With an increased turnout of 88.6 per cent, Carron won the seat with 31,278 votes and Ken Maginnis was runner-up with 29,048, almost exactly the same as Harry West's vote in April.

On August 23rd, in the wake of the electoral triumph, Provisional Sinn Fein announced they would contest future Ulster elections, including the Westminster seat of West Belfast that was held by Gerry Fitt, who had been a strong opponent of the hunger-strike.

Devine was the last hunger-striker to die. The same day, the wife of one of the remaining hunger-strikers agreed to her husband receiving medical attention. By the 6th September four hunger-strikers were being given medical attention, and by the beginning of October the remaining hunger-strikers ended the fast. Moreover, despite the ending of the hunger-strike, republican prisoners in the Maze continued to protest, but although they did not achieve special category status, in the months ahead they did win substantial concessions on several issues.

In the seventh month of the hunger-strike, Mr James Prior became the new Secretary of State for Northern Ireland on the 13th September. Lord Gowrie became the new Minister of State, and Nick Scott became the new Prisons Minister. When Prior arrived in the Province, one of his first duties was to visit the Maze prison. Speaking about the prisoners' announcement on the 3rd October in which they called off the hunger-strike, Mr Prior promised that he would look carefully at reform in the prison.

Three days later the Secretary of State conceded to one of the prisoners' demands by announcing that they would be able to wear their own clothes at all times. He also made partial concessions on some of the other hunger-strike demands, by stating that 50 per cent of lost remission would be restored, association would be permitted in adjoining wings in the blocks and also in the recreation rooms and exercise yards. Association in adjoining wings basically meant that prisoners would be allowed to associate between the opposite wings on each side of the H Block. For example, they could move between 'A' and 'B' wings, or 'C' and 'D' wings, but not across the circle area of the block. A greater number of visits would also be allowed to each prisoner.

By the 25th October all but 10 of the 399 prisoners who took part in the dirty protest were wearing their own clothes and on the following day a bomb exploded in Oxford Street in London, killing a police explosives expert who had tried to defuse the device. Although the issue of prison work remained a matter of disagreement, it was a subject that was left open at the time. The possibility of widening the whole question of employment in prisons could be examined. In fact sometime later the NIO did concede on the work issue, and all the workshops in the Maze were closed down. But despite meeting the substance of the demands, no formal recognition was ever made of the prisoners' right to political status. Nevertheless, there is little doubt that Special Category Status was achieved by the prisoners in everything but name. It was a total reversal of prison policy. I believed at the time that although the Government had won the battle, they had lost the war. As one politician put it, whilst speaking in the House of Commons, "The Government has grabbed defeat out of the hands of victory!" But I think it has to be said that the one person who did most to end the hunger-strike, and who paid dearly for his efforts, was Dennis Faul, who was ostracized by his flock in the Maze.

While the hunger-strike lasted, ten prisoners had starved themselves to death and, in the violence that accompanied the protest, sixty-one people had been killed, thirty of whom were members of the Security Forces. Since these events, much has been written about the hunger-strike, and much propaganda made. On October the 31st 1981, at the Provisional Sinn Fein ard theis, a leading republican, Danny Morrison, confirmed the party's intention to contest elections, by stating: "Who here really believes we can win the war through the ballot box? But will anyone here object if, with a ballot paper in one hand and the Armalite in the other, we take power in Ireland!" Perhaps it should be noted that Morrison did not refer to Northern Ireland, but to Ireland.

On the 14th November the Ulster Unionist MP for South Belfast and Methodist Minister, The Reverend Robert Bradford, was murdered by the IRA at a community centre in his constituency at Finaghy in Belfast. The caretaker of the building also died in the attack. After the murder Dr Paisley commented:

"The blood of the murdered not only lies on the skirts of those who did the evil deed, but on the Government whose political and security policies have created the circumstances in which such crimes can be committed with impunity!" Three days later, on the 1st November, I attended the Reverend Bradford's funeral, accompanied by a colleague and his wife. The Secretary of State, Mr James Prior, also attended the service, and received an unfriendly reception of sustained hissing before the commencement of the funeral service.

At the end of the hunger-strike the republican movement made a statement, claiming that as a result of 'mounting pressure and cleric-inspired demoralisation, the hunger-strike was for tactical reasons suspended!'

Throughout the hunger-strike, doctors were on call 24 hours a day. They carried out observations and recorded all abnormalities in each prisoner. At the end of the fast, all notes and observations provided invaluable information to the medical profession regarding the slow deterioration of the human body, and the effects of starvation right up to death in each case. A consultant who specialised in metabolic disorders was in charge of the patients throughout the progression of the fast, and recorded details and itemized the sequence of events until death.

Daily statistics were also kept of the prisoners' condition, which included: weight, temperature, blood pressure, pulse, body functions etc. The slow deterioration of the prisoner's skin was another factor that was closely observed, as it became pale and dry. As a result of the diminishing levels of body fat in each patient, they always felt cold. The first two to three weeks on hunger-strike proved to be the most uncomfortable time, with pain arising from wind and colic. Excruciating pain was also caused by the stomach reducing in size. However, after this period had passed, the prisoners found it less painful and more bearable, as the body's metabolism adjusted to the condition. It was at this point, as the body's resistance to disease diminished, that the Prison Governor decided that the patients should be supplied with natural spring water, because he feared that tap water might be contaminated with bacteria, and therefore hasten death.

In each case as the strike progressed, the extremities of the body became bloodless and numb, and the prisoner in turn developed slight stomach infections, which produced poisonous gases that assisted in the eventual cause of death. After approximately 30 days on hunger-strike, each prisoner became confused and lapsed into a semi-coma, and then regained consciousness and was able to converse with the hospital staff. At about this stage in the fast, their vision became blurred and their eyes started to oscillate, making it impossible for them to focus their sight. As time went on, they fell into deeper comas and eventually into full comas without regaining consciousness.

Whilst on hunger-strike, each prisoner was allowed to have regular visits, and when it became evident to the doctors that he was nearing death, it was decided to allow close relatives to remain at his bedside until death occurred. A visiting room was prepared, complete with tea-making facilities, and trays of sandwiches supplied by the prison kitchen staff. The decision to allow relatives to remain in the prison hospital overnight caused some dissent among the hospital staff, particularly in regard to female relatives. For example, a question that was asked by the 'medics' was: what would the staff do if a female became hysterical and aggressive towards a prison officer in the middle of the night?

The hospital staff in the Maze at the time were all male, and according to the law, were unable to restrain a female, fortunately, no such problem arose throughout the hunger-strike. At the end of the hunger-strike, the next-of-kin signed the document allowing the doctors and hospital staff to administer immediate treatment to save the prisoners' lives. Each prisoner was transferred to the Royal Victoria Hospital for intensive care therapy, and later they were returned to the Maze in good health.

Prisoners all over the world have, at times, seen the hunger strike as a means of obtaining their objective, whether for better prison conditions or something else about which they feel strongly. But it is only when a hungerstrike takes place in one's own country that people begin to wonder what kind of person is prepared to take his own life for a cause. It is now known that during the Maze hunger-strike. the Chief Medical Office was in constant contact with prison doctors in other countries where hunger-strikes were in progress at that particular time.

The official U.K. Prison Service definition of a hunger-strike in 1981 was that when a prisoner refused food, for at least 24 hours, it was deemed a hungerstrike. The prison service strategy for dealing with such a situation was, after two days if the prisoners were still refusing food the Governor of the prison would interview him to establish the reason for his action. If at the end of the interview it was clear that the prisoner was to remain on his fast, the facts would be reported to the Prison Department. At this stage the medical officer would take charge of the case, and explain to the prisoner the effects of starvation on his health.

The consequences of self-starvation will vary with every case, as highlighted in the Maze fast, when one prisoner lived for 73 days and was conscious up until about two hours before death. Another prisoner only survived for 45 days before high blood pressure and kidney complications caused his demise. One significant factor illustrated in the Maze hunger-strike was that the prisoner who keeps his body in good physical condition will withstand starvation longer than one who is less fit.

The hunger-strike had been over for a few weeks, when the prison authorities suddenly realised they had a problem on their hands. Far from the prison system in the Maze going back to what it was before the protest, the paramilitaries were now better organised and resourceful, and they could always depend on the help of their dedicated friends and associates on the outside. By now total segregation had taken place and the main paramilitaty organisations occupied their own wings and blocks. We didn't realise it at the time, but the first stone had been cast for worse to come.

A new Number One Governor had taken charge of the Maze. His predecessor had been promoted to Director of Prisons and Security, and was now based at the NIO. The new man was one of the few Governors in the Maze who had come up through the ranks. He was a quiet, dignified man, in his early sixties. He had the manners and appearance of a country gentleman, a man I had much regard for. He wore a slightly dilapidated hat and his Christian name was William. As a result the staff nicknamed him 'Box-car Willie', after the famous country and western singer. After his retirement, those who followed him in the job perfectly illustrated the decisive shift in the NIO's centre of gravity.

There was not enough activity to occupy the large numbers of prisoners who were now in the wings. As a result many of them took up further education courses through the Open University. As has been seen, the large numbers of young men who entered the Maze without any kind of educational qualifications, and emerged with University degrees, including Honours and Masters degrees, illustrate a more compassionate regime than that portrayed by the IRA propaganda machine. The education facilities were firstly and typically exploited by the republicans. But from the early days, loyalists, mainly under the influence of Gusty Spence, also became involved in the option. The Maze has been described as a university of terror, but it certainly was a university campus for many who would not otherwise have had the opportunity to study on the outside. I have to admit, it was a lesson for me and many of my colleagues in the prison service, and we decided to have a go at further education ourselves. After some years of intense study, I achieved a Diploma in Applied Social Sciences, and before retiring from the service in 1999 I attained a Bachelor of Science (Honours) Degree.

It was the normal procedure in the blocks, when we were detailed duty on a bank holiday to have a day in lieu at a later time, provided the duty office staff agreed with the duty change. On Thursday 8th April 1982, I applied to the duty office for five bank holidays that were owed to me. When I saw the duty roster for the following week, I had been detailed four of the days, but as the fifth day's duty had yet to be displayed I assumed I had been assigned the five holidays so I took the five days off. When I returned for duty, the duty office PO sent for me and explained - in no uncertain terms - 1 had not been detailed the fifth day. When 1 explained I had assumed I was detailed all five days off: he raised his voice and started swearing at me.

Since I joined the service, I thought I had got used to that kind of language. It seemed to be a prerequisite for advancement in the service. But when it is directed at you with such venom, it becomes intolerable, although it was in keeping with the man's mentality. His office was run chaotically and he had the tendency to surround himself with a bunch of yes-men, probably to soothe his own insecurity and portray himself with a sharper edge. They were like courtiers around their King. But I have to admit his feelings towards me were reciprocated in full measure.

I decided to report him to the Chief Officer, but soon afterwards I realised I had committed the ultimate sin. I had made a formal complaint about a senior officer to another senior officer. a transgression that would haunt me for the rest of my career in the prison service. I soon found myself ostracized by the nudge-and-whisper brigade. A few days later I was ordered to report to the Chief Officer's office, and as I walked towards the admin building, I wondered about the fate that awaited me. Every time I walked into the admin building the surroundings conveyed to me a feeling of not belonging, as if I were trespassing. But I was content that I didn't belong there, because that was where the phoney people resided, the Chief Officers and Governors who ran the prison and pretended they actually cared about the place. I could never have fitted into that company, because I wasn't their type of officer. They preferred the mealymouthed crawler, who deferred to their superior status. I was much too forthright for that.

The office door had a tapered panel set into its upper portion, which bore a small name-plate with the words: 'Chief Officer 1'. The door was slightly ajar and he was sitting at his desk. I knocked on the door and he got up and walked towards me. Speaking in his Chief Officer's voice, he said: "McKane, wait there!" He indicated with a pointed finger to the very spot on the hallway floor where I was to stand. He stepped back into the office and closed the door behind him. Presumably, I was to stand and wait for him like an errant schoolboy, while he returned to his desk and continued to write. After some time had passed, he shouted: "Come in!" His voice penetrated the door panelling like a blast from a twelve-bore shotgun, which echoed down the corridor to the astonishment of some members of staff who were standing at the far end. I opened the door and walked slowly into the office. The Chief was still seated behind the large, leather-covered desk, hunched over a file and scratching it with a biro pen. A desk tidy with the words 'Chief Officer 1' was displayed prominently in the centre of the desk, and a small forest of pens stood tidily in a plastic holder. He did not look up, but continued to write for a couple of minutes. The folder lay open on a large platter and next to it a telephone.

It was a neat and tidy desk, and from what 1 could see it was more of a status symbol than for any practical use. He stopped writing, bent over the folder to read for a moment and then said, "Take a seat!" without looking up. I sat in a chair directly in front of the desk. I settled back and studied him, unobserved. He was a small, dapper man in his late fifties. His well-oiled hair, what little remained of it, was brushed over the top of his head in an attempt to cover the baldness. His clean-shaven face spoke of a fastidious manner. He finished reading, set the folder, still open, back on the desk, removed his glasses and placed them on the folder. Each task was done in a slow, methodical fashion. Then he looked up into my face. I was the next task to be dealt with.

"Mr McKane," he said, apparently reminding himself who I was, with a quick glance at the folder: "This complaint about the duty officer PO." He paused for a moment, his speech clipped and precise, his tone mellow and in an assumed, middle-class accent. "Yes, Sir, "1 replied, sitting up in the chair and folding my hands in my lap. Then seemingly changing the subject, he said, "I see all your service has been in the Maze, hasn't it?" As his eyes flitted back and forth between the folder and my face, I took it to be a veiled threat that 1 was in danger of being transferred to Magilligan or somewhere. The innuendo hung in the air. I didn't know if it was a statement or a question. Whatever it was, I didn't feel I Owed him an explanation of my record of service.

He looked at me more intently, as he made a mental note of my reticence. He was used to staff answering all his questions. For a second I thought our meeting was in the balance. He toyed with the idea of repeating the question. But coming to a decision, he slowly placed his elbows on the desk, and lifted a pencil from the plastic holder. He held an end between the thumb and index finger of each hand. His eyes narrovved as the pencil rotated between his fingertips, and he scrupulously examined its contours.

He spoke again. "The situation is, as you know, the duty office staff have to detail about twelve hundred staff each day and I'm sure you will agree it is difficult to please everybody, all the time. I have spoken to the PO, and he has assured me he will moderate his language in the future." He paused for a moment, waiting for a response. But 1 just looked him straight in the eye. "So I think it might be best to let the matter rest at that." His eyes met and held mine, as he waited for my reaction. 1 nodded in agreement, as unspoken words passed between us. Then the moment had passed. He returned the pencil to the holder, clasped his hands and sat back in the chair. "Any other problems Mr McKane?" His tone was brisk and business like again. "That's fine," he replied and nodded. It signified the end of the interview.

I was clearly forgotten. I stood and walked out of the office. I knew I hadn't handled the interview very well, but it didn't matter. I had a feeling that had I pushed the issue, it could have rebounded on me. It was the lesser of two evils, but to concede to every pompous upstart was something else entirely. I intended to keep my dignity, no matter what.

Chapter 14

I was shocked to hear of the murder of my friend and colleague Trevor Elliott on Wednesday 14th April 1982. I knew Trevor when I was in the Royal Irish Rangers, and our unit was assigned guard duties at the Battalion Headquarters in Armagh. Trevor was a Sergeant in the regiment, and was murdered by the IRA as he left the grocery business he managed at Keady in South Armagh. He had joined the Battalion in 1973 and was based at the Headquarters in Armagh City. He was an enthusiastic soldier and was promoted to Lance-Corporal in 1974, and again promoted in 1976, to Full Corporal. In January 1982 he was once more promoted, this time to Sergeant.

Trevor was 38 years of age, and was married with a family of five. He had just left the grocery shop in Main Street, Keady and was about to get into his car, which was parked outside the shop, when he was confronted by a masked man armed with an Armalite rifle. The terrorist opened fire from close range, hitting Trevor in the head and chest. As he fell mortally wounded, the gunman ran off towards the town centre. Several bystanders ran to his aid, but Trevor was dead within seconds.

He lived in Armagh and was survived by his wife Josephine, and children aged between 18 months and 14 years - Deborah, David, Jonathan and twins, Gary and Paul - who at the time were being comforted by relatives. It was the usual kind of cold-blooded and calculated murder the IRA were famous for carrying out, and it was part of the campaign of genocide mounted against the Protestant people living in the border areas.

Trevor was a talented musician. He played the pipes and drums in the Regimental Band and was the lead drummer in the Colour Parade in 1981 . A qualified NBC Instructor, he had completed a Soviet Army Studies Course at the School of Army Service Corps. He was a cheerful and loyal SNCO, whose enthusiasm showed in civilian life, where he took an active interest in his church, The Free Presbyterian Church. Although the T.A.V.R. was never involved in the fight against terrorism in the Province, Trevor was the second T A Officer to be murdered in a little over two years. Colour Sergeant Major Hugh McGinn was shot dead by the INLA at his home also in Armagh City. The IRA claimed responsibility for Trevor's murder and warned of a major onslaught against members of the security forces in the South Armagh area.

In the Maze each morning a cleaning party of orderlies from H Block 6 were assigned to clean the offices, the tally lodge and around the main gate complex. Two orderlies were also taken to the uniform stores, which were situated about 100 yards from the tally lodge, inside the prison.

Some mornings I was detailed to collect the work party from H6 and escort them to their places of work. From the tally lodge the road ran straight to segment gate 1, which operated the admin, area from Phase 2 and the H Blocks. I would leave the tally lodge and walk past the stores to the admin gate, where 1 would have to show my pass to the gate officer. Then after walking past the admin block and the prison hospital, I would arrive at the segment gate, which was also manned by an officer. From here I proceeded to the gate of H6 and then into the block. It was only about 500 yards from the tally lodge to H Block 6, a short distance in comparison to the extreme parts of the prison at Phase 1, which housed H Block 1 and H Block 2. In fact, staff who worked in these two blocks were allowed 20 minutes' walking time from the tally lodge to their blocks. Or, at certain times of the day, officers were transported in a minibus from segment gate I, to H I and H2. At that time the entire prison complex of the Compound Maze, and the Cellular Maze, covered an area of 260 acres.

The work party consisted of four prisoners, two of whom had to be left with the staff in the stores, and the other two were the tally lodge cleaning party. I collected the four security books from the block control room and called out the four names to the grille officer, and as 1 waited, I wrote the details in the books. When the four prisoners arrived in the circle, we headed off for the tally lodge, the four cons walking in a straight line and myself at the back with the security books. As we arrived at segment gate 1, the gate officer radioed the ECR and asked permission to allow the four prisoners into the admin area, and when permission was given, he opened the gate and we all filed through. When we arrived at the admin gate, the officer went through the same process; and when he got permission from the ECR, he opened the gate and we proceeded on through towards the tally lodge. When we got to the stores, I left two of the cons with the gate officer and walked the other two on down to the tally lodge and their work, where I kept an eye on them in case they got up to some of their tricks.

There was one con I will always remember. When I opened his security book, his face stared morbidly from the page with its dishevelled appearance. The most memorable thing about the man was his extraordinary outbursts of giggling, which was such a contrast to the photo in the book. It was almost as ,if it were a defence mechanism, a way of easing the burden of jail tension. Every time I saw him his first words were, "What's the scale?" Always looking for news, he was an obsequious individual, plump, in his late 20's, with constantly moving eyes that gave me an innate suspicion about him.

He was doing a three-year-stretch for burglary. An old timer in jail terms, he had done two stretches before, one in the Crum and I had run into him when he was doing an 18-month stretch in HI in 1976. A compulsive talker, he was engaged in conversation all the time. It was probably a case of thinking out loud, rather than any urge to talk to a prison officer. He would talk endlessly about the video recorder and a comparatively recent innovation to the machine, the VHS system that he had been reading about in a magazine. "I'll get one when I get out!" he would repeat to himself. Then when he thought I was not in range of hearing, he said, "I'll get one when I get out, should I have to buy it!" He glanced at me as though he suddenly realised I was in earshot. Clearly prison was no deterrent to this guy. It didn't look good for any of his neighbours who happened to own a video recorder with a VHS system.

I was deeply saddened to hear of the murder of my friend and former colleague Gerry Cathcart, whom I had served with on the police in Bessbrook in 1962. Gerry was still in the police and he was attached to the technical branch at RUC Headquarters, in charge of radio communications equipment.

A 49-year-old married man, Gerry was shot in the back of the head after a gunman approached him casually from behind, as he locked his car door outside his home in the Upper Malone area of Belfast. Gerry's 18-year-old daughter Carol, whom he had collected from Victoria College, watched in horror as her father was murdered, and saw her mother Kathleen running out into the street shouting, "Gerry, my Gerry!"

The assassin fired four shots from a handgun before running across some waste ground, where an accomplice was waiting on a motorbike, and they both took off at high speed, leaving their victim lying in a pool of blood. Shortly after the murder the IRA claimed responsibility for the killing. But even before the claim, police chiefs suspected it was the work of the IRA, as similar tactics had been used before by the same murder gang. A stolen motorbike and a revolver had been used in a number of murders in the Belfast area. Some time later the motorbike was found abandoned in the Finaghy area. Police later established the killers' escape route, which was along Malton Drive, Finnis Drive, Sicily Park and across the main Lisburn Road. A 13-year-old boy who was playing in a nearby street when the shooting occurred claimed to have seen the gunmen as they fled. He described them both as young, one wearing a white safety helmet and the other a green duffel coat. Shortly after the murder of her husband, Mrs Cathcart had to be sedated, while friends and neighbours comforted her two daughters Carol and 24-year-old Linda, who was expecting a baby at the time.

Gerry had served 22 years on the police. Two years before his death he narrowly escaped a murder bid when an INLA bobby trap bomb was found attached to his car. It was defused by an army bomb disposal team. He was the fourth policeman to be murdered in 1983, and his death sparked a flood of condemnation. One comment was from the Workers Party Representative in South Belfast. He said that the murder was a conscious decision to engage in a vicious campaign of sectarian conflict in order to heighten tension in the city.

He also stressed that only by the development of anti-sectarian, progressive policy could this type of terrorism be eradicated from society. Three weeks after the murder, on the 8th June, a 34-year-old Andersonstown man was remanded in custody at Belfast Magistrates Court, charged with Gerry's murder. He was Robert Joseph Lavery. He was also accused of attempting to murder police in the Ravenhill Road area of Belfast, and possessing a revolver that was loaded with six rounds of ammunition. These charges followed an incident in which police chased a man on the Ravenhill Road.

Since I served with Gerry in Bessbrook, as a mobilized B man, I had lost contact with him over the years until I saw his photo in the paper after his murder. I had last seen him when I left the police in May 1963, exactly 20 years to the day of his murder.

Since my skinnish with the Chief Officer I found myself being detailed less to the tally lodge and more frequently to the visitors' car park. As the visitor's car park was situated outside the prison, I wondered if the Chief Officer were trying to convey some sort of message to me, in his own surreptitious way. However, I have to say I enjoyed working in the car park. It was probably the fuss and excitement of the place, with large numbers of visitors passing through each day.

All the visitors were processed at the front desk in the reception building and, after being searched, they were passed through into a waiting room to await transport to the visits complex inside the jail. All male visitors were searched by prison officers, and female visitors were searched by pairs of specially-trained female, civilian searchers. Two officers occupied each male search cubicle, one officer to give the visitor a rubdown search and his colleague to take details of all items in his possession.

It was always recognised that visitors entering the Maze presented a serious threat to the security of the prison. Certainly some visitors showed themselves more than willing to smuggle contraband into the jail and there is little doubt that some visitors would be prepared to smuggle weapons and ammunition into the prison, too. The staff therefore faced very considerable difficulties because, unlike any other top security prison in the UK, the Maze had at the time some 800 prisoners with paramilitary association. Particularly when it was taken into account that each prisoner was allowed one visit per week, and as each prisoner was allowed up to three visitors at anyone time, the total number of visitors who came into the Maze each week averaged 1,800.

To completely eliminate smuggling would be to subject visitors to the most vigorous body searches before they were allowed contact with the prisoners. However, many visitors are law-abiding citizens, and if they were subjected to such intensive security measures, there would be a public outcry. Similarly, security measures which would affect the quality of a prisoner's contact with his family would be likely to be resented by both the prisoner and his family. In the past, such issues had become a focus of discontent and had led to protests and civil disorder. Experience in the Maze over the years had shown, too, that staff who were faced with such hostility would eventually allow security measures to lapse. This illustrated the dilemma that faced the authorities in the Maze in their efforts to establish an effective searching system.

Similar problems were experienced in the main visits complex inside the prison. The degree of supervision applied to visits at the Maze varied between the three different visiting areas. All prisoners had their visits in open conditions in the two main visiting rooms, A Block and B Block, each of which contained 20 tables, separated by partitions some five feet high. These partitions divided the rooms into semi-private cubicles, which actually prevented the staff from supervising the rooms effectively. As a result, any attempt to transfer contraband, or even a weapon, from a visitor to a prisoner would have been difficult to detect.

Special arrangements were made in the Maze for visitors who had professional business with prisoners. These included legal people, doctors, clergymen, probation officers and social workers who were not actually part of the prison staff. It was sometimes suggested that the professional standing of this group precluded the kind of precautions that were applied to other visitors to the prison. However, international experience indicated that such visitors could be actively sympathetic to a terrorist cause, and they could still pose a threat to the security of the prison, particularly as their visits took place out of the hearing of prison officers. Our instructions for searching professional visitors in the Maze stated that they and their baggage should receive the same, thorough search as domestic visitors. It was always emphasized that special precautions should be taken with professional visitors who arrived at the prison outside normal visiting hours, and therefore did not go through routine searching procedures. These precautions were strengthened after an incident in 1981, when eight IRA prisoners who were on remand for murder and the possession of firearms shot their way out of the Crum using three handguns.

According to the emphasis placed by the Council of Europe on prison visits, the need to preserve confidentiality between the legal adviser and his client was paramount. This ruled out the use of open visits accommodation for professional visitors, as the visit would have been held in hearing of the prison staff. To accommodate such visits, closed cubicles were available with glass panelled doors, in sight and out of hearing of the prison staff.

The high outer fence between the car park and the visitors' reception area contained three turnstiles. One gave access to the parcel censors, one to the car park reception, and the third allowed people to pass out one-at-a-time from the prison precinct to the car park. It was through this third turnstile that prisoners were released from custody, either on parole or time served. Since the turnstiles presented a possible breach of security, it was decided that no cleaning party of orderlies would be permitted into the area, so a civilian sweeper was employed to clean the enclosed area around the offices and the car park. He was a small, stout man with a round face, who walked with a slight limp, the result of an accident when he fell off his motor scooter. He was a likeable character. He carried a tobacco tin and rolled his own cigarettes. When someone spoke to him, his face was immediately transformed with a smile that went from ear to ear. His manner had a happy-go-lucky openness about it. A compulsive tea drinker, he spent most of his time in the small officers' mess beside the back waiting room. Each time the PO would catch him at a cup of tea he would hunt him back to his work by saying, "Take your brush and clean up those loose papers along the side of the car park." The quick reply would be uttered, "Yes, PO, I was just goin' to do that, when I get this wee cup of tea!" At other times the exasperated PO would exclaim, "Take your brush and brush up them papers around the turnstiles," at which the reply would be, "Yes PO, I just done that before I poured myself this wee cup of tea!" One day when I was talking to the PO, I passed a remark about the efficiency of the sweeper, and he replied, "He's either just going to do something or he's just after doing it. But you rarely actually catch him doing very much. Most of the time he just stands around with his arms folded in front of him like the Genie from Aladdin's lamp!"

The visitors' car park closed at 5.30 each evening, except for the parcel censors' department where the staff had to prepare the day's parcels for delivery to the blocks. The car park staff were detailed two or three associations each week in the blocks, which meant they had to stop work an hour early to allow them to have a meal in the officers' mess. But when I was on association duty, rather than go to the officers' mess I had a cup of tea and a sandwich in the car park mess, before making my way up to the prison and the blocks.

On Saturday the 24th September I was detailed on association in H Block 4. I had a cup of tea in the car park as usual, and a short time later the central alarm at the Army Guard Force Operations sounded. It was a very loud, whistle-type alarm and it could be heard around the area, as far as Hillsborough to the south of the prison and Lisburn to the north. I remained in the mess and one of the staff shouted, "It's alright! It's only a 'Vespa' exercise." Vespa was the code name for a Prison Guard Force contingency operation that was put into effect, in the close precincts of the jail, in the event of an escape or serious disorder in the prison. Basically, it entailed an army truck which contained several units of 'squaddies' circling the prison, and at intervals of about 100 yards a 'squaddie' jumped out of the back of the vehicle. He immediately took up his position on the opposite side of the road from the perimeter wall, came to attention facing the wall and held his rifle at the 'command slope'.

Periodically, the exercise was put into effect purely as a training drill, and when it was called off, the truck collected the soldiers and took them back to their base. However, on that Saturday evening, there was a slight variation to the normal practice. The alarm had stopped sounding, which indicated the exercise was over, and a few minutes later I left the car park and was driving towards the main gate. To my surprise, all the soldiers who had taken part in the drill had formed up and were marching down the road towards the army camp. It was something I had never seen before. They were an impressive sight, as the formation marched in the autumn sunshine.

There was also a contingency plan with a wider dimension, that involved the other branches of the security forces. When the alarm sounded and it was clear that prisoners had escaped, both the army and the RUC brought this plan into effect. The operation was designed to prevent the escaping prisoners from getting away from the immediate vicinity of the prison. The plan depended on the establishment of a series of cordons at ever-increasing distances from the prison. Between the cordons movement would be strictly controlled. The inner, and most immediate cordon was provided by the soldiers of the Prison Guard Force, deployed around the perimeter wall. Outer cordons would consist of army patrols and police check points (VCP's), which would be set up and manned by the RUC, supported by the Ulster Defence Regiment.

In 1983 an incident took place in the Maze prison that rocked the United Kingdom prison service to its very foundations, an incident that would later be described by the Prime Minister, Mrs Thatcher, as, "The darkest day in the history of the British penal system." It was an incident that up to that time would have been deemed impossible. It was the escape of 38 IRA prisoners, and resulted in the death of one prison officer and the serious injuries to many others.

That day started for me about 6.30 in the morning. The 25th September, 1983, was a Sunday and it was the day on which the Harvest Thanksgiving Service was held in our church. I always made a special effort to attend the harvest, because 1 believe it is one of the most important events in the church calendar. So, before leaving home that morning, Delta and I decided that, all being well, when I would get home early, we would get along to the harvest.

As the car park was closed to visitors on a Sunday, and the sweeper did not work at the weekends, three members of staff were detailed to sweep and mop out the offices and the waiting rooms, which usually took up to about lunchtime. The day was routine and uneventful, and at lunchtime I went for my usual two-mile walk around the prison. This took me past the extern gate, where the area was busy with the constant flow of both military and civilian traffic. The army camp was just around the corner, with its scattering of prefabricated huts, surrounded by concrete blast-walls and sandbag emplacements. As I walked along the road that meanders around the prison, I noted that the perimeter wall had recently been fitted with a plastic oval canopy. It was like a big plastic pipe which had been grooved, so that it fitted snugly on the top of the wall, each length with a flange which joined it with the next, making it look like a continuous length. It ran along the length of the wall as far as the eye could see. The purpose of the canopy was, by its rounded smoothness, to prevent a rope or hook from catching onto the top of the wall.

The main activity of the afternoon centred next door in the parcel censors, when the Sunday papers were delivered. Each paramilitary organisation that was represented in the prison supplied its members with copies of all the main Sunday publications. The papers were delivered in large bundles, and on most of the copies they had scrawled the name of the prisoner, which meant we had the laborious task of checking the name with the block information boards, to find where each prisoner was housed. The copies were then placed in separate piles, one for each of the eight blocks. When the job was completed, the bundles were tied up and one of my colleagues rang the transport to let them know the papers were ready for collection. A van soon arrived to collect the papers for delivery around the blocks, and when it left, we decided to lock the place up and leave the keys back in the keyroom in the administration building.

It was about 4.30 pm, and I was the only straight day man, as my two colleagues were both detailed association duty that evening. One of them decided that if I would drive him up to the main gate he would lodge the keys, before going to the officers' mess for a meal. I agreed and I asked him if he would check my detail for the following Tuesday, when he was in the admin building. I drove him up to the main gate in my car, which I had recently bought, and it was our main topic of conversation. It was a green, Toyota Corolla Hatchback. An economical car to run; I enjoyed driving it. When I dropped him at the gate, I turned the car and headed it towards the extern gate, the direction I would be driving as soon as I got my detail. I was parked for about 15 minutes and everything seemed normal. Evening duty staff were returning into the prison, through the tally lodge, after their tea meal. But I couldn't understand what was keeping my colleague, as it was about a five minute walk from the tally lodge to the keyroom in the admin building and he should have been back by now. I have to admit my only concern at that moment of time was that he would return and give me Tuesday's detail and I would get away home and later attend the harvest service.

But within a few minutes, events started to take a disturbing turn. As the evening staff were returning to the prison in ones and twos through the pedestrian door at the side of the main gate, one officer who was on his own walked to the door. But when the door opened, instead of walking through, he suddenly ran back onto the road, in a very excited state. He started to give loud blasts on his whistle, and I wound the car window down and shouted at him, "What's wrong?" "There's an escape!" Came the first frenzied words. "The IRA have taken over the tally lodge. McFarlane's standing in there, in prison officer's uniform!" I couldn't believe what I was hearing. 1 knew Brendan 'Bic' McFarlane was the IRA's so-called commanding officer in the Maze. He was 31 years of age and came from the Ardoyne area of Belfast. He was sentenced to life imprisonment for a bomb attack in Belfast, in which five people were killed and over 40 injured. McFarlane had made a previous escape attempt in March 1978, and he led the IRA prisoners on the streaker protest and the hunger-strike. If what I was hearing was true, the unimaginable had happened. A wave of anxiety passed over me. And I decided to do my best to stop them, should it cost me my life.

At that moment the large, vehicle door started to open and the officer shouted again, "They're all in the kitchen wagon, in the airlock!" And as the door opened further, I could see into the airlock from where 1 was sitting in my car. 1 could see part of the front of the kitchen lorry. I started the car, moved forward and spun round on the road and put the front of the car up close to the opening door. When the door had opened about half way, there was enough space to allow the car into the airlock. I drove slowly in and up to the front of the kitchen lorry. I got out of the car, took the keys and locked the door, and it was at this moment that I looked through the windscreen of the lorry. 1 could recognise the driver. He was the officer who was the normal driver of the kitchen lorry, but I did not recognise his passenger who was a clean-cut chap in officer's uniform.

As I paused and looked around the tally lodge and main gate area, I was surprised, because nothing seemed to be out of order, but there was an eerie silence about the place. The lorry seemed innocuous as I looked again at the passenger, who was sitting motionless and calmly looking at me. Although I did not recognise him, he could well have been a prison officer, because during the previous few weeks there had been an influx of new recruits into the service, and it was possible he had arrived from the college and I had not seen him before. However, I decided to challenge him. I drew my baton and walked forward to the passenger door of the lorry. I grabbed the handle, opened the door and said to the passenger, in a stern tone of voice, "Right, get out!" As his body pivoted around towards me, I saw an automatic pistol in his hand, and he pointed it at me and said, "F --- off, or you're dead!" I immediately backed off and continued walking back towards the main gate, which was by now fully open. A few seconds later I watched with disbelief as prisoners piled out of the back of the lorry, whilst others ran out of the tally lodge, and they all came walking down the airlock towards me. There were about 40 or 50 of them altogether. I recognised some of them who had been on the streaker protest and had been in the jail for years, but there were others I did not recongise. Some of them were dressed in prison officers' uniform, some in part uniform and some in civilian clothing.

I raised my baton and shouted at them, "Get back!" Then one of them who was in front of the crowd pointed a pistol at me and shouted, "Get back, or I'll blow you away!" I stepped backwards, and suddenly they all stormed past me, through the main gate and out onto the road. At this point total pandemonium broke out. Members of staff who were returning to the prison for evening duty, recognising some of the prisoners, realised it was an escape and drew their batons and there was a free-for-all. This quickly developed into such a confused melee, that the squaddie in the watch tower at the main gate radioed his operations room and reported that a big fight had broken out between prison officers at the gate.

An unsuspecting officer who was on his way home in his yellow, Toyota Celica car was driving past the gate as the rumpus started. When a bunch of prisoners ran in front of the car and caused him to stop. Others opened the car door and dragged him out. As he was leaving the car, he had the presence of mind to grab the ignition keys and take them with him, and as they punched him to the ground, he threw the keys away. But as he was lying on the road, a couple gave him a kicking whilst another one retrieved the keys. About 5 or 6 baled into the car, started the engine, and as they moved off, I dashed forward and crashed my baton into the windscreen. The glass shattered, sending small pieces in all directions. The car swerved to the left and sped off at high speed towards the extern gate.

Simultaneously, the mass of the escaping prisoners had run across the road to the outer fence. Some of them had clambered through the barbed-wire coils and were running up the field, in a wild burst for freedom. I ran to the place in the fence, and as I got there, one of my colleagues had grabbed one of the escapees, who turned and shouted, "Let go or I'll shoot!" And as the officer continued to drag him back, he raised his right hand and there was a shot. The officer instantly grasped his thigh as he fell backwards and screamed out in pain, "My God, I've been shot!"

At the same time the prisoner turned and awkwardly staggered, and as he did so, he dropped the weapon on the ground, before making a dash after his mates. Seeing this, I hurled myself into the fence, grabbed the gun, which was a small calibre pistol with a silencer that had been attached to the end of the barrel, but the impact on the ground had broken it loose. I pointed it at the fleeing gunman, but as I pressed the trigger, the weapon jammed. I cocked the gun again, pointed it after him and fired. I missed him and tried to fire a second shot, but the pistol was empty. There had only been one last round left in the magazine. At that moment the soldier in the tower, who had been overlooking the scene, suddenly realised it was an escape. He lifted his rifle and shouted at the prisoner, "Halt or I'll fire!" As the prisoner continued to run, there was a loud crack and the prisoner collapsed to the ground, with a bullet through his leg.

While all this was taking place, a member of staff with a radio had called the ECR and ordered an ambulance to take the wounded officer to hospital. At the same time one of the prison drivers took a minibus out of the transport pool and drove round to where the officer was lying. We lifted him into the back of the bus, and he was driven to the extern gate where he was collected by the ambulance, and taken to the Lagan Valley Hospital in Lisburn. I felt hopelessly inadequate as I looked around at the staff who were standing in a state of bewilderment, each with an incredulous expression on his face. I took a deep breath as I realised how a shooting incident like that makes you appreciate life.

I wondered how McFarlane had done it. The original plan had obviously been to drive out of the jail; and up until I blocked the gate, their success must have been beyond expectations. But in all escape plans there must be a big element of luck, and at the main gate their luck ran out. When the driver returned from taking the wounded officer to meet the ambulance, he told us that the escapees who hijacked the officer's yellow Celica car had crashed it into the extern gate, where it was still wedged between the two parts of the gate. He said that the five prisoners had escaped through the gate, and the army had fired warning shots and had captured one of them.

We were still standing around the main gate when suddenly the Security Senior Officer dashed out of the pedestrian gate. Almost in a state of panic, he started to shout, "What happened? What way did they go?" He was chafing at the bit, as it took a few minutes for the confusion of the moment to melt into an organised response. "After them!" came the roar from the SO. "After them! Don't let them get away." After the initial shock of the events, the staff who were there threw themselves enthusiastically into the task of re-capturing as many of them as we could. Followed by a bunch of officers, the SO dashed forward through the gap in the fence the prisoners had made in their getaway.

As we ran up the field and along the side of a deep impression that had been a heavy gun emplacement during the Second World War, we found some articles of prison officers' uniforms that had been discarded by the escaping prisoners. As we continued across the fields in the direction of the River Lagan, I shouted to the SO and asked him if any of the staff had been killed. He glanced across at me and shouted, "I don't know about the rest of the jail, but Jimmy Ferris is lying dead in the tally lodge!" I was by now becoming exhausted, as a wave of emotion swept over me. My eyes grew hot and moist and I felt a lump in my throat. Emotion had played no part in my career in the past. But now I felt it overwhelm me.

We came to a gate that lead to a side road, and as we clambered over it, I looked round to find we had outpaced the others and there were now only four of us, the SO, myself and two other officers. We started to run along the side road towards the Halftown Road, and we hadn't got far when a police land rover came round the corner with two policemen in it. They stopped, and the four of us clambered into the back. They told us they were going down to the bridge over the Lagan, on the Half town Road. We went with them, and when we arrived at the bridge, we found more police and army. They had set up a vehicle checkpoint, and were stopping and searching all traffic on the road. The SO then ordered me to come with him to search the southern bank of the river, and the other two officers were ordered to search along the northern bank. At about 300 yards upstream from the bridge, one of the men on the opposite bank shouted across to us, "There's some in the river!" And as we ran to the spot, three IRA prisoners were wading, with their hands up, towards my colleagues on the far bank. I instantly recognised the three of them because they had been in the Maze for years. Their names were Hamilton, Simpson and Storey. The police and army on the bridge, on hearing the shouts, sent a unit to assist in the recapturing of the three escapees.

At our side of the river the SO and I were still searching along the reeds when suddenly I saw another prisoner, who, when he saw me, put his hands up. I pointed the pistol that I had recovered earlier at the main gate at him, and shouted at him to come out with his hands up. He clambered out of the bank, and walked over to us with both hands on his head. I instantly recognised him as Sean McGlinchey. He, too, had been in the Maze for a considerable time. We walked him back to the bridge, where we put the four prisoners into a land rover and the police drove us back to the Maze. The four of them had been in the river for some time, and as it was late September and the river was in full flow, they were trembling with cold. I thought at the time, they had accepted the futility of the whole thing, and they were only too glad to get out of the water. When we arrived back at the main gate, the four prisoners were taken from the land rover and brought up to the reception building, where we left them with the PO and his staff. As the SO and I left the reception, we could see the Chief Officer standing on the steps of the administration building. The SO decided we should report to him that we had recaptured the four prisoners and show him the pistol I had retrieved during the ruction at the main gate. We walked over to him. He had an expression on his face that resembled a tortoise that had just woken up after hibernation. The very thought that the largest escape in the history of the prison service had just taken place in his prison had not yet seemed to register.

The SO explained to him the sequence of events that had taken place at the main gate, how we had followed the prisoners to the Lagan, and recaptured them. The Chief listened intently and then said, "Come with me and explain your courageous actions to the Director of Prisons. He is in the No I Governor's office at the moment." He laid the way into the admin building, up the stairs and into the Governor's office, where the Director was in conversation with the No I Governor, his Deputy, and a couple of senior policemen. The Director looked up as the Chief approached and started to explain how I recovered the gun and the recapture of the four prisoners.

I stepped forward and handed the weapon to the Director, who then passed it to one of the police officers. He examined the gun and placed it on the side of the desk, close to where the Deputy Governor was standing. The Deputy suddenly lifted the pistol, turned round to face the wall, removed the clip, drew back the mechanism, and cleared the breech. Then he placed the weapon back on the desk. The whole stunt was a transparent attempt to justify his presence. I immediately said, "1 have already cleared the weapon, sir." The Director then turned to the Deputy and said in a very sharp tone, "Has any more been recaptured?" "1 will see, sir!" Came the Deputy's reply, clearly surprised by the question as much as the tone. He turned, dropped his head and left the office like a schoolboy who had just received a severe reprimand from the headmaster.

Needless to say I didn't make it to the Thanksgiving Service that evening.

It was in the early hours of Monday morning when I got out of the Maze. As I was driving home, I switched on the car radio, and tuned in to a foreign station to hear if there was any news about the escape. 1 picked up a station; I believe it was in the United States. I have to say I felt a little bit 'chuffed' when the newsreader, reading out the breaking news about the escape from the Maze prison, said, "An alert prison officer drove his car into the main gate of the prison and blocked the lorry containing the escaping prisoners."

A few days later the largest assembly of prison officers ever to convene in Northern Ireland outside a prison establishment gathered in the small town of Donaghadee for the funeral of my good friend and colleague, Jimmy Ferris. It was at First Donaghadee Presbyterian Church and the building was filled to capacity. The crowd included members of the other branches of the security forces and friends who knew the dead officer. I had first met Jimmy when I joined the service, eight years before. We had worked together in the compounds before the blocks were built and then later in the cellular side of the Maze.

Jimmy was killed during the takeover of the tally lodge, when a clash took place between some officers and the IRA men. He saw the opportunity to dash the 20 yards to the officer on the pedestrian gate, and warn him the escape was in progress. But as he broke loose, and ran out of the tally lodge, shouting, one of the prisoners charged after him and stabbed him with a quarter-inch wood chisel. The chisel had been taken from the hobbies room in H7.

Some time later a number of prisoners who were recaptured were charged with Jimmy's murder, but during the trial the charge of murder was ruled inadmissible, as evidence was given that he had died as the result of a heart attack. We all knew Jimmy had a heart complaint. The Prison Department was very aware of his medical condition, because he had attended a Medical Board shortly before the escape. According to the doctors his health was sound, and he was cleared for his work but there can be no doubt that the stabbing exacerbated the heart problem which caused his death. Clearly, had Jinmy not have been stabbed by that IRA man on 25th September 1983, he could have been alive today.

Four days after the escape, the manhunt for the escaped prisoners had moved to the Castlewellan area, in an attempt to flush out more of the fugitives that were believed to have gone to ground in the surrounding countryside. The landscape provided thousands of natural hiding places, making it extremely difficult to search thoroughly. Tracker dogs were out in force to back up police and army personnel, as a yard-by-yard search of the region took place, although fog and low cloud hampered the search and prevented helicopters from joining in the hunt. However, two of the escapees, Paul Anthony Kane and Brendan Meed, were arrested by police on a country road, and another two, Hugh Carey and Patrick McIntyre, were recaptured after a siege in a house in the foothills of the Mourne Mountains. The two IRA men had held a 55-year-old widow hostage in her isolated home. It was believed they had arrived at the house in a car that was hijacked near the Maze, shortly after the escape. The car was later found abandoned in Castlewellan, and police said that when it was hijacked, a number of IRA men were in it.

Of the prisoners who got away, three were later shot dead in three separate shoot-outs with the security forces. They were Kieran Gerald Fleming, who was 23 years-of-age and came from Londonderry. Fleming was detained at the Secretary of State's Pleasure (SOSP), for the murder of a policewoman, Linda Begley, in an ambush in 1976. SOSP is the same as a life sentence except where the murderer is under 21 years-of-age when the crime is committed. In a similar case on the mainland the murderer would be sentenced to Her Majesty's Pleasure. The second man was Seamus McElwaine, who was 22 years-of-age and came from Knockmacullion, County Monaghan. McElwaine received a life sentence in 1982 for the murder of a UDR man, and a Reserve Police Constable two years previously. The third man who died was Patrick Oliver McKeamey, who was from Benburb Road, Moy. McKearney was 29 years-of-age and he was sentenced to 14 years in 1981 for the possession of firearms. The three men were killed on, what the IRA called, active service.

I later discovered the name of the IRA man in prison officer's uniform who had been the passenger in the front of the lorry. He was Gerald Kelly from Moyard Crescent in Belfast. Kelly had received a life sentence in 1973, for his part in the bombing of the Old Bailey in London. He and his fellow bombers, the Price sisters, were later transferred to prisons in Northern Ireland. Kelly was the key member of the IRA team who planted the first bombs in London. At 6.00 am on the 8th March 1973, bombs were placed at four targets in the capital, and one was defused outside Scotland Yard. The members of the bomb team were later arrested at Heathrow Airport.

On the 16th January 1986, both McFarlane and Kelly were arrested in the Netherlands, where they faced extradition warrants from the UK Government, relating to the escape from the Maze almost two-and-a-half years before. On December the 3rd of that year both men appeared at a court in Lisburn, after being extradited from Holland, charged with escaping from the Maze Prison. They were both remanded in custody and returned to the Maze, and to H Block 7, from where they had absconded just over three years earlier. Kelly was extradited on the agreement that he should not serve the remainder of his life sentence for the bombing of London in 1973. He was sentenced to five years for his part in the escape, but served only 13 months after his time in custody in Holland was taken into account. So, it could be said, it was well worth Kelly's efforts to escape from the Maze. At the time of writing, Gerry Kelly has been elevated to the status of respectable politician and is currently a prominent Provisional Sinn Fein spokesman in the Northern Ireland Assembly.

Who precisely was to blame for the escape was soon lost in the bureaucratic jigsaw of responsibility, as we were told that important lessons had been learnt. But it was the general opinion of the staff in the Maze that the main lesson that had been learnt was that the people who were in charge of the prison at the time should have been sacked on the spot. The calibre and ability of the senior staff in the Maze probably originated in the early 1970's, when there was a sudden increase of promotions in the service.

Since the end of the hunger-strike the prison regime in the Maze had been less restrictive and more relaxed, until security had reached such a point that it was inevitable something serious was going to happen. In order to placate the demands of the prisoners, Principal and Senior Officers who had been in charge of the blocks before the hunger-strike, and were perceived to be too authoritative and over-zealous, were moved out of the blocks to run visits and other off-beat areas of the jail. A bunch of brilliant officers, were lost forever in the mists of expediency, and a remodelled prison regime. These officers had been replaced by weak, subservient men. It seemed to me that the prison staff were continually criticized for being too austere in their work, and at the same time they were criticized for not doing enough to prevent disorder in the prison. The morale of the staff on the ground had also suffered when the prisoners were given segregation and most of the hunger-strike demands were met. As a result, the security of the prison gradually drifted into a languid state, as many of the staff had lost interest in the place, and just wanted to get their day in and get home at night.

In H Block 7, which was an IRA block, the prisoners had embarked on a psychological strategy to manipulate the staff, the result of which proved they were past-masters in psychology. They had developed the subject into an art form. They began by adopting a deliberate policy of conditioning the prison officers, in order to reduce their alertness. This was achieved by lowering the level of tension in the block and avoiding confrontation with staff. As a result, the staff-prisoner relationship in H7 improved and the number of incidents between staff and inmates declined. There was, on average, only one adjudication per week on an H7 prisoner, when he was charged under the Code of Discipline, whereas the prisoners' charges in other blocks averaged almost three times that number. The IRA's strategy of diverting the attention of the authorities from H7 had been so successful, that an atmosphere had been created in which the abuses of normal security procedures were regarded, by the majority of staff in the block, as routine. This rather skilful manipulation would take the form of a prisoner approaching an officer at a grille. The prisoner would grab the grille and pull, to give the impression he thought the grille was not locked. The officer, in the other hand, would have taken the notion that the grille should not have been locked, although he was aware that regulations stated it should be locked at all times. Eventually, the officer would leave the grille unlocked, in the knowledge that if a senior officer appeared, he could lock it. The ending of the customary searching of prisoners and the failure to supervise orderlies correctly was considered by some officers as a practice that did no harm, provided everything was OK. The regular Block PO encouraged this lackadaisical behaviour from his staff, by putting increased emphasis on 'prisoner co-operation'! And over a period of time, H7 had acquired the reputation of being 'liberal', which in staff grapevine terms meant the cons had almost taken over the place.

For some of the staff in H7, the everyday controlling of the prisoners had become more trouble than enough. In some cases they believed it was prison policy to appease the IRA men and that they were required not to 'rock the boat'. The behaviour of the prison staff in H Block 7 not only reflected the reality of life in the block, but it also reflected the reality of life in the Province at the time, as many prison officers and their families had found to their cost. So perhaps it was understandable if staff were reluctant to put themselves or their families at risk by taking disciplinary action against members of the paramilitary organisations. Therefore, it was not difficult to see how a group of seasoned prisoners like the IRA, under the control of a highly intelligent leader like McFarlane, could manipulate staff in the way they did.

Having reported the events in H Block 7 to the Security Department a number of times, which resulted in little or no response, it seemed to become the accepted attitude among the more experienced prison officers in the Maze that, after you have intervened a number of times to try to prevent a man from cutting his own throat, there comes a time, perhaps through exhaustion, when you are inclined to stand well back and view the whole matter with a certain detachment. The many reports about the lapses in security had impacted on a rubber wall of indecision, or for some unknown reason were totally ignored, without a single reply. This caused predictable fury and alarm among the staff after the escape.

Although I had been involved at the main gate of the prison in trying to frustrate the escape, it was not until some days later, when I had spoken to other officers who had been on duty, that I began to form a broad picture of the events in the prison and particularly in H7 on that day. The total number of staff in the Maze in 1983 was about 1,200, the majority of whom had served less than four years in the prison service. The reason for this high proportion of young and relatively inexperienced staff was characteristic of the service, since the outbreak of the terrorist campaign with a rapid increase in the size of the service from 300 officers in the late 1960's, to 3,000 in a period of less than 15 years. Despite this large increase in the numbers of prison staff, there was still a shortfall in relation to the numbers of prisoners. As a result, the average overtime for all disciplined staff was about 16 hours per week. In September 1983 the blocks contained 833 inmates altogether; 541 Republicans and 292 Loyalists. Seven of the eight blocks were occupied, and of the twenty-eight wings, fifteen accommodated Republican prisoners, six Loyalist prisoners, and seven had a mixed population. That is, they were from both communities, and the majority of whom had been sentenced for non-terrorist crimes. Therefore, the largest part of the inmate population at the Maze had been convicted of offences connected with terrorist activities, and was therefore quite unlike the prison population in any prison on the mainland.

This was demonstrated by their allegiance to their particular paramilitary organisations. The one thing they all had in common was their determination to try to escape from lawful custody. The background of the 125 inmates who occupied H Block 7 on the day of the escape can perhaps best be illustrated by a breakdown of their convictions: 44 had been convicted of murder, attempted murder, or conspiracy to murder, forty-six had been convicted for the possession or use of explosives, and 23 had been sentenced for the possession or the use of firearms. Twenty-four had been given life sentences or the equivalent, and 88 were serving sentences of ten years or more. All these prisoners were comparatively young as 98 were in their twenties and only seven were over 35 years of age. Of the 38 prisoners who attempted to escape, 28 had been convicted of murder or an associated offence. Five of offences related to firearms, and a further five for offences related to explosives. Twenty-one were serving life sentences, and the remainder were serving sentences of fourteen years or more. None of these prisoners, like the rest of the IRA population at the Maze, was ever prepared to settle down and serve his sentence.

Five guns recovered after the escape.

Chapter 15

As the workshops in the Maze were closed on Sundays, the prisoners remained in their blocks, where they could engage in association and recreation activities. This was known as normal Sunday routine, and in H7 on the 25th September 1983, most of the 125 prisoners in the block were engaged in this comparatively relaxed regime. The movement of prisoners between the wings of the block was freely allowed, and normal. There were 24 orderlies in the block at the time, cleaning and perfonning their tasks as usual. In the four wings of the block, orderlies were employed to clean the landings, ablutions and the dining hall. In the circle area there was a mess orderly, a stores orderly and a circle orderly. There were also two yard orderlies, to sweep the exercise yards.

The full complement of prison staff in H7 was 24, and consisted of two Senior Officers who were in charge of the Block, one of whom was acting Principal Officer, as by a strange coincidence the regular Principal Officer who was in charge of H7 had the day off. There were sixteen officers supervising the prisoners in the wings and six officers were manning the static posts~ the two grille officers, the circle officer, the hall guard officer, the control room officer and the officer on the block gate. These six officers were controlling movement throughout the block. There was also one medical officer, whose duties were normally to give medical cover to the three H Blocks in the phase, H6, H7 and H8, but he happened to be in H7 when the IRA seized control of the block.

This pattern of activity-the staff on their posts and the inmates engaged in recreation activities-would normally have continued until about 4 pm, when the tea meal would arrive from the kitchen and be served to the prisoners. However, at about 2.30, five of the orderlies were in the circle area, and they were each armed with an automatic pistol. It was at this moment that the IRA started to put into motion the plan that would enable them to take over the block.

Firstly, each member of staff in the circle area was shadowed closely by one of the IRA men. A prisoner was also detailed to stand close to every alarm button in the block, and be ready to prevent it from being activated by an officer. The signal to put the escape plan into effect was a shout from McFarlane to the wings for the bumper to be sent out to the circle. This was jail slang for an electric floor polisher, which was used to polish the floors in the block. As there was only one machine supplied to the block, it was not unusual for an orderly to call out for the appliance. One of the orderlies walked into the PO's office and asked to speak to the Senior Officer in charge, about a personal problem. The Senior Officer agreed, and the prisoner closed the office door behind him, which effectively allowed him to cover both Senior Officers in the office. Similarly, other prisoners took up their pre-planned positions, and simultaneously they produced their weapons and held up the staff. Four members of staff were in the small officers' mess when an orderly walked in, pointed a gun at them, and ordered them to "Keep quiet!" An orderly told the circle officer he was wanted in the mess for a moment, and as he stepped through the door, he too was immediately overpowered. At the same time the medical officer who was in the medical room was sitting at his desk and heard the door open. He looked up to find a prisoner standing in the doorway with a loaded gun. The prisoner ordered him to crawl on his hands and knees, across the circle to the officers' mess where he was overpowered and held with his five colleagues.

The control room door was open for ventilation purposes, although the grille on the outside was locked. The problem of lack of ventilation in the control room had been brought to the attention of the Governor by staff in HI some eight years earlier, and nothing had been done about it. A prisoner approached the control room grille, pointed a gun at the control officer, and ordered him to unlock the grille and lie on the floor. The control room contained the central alarm system and all the keys for the block. This was a vital area for the prisoners to secure, enabling a successful takeover of the Block. However, the entire plan was briefly put at risk when the control room officer quickly raised himself from the floor in an attempt to reach his baton which was on a shelf. But before he could grab the stave, his sudden movement had attracted the attention of the gunman, who turned quickly and fired two shots. The officer immediately collapsed to the floor with a bullet through his head. At the same time as these events were taking place, the hall guard officer, at the front grille to the block, was also ordered at gunpoint to lie down on the floor, and he was immediately relieved of his keys.

While the staff in the circle area were being overpowered and taken captive, similar actions were being taken by the prisoners in the wings. The two officers who were manning 'A' and 'B' grille, and 'C' and 'D' grille, which lead to the wings on either side of the circle, were simultaneously overpowered by two armed orderlies who had entered the grille airlocks at the same time. In 'C' wing an officer who refused to hand over his keys was clubbed to the ground with a heavy blow to the back of the head. He later required a number of stitches to a serious head wound. In 'D' wing, an officer who was similarly slow to obey the orders of the IRA men was stabbed with a handicraft knife. The remaining officers in both wings were overpowered or surrendered themselves at the sight of the guns.

The officer who was on duty at the block gate was totally unaware of what was unfolding inside the block. Three orderlies, using the keys they had taken from the hall guard officer, let themselves out and walked down the courtyard to the block gate. They told the gate officer they had been sent down to clean the gate area, and asked him to let them into the airlock. Suspecting nothing out of the ordinary, the officer opened the gate and gave them admission. Once inside the airlock they produced their guns, took the officer prisoner and relieved him of his keys and uniform. The gate officer was quickly escorted into the block, where he joined the rest of his colleagues, who were by this time being held in the two classrooms. Here most of them were stripped of their uniforms, which were to be used by the escapees. Pillowcases were tied over their heads and some of the officers were forced to hand over their car keys, and explain exactly where their cars were parked in the car park, in case the prisoners would need them to further their escape. In order to disorientate their captives further, the officers' hands were tied behind their backs, loud music bellowed out from transistor radios, and they were made to walk repeatedly around the room. As a result, when they were eventually placed on the floor, they were so confused they didn't know the direction of the room door. The prisoners were in complete control of H Block 7 without a single alarm being raised. There is not a doubt in my mind that the relaxed regime, introduced at the end of the hunger-strike, created the environment in which the plans for the take-over of H7 could have been practised until they were carried out with the precision that gave them such success.

It was relatively quiet in the block as the prisoners waited for the arrival of the lorry with the tea meal. About a dozen of them had put on officers' uniforms and had taken up their positions at the static posts, in order to give the impression that everything was normal. Meanwhile, inside the block, the armed prisoners kept guard over the captive officers, whilst others removed all documents, security books and photographs of prisoners, from the control room. All this material was piled in the circle, doused with petrol that was supplied in tins for their cigarette lighters and set on fire, in an attempt to obliterate the identities of the prisoners concerned and to hinder the inevitable follow-up searches.

It was about 3.30 when the kitchen lorry arrived at the gate of H7. The gate was manned by two prisoners in officers' uniforms, who opened the gate and admitted the lorry, apparently without arousing the driver's suspicions. When the lorry arrived at the front grille, a uniformed prisoner who was on the hall guard post opened the grille and admitted the driver, who was immediately seized at gunpoint and taken inside. He was escorted to the medical room, where he was briefed by the IRA men about the escape and the part he was to play in the breakout. He was given precise instructions about the route he was to follow and how he was to answer any questions and generally behave in the event of being challenged. The prisoners seemed to show remarkable knowledge about the layout of the prison. How they came to obtain such infomlation is a mystery, and was never addressed by the Hennessy inquiry.

After some time the driver was taken back to the lorry, which had by this time been emptied of all food containers. His left foot was tied to the clutch and his door was locked. A length of cord protruded from beneath his seat and he was told it was attached to a hand grenade, but it was later discovered it was tied to the frame of the seat. One prisoner, who was dressed in prison officer's uniform, got into the passenger side of the cab, and lay on the floor with a gun trained on the driver. At this point 36 prisoners clambered into the back of the truck, and the aluminium roller shutter was pulled down to conceal the human cargo in the back.

As the lorry slowly left the block, and crawled out through the gate, the last prisoner to leave locked the gate behind him, and jumped into the back along with the others. The prisoners who remained in the block continued to watch over the captured prison officers until they thought their mates were clear of the prison. They then ran amok throughout the block, smashing up furniture and fittings, before setting fire to uniforms, papers, bedclothes and anything else that would burn. Having finished their wrecking spree, each prisoner walked into his own cell and slammed the door behind him. It was only when everything became quiet that the staff started to free themselves from their bonds.

As the lorry left the block gate, it turned left and followed its normal route, which took it to segment gate I. This was their first obstacle and the first gate that was manned by a prison officer. Segment gate I divided the Phase II area from the administration and the prison kitchen. As it was the normal procedure for the lorry to be travelling through the gate to the kitchen at that time of day, the officer, on seeing the vehicle approaching and recognising the driver, opened the gate and allowed the lorry to continue without searching it. The lorry was then driven into the administration area, but rather than turn right into the kitchen, which would have been its normal route, it continued on until it reached the admin gate. As the lorry drove past the prison kitchen on the right, a prominent building on the opposite side of the road was the prison hospital. I often thought, as McFarlane and his men were standing in the back of that lorry, that had they known they were driving past the place where only two years earlier the hunger-strike drama was played out, they would have seen the irony of the moment.

As the lorry approached the admin gate, and the officer on duty recognised the driver and, seeing nothing was amiss, he opened the gate and waved the driver through, without challenging him. The lorry continued on the final leg of its journey that took it to the main gate complex. The tally lodge was manned by an SO and five or six officers, whose duty it was to check the identity of all pedestrians through the security system, to prevent any unauthorised persons from entering or leaving the prison. It was generally believed that the prisoners intended to take control of the main gate complex, before the lorry could be driven out of the prison and onto the road leading to the extern gate, where they would apparently try to bluff their way out.

As the vehicle came to a stop at the prison side of the inner fence gate, some of the prisoners who were armed and wearing officers' uniforms left the lorry and walked into the tally lodge. They ordered the staff at gunpoint into a back office where they were tied up and made to sit on the floor. There was some confusion at this point as one armed prisoner who thought he was going into the tally lodge walked into the transport office and surprised a driver who was on a rest period. The officer was taken at gunpoint to the tally lodge, where he was tied up and dumped on the floor with his colleagues. At this point the plot was beginning to unwind, as more and more evening duty staff were reporting for duty after their tea break; and as each officer entered the tally lodge, he was immediately seized and taken captive, tied up and put in the back office. One of the first officers to be seized by the IRA escape gang was my colleague whom I had been working with all that day in the car park. I last saw him when I left him at the main gate to take the car park keys to the key room. As he entered the tally lodge, he was grabbed, tied up and dumped in the back office. At this time a prisoner who was in uniform approached the officer who was manning the inner vehicle gate, produced a gun and ordered him to open the gate. Fearing for his life, the officer obeyed the instructions and opened the gate. The driver was then ordered by the prisoner, who was lying on the cab floor, to drive the lorry into the vehicle airlock. The officer was then taken at gunpoint into the tally lodge, where he joined the ever-increasing crowd of prison officers.

At this moment of time, there was only one prison officer on duty and still at liberty in the entire main gate complex. He was the officer who was manning the pedestrian gate, which was situated at the opposite end of the tally lodge and about 20 yards from the building. He therefore had seen none of the events in the tally lodge or at the inner fence gate, and he was continuing to admit evening duty staff into the prison. Meanwhile, by now some of the staff in the tally lodge had recognised some of the IRA men, and there were now more staff tied up and lying on the floor than there were IRA men to look after them. The staff were beginning to show resistance to their captors. This was effected, firstly, by refusing to take orders from the prisoners. But whilst they continued to protest, the argument developed into a shouting match, and while this was going on, an officer who was in the background and unnoticed by the prisoners edged over to an alarm button and pulled it. The alarm sounded in the ECR, at which the control room staff immediately responded by the intercom communications system, which was a direct link to the tally lodge.

When the staff were alerted by the buzz of the intercom, a prisoner put a gun to the head of the Senior Officer and told him to bluff the call. The SO's voice quivered with fear as he spoke into the intercom. He told the ECR staff that the alarnl had been set off accidentally and the control room staff were satisfied with this explanation, and rang off. The security system in the Maze was operated by the control room staff, men who were specially trained for the job. Sadly, when the alarm was sounded, it should have been checked, but it was probably 'situation normal', in the control room.

The IRA were in total control of the situation once again. It was at this time that Jimmy Ferris, who was close to the back door of the tally lodge, glanced out and saw the officer standing at the pedestrian gate. Realising the officer knew nothing about what was taking place in the tally lodge, Jimmy knew it was vital that the officer should lock the gate and therefore seal the prison. He observed the area, and waited for the moment when he could make his move and take advantage of the situation. Suddenly, he burst out through the door and dashed towards the pedestrian gate, shouting at the top of his voice to the officer manning the gate, "Lock the gate! Sound the alarm!" However, before he could reach the gate, a prisoner who had bolted after him caught him around the neck, swung him round and stabbed him three times in the chest. Jimmy Ferris collapsed and died a few minutes later. The prisoner then dashed forward to the astonished gate officer, and before he could secure the gate or sound the alarm, he too collapsed with a stab wound to the chest.

The two officers were then carried into the tally lodge, and a prisoner in uniform took up position at the pedestrian gate. It was at this point that the officer who was returning to the prison recognised Brendan McFarlane at the pedestrian gate and shouted to me. A few moments later I drove my car into the airlock and blocked the lorry.

Within hours after the escape, the greatest manhunt in the history of the island was put into operation in both jurisdictions. All contingency escape plans were put into operation and the series of cordons, or rings, were established around the prison and extended for miles from the jail. Some permanent vehicle checkpoints were set up across the Province and all vehicles travelling in the direction of the border were stopped and searched. It was later stated by the police that they had been able to set up the checkpoints quickly because the escape had taken place shortly after a changeover between shifts and extra police happened to be on duty and available at the time.

Although it had been the IRA's plan to get as far away from the Maze as fast as they could, the police contingency plan had some success in preventing this. One VCP stopped a taxi carrying a man in prison officer's uniform, who was promptly arrested and returned to the prison. At another VCP a Mercedes car was stopped, and when the registration was checked, it was discovered the vehicle had been hijacked. The two men in it were immediately arrested, and it was soon established they were two of the escapees, and were also returned to the jail.

When the contingency plans were drawn up, it was emphasized that if the VCP's were to be effective, it was important there should be no delay in providing both the police and the army with a photo montage of all the prisoners who had escaped from custody. But because the prisoners who remained in H7 after the escape burnt all the security books and photographs, it was difficult to establish which prisoners were missing. As a result the security forces were unable to circulate photographs of the prisoners who had escaped, until some hours after the event. However, it has to be said the usefulness of the photographs was limited because in the days before the escape, the prisoners in H7 had set about changing their personal appearance. Thus, those who had been photographed with long hair had their hair cut short, whilst those who were photographed with short hair had grown their hair. Prisoners with beards had shaved then off, and those who were clean-shaven in their security photographs had grown beards. In the hours before the escape, some of the inmates had dyed their hair, and others had made a white creamy substance out of chalk that had been stirred in a small drop of water. This was massaged into their hair to give a greying effect to make them look much older than they were.

Meanwhile, newspaper and media reports the next morning showed the scale of the escape. Not only had 38 IRA men escaped from the Maze, which was devastating enough, but also the fact that a number of automatic pistols had been smuggled into the prison provoked a crisis of confidence in the Secretary of State, the Prisons Minister and the entire Prisons Department. The political flak was so bad that the number one Governor offered his resignation, but the Prisons Minister refused to accept it and instead, the Secretary of State, Mr James Prior, ordered an immediate inquiry into the security arrangements at the Maze. On the same day, Monday the 26th September, the Chief Inspector of Prisons, Sir James Hennessy, arrived in Belfast and went straight to Stormont where he met Mr Prior.

The Secretary of State instructed Sir James to interpret his brief as widely as possible and to look at all aspects of security in the prison. On the 28th September the Secretary of State set out in a letter to Sir James, the terms of reference of the inquiry: "To conduct an inquiry into the security arrangements at Her Majesty's Prison Maze, relative to the escape on Sunday the 25th September 1983, and to make relevant recommendations for the improvement of security at HMP Maze."

When I reported for duty on Monday morning the 26th, I was instructed to report to the admin building, where a team of detectives was taking statements from all the officers who were on duty the previous day and had been involved in any way in the circumstances surrounding the escape. Although I had made a full written report to the Governor in the early hours of Monday morning before I had left the prison, the SO, myself and the other two officers were taken to the security office and told to fill in 'half sheets' about the escape. A 'half sheet' was a sheet of paper that was folded in the centre. It was the standard official report sheet in the prison service, which had to be filled in to describe an event or incident. The security office or the Security Information Centre (SIC), to give it its full title, was based in a small room on the first floor of the admin building. It had one back window that looked out over the football pitch beyond the roof of the Officers' Mess. In this 14 foot by 9 foot room the collection of all information and the monitoring of all prisoners was supposed to take place. The PO in charge was an improviser who did his best, in an uphill struggle, to keep tabs on the most sophisticated terrorist organisation in the world. It was a security system that stumbled on from one day to the next, and was overseen by a security Governor whose arrogance and self-importance would have viewed any attempt to update or modernise the office as an affront on his competence and authority. The SIC failed to see what was crying out to be seen. The jail cat knew something was about to happen.

I went into the office and made a lengthy statement to the detective. He asked me a number of questions about the incident at the main gate when I blocked the lorry, and he took the names of all the prisoners whom I recognised in the escape. As the interview ended and I left the office, I felt extremely exhausted, and on my way out of the admin building 1 called at the duty office and told them, that I was going home to see my doctor. On my way home I called to see our family doctor. He was Doctor Deeny and I told him how I felt. He knew where I worked and he asked me about the escape the day before. I told him about it and about the part I had played in the episode, at which he shouted, "You're a bloody hero!" He diagnosed that I just needed a few days' rest. He gave me a line for two weeks and I left the surgery and went home. It was my first period of sick leave since I joined the service.

Sir James Hennessy and his team set up their headquarters in the education building in the Maze on September the 27th only two days after the escape. The full team was: Sir James Hennessy, KBE, CMG, HM Chief Inspector of Prisons for England and Wales, Mr G H Lakes, MC, and HM Deputy Chief Inspector of Prisons. There were eleven other people, two of whom were former Senior Prison Governors, a former Administration Officer, and two former Chief Officers. All were members of HM Inspectorate of Prisons, and all had wide experience in prison work. The inquiry took four and a half weeks, during which time they examined the whole Maze complex, from the ground as well as from the air. They reconstructed the events of the escape, and inquired into all aspects of the routine and procedures practised by the staff which had the slightest bearing on the escape. The inquiry team interviewed the Governor and 115 members of staff, both serving and retired.

On Tuesday the 11 th October a messenger from the Prison Department called at my home and told me about the inquiry that was taking place in the prison. He told me they wanted to speak to me, to get a statement and hear about my experiences on the day of the escape. I told him I would go down to the Maze the next day and talk to the inquiry team. It was about 9 o'clock the following morning when I walked into the education building. I was met by an officer whom I knew very well. He was usually employed as the Chaplain's Clerk but he had been seconded to the inquiry team. He had a list of people who had to be interviewed. He marked my name off the sheet and directed me to a side office beside the main teachers' hall.

The door was open and I gave it a knock and stepped into the office. The two men who sat behind a desk introduced themselves, and a secretary sat at a small desk close to the office door. We had a few pleasant words before we got down to the business of the escape. They explained they wanted to hear about the events of Sunday 25th September, and the part I played in attempting to prevent the escape. I explained the sequence of events at the main gate of the prison and the chase across the fields to the river and the subsequent capture of the four prisoners. They asked me a number of questions which I answered frankly and to the point as the secretary wrote all the information down in shorthand. As the interview came to an end, they asked me if I had any questions I'd like to ask them. I asked how many weapons were recovered altogether, and they told me that five automatic pistols were recovered, one with a silencer that had been brazed to the muzzle. They said they thought the modification to the weapon had been carried out in the metal shop that was part of the workshops. The five guns were very small calibre weapons, and they had been-as it was later discovered-purchased abroad and smuggled into the country.

As I got up to leave, one of the men, a Mr Wilson, shook hands with me and congratulated me on the action I had taken to try to stop the escape. He said that the inquiry had found that the whole operation at the main gate and tally lodge area had been marked by great courage and daring of the prison staff. A few days later I returned to duty, and the place was running just the same as if nothing had happened. The crisis was clearly over and the higher ranks were in damage limitation mode. It was through these experiences I learnt that the prison officer was subtly divorced from the outside world of normality. Working in the Maze ensured that contact with friends and neighbours was kept to a casual level, where I had to remain distant; and part of me could not be shared, even with my own family-a separate element, which was inherent in the very nature of the job.

Within days of the arrival of the Hennessy team, new security improvements were introduced that had never been seen before in the Maze. Hand-held metal detectors were supplied to the search teams in the visitors' reception area, to be used in the searching of both men and women visitors. Large arch-shaped detectors were fitted at the entrance door to the reception area and to the entrance to the waiting rooms. All visitors to the prison had to pass through the detectors, which set off an alarm if a metal object was detected on a person. In the parcel censors a conveyor belt x-ray machine was installed with two colour monitors. The belt carried all parcels, hobbies material and newspapers through a concealed compartment which did not only x-ray every item, but identified every object through a colour intensity apparatus that identified by different colours the acute intensity of a solid object, like a book or the heel of a shoe.

Obviously, the urgency that had been placed on the introduction of metal detectors, and the detection of metal objects on visitors passing through the visitors' car park, was the result of so many guns being used in the escape, and the fear of history repeating itself.

The monitoring and searching of all visitors to the prison was always an extremely important assignment, particularly in regard to male visitors. One morning I was on male search duty when a visitor arrived to have his prearranged visit with a prominent IRA figure. After being documented at the reception desk, he was passed to a colleague and myself to be searched before being transferred to the visits area inside the prison. As he stepped into the search cubicle, I asked him to empty his pockets onto the table, which he did, and the contents were recorded on a search sheet.

Each visitor to the prison had to produce some kind of identification before he or she was permitted into the prison. All documents were then removed by the search team, placed in a sealed envelope and held in a property room, where they were collected by the visitor on return from the prison. He was a tall, well-dressed chap in his early thirties, and before I gave him a rubdown search I thought 1 would try to get into conversation with him. I passed a remark about the weather and as he answered, he spoke in a very plausible tone but with an unusual accent. At first I thought he was an Australian, and I said, "0, you're an Australian." But he quickly replied, "No, I am from Zimbabwe." As he spoke, I thought I detected a sudden pause in his voice and a slight tensing movement of his shoulders. His body language indicated to me that as the words left his lips, he realised he should not have told me where he was from.

I gave him a quick rubdown search and showed him into the waiting room. I quickly returned to the search cubicle and examined his property. The identification document which he had used at the reception desk to gain access into the prison was his passport, which was with his property. As I lifted the passport and opened it, everything seemed to be correct, with his photograph, the passport number, country of issue and his name and address. As I turned the pages, I was surprised to see it had been stamped in a number of countries where there had been civil wars or armed insurrections. The country of issue was Zimbabwe - true enough - which had only got its independence three years before, after a long guerrilla war and a cease-fire that was monitored by commonwealth forces. But it was the countries he had visited that attracted my attention, countries like Vietnam, Cambodia, Egypt and Palestine. I took the passport and rang the security department and explained my suspicions, and they took note of the situation. A few weeks later I had forgotten all about the incident, when 1 was talking to one of the security staff. He reminded me about the episode, and explained that the character in question had been traced by the police and they had discovered he was an international, terrorist liaison officer, who travelled around the countries of the world that were hotbeds of insurrection or had terrorist problems. His job was to establish contacts and set up a communications network between the various organisations to ensure unity of purpose between them. His visit to the Maze was with a top IRA man. It made me wonder what the Special Branch and their sister clandestine services were doing, when the existence of such a high profile character had to be drawn to their attention by a prison officer in the Maze.

In the visitors' reception of the car park area the normal Sunday routine continued, and on Sunday the 20th November I was detailed the cleaning squad once again. I was assigned an association that night in H2, and as I made my way into the block, 1 was surprised to see the changes that had taken place at the grilles. Between the two wings on each side of the circle a new grille had been fitted. It was called the 'association grille' and it crossed the landing between the two wings. A long bar at each side, that was nicknamed the 'baconslicer', allowed the wing grilles to be opened or closed to give the prisoners access from one wing to the other, and at the same time seal the grille officer off from the cons. This was the free association that was given to the prisoners after the hunger-strike. At the same time as the new system was introduced, staff manning levels in the wings were reduced and the only time a full quota of staff was allowed into the wings was at lock-up, when the officers were needed to carry out headcounts. It seemed to me the Maze was being reduced more and more to a holiday camp status, rather than a high security prison. But the normal procedure took place when lock-up was called by the PO, and the prisoners were locked and counted and the numbers returned to the circle. Then when all the block numbers were in, they were rung through to the ECR and soon afterwards we were ordered to "stand down."

H2 was situated in Phase I, and therefore the furthest block from the prison main gate. Each night after lock-up a minibus was assigned to convey the staff from the block to segment gate I, and when the night guard took charge of the block, all the day staff walked briskly out to the block gate to catch the minibus. Sometimes when the bus was full some of the officers would start walking in the direction of the segment gate, and then catch the bus on its second trip from the block. That Sunday night I missed the minibus as it left with the first load of staff, and as I was joined by a couple of other officers, we started to walk, but a few minutes later the minibus returned and collected us.

It was a few minutes after 9 pm when we walked into the tally lodge, and some of the night guard staff were talking about a shooting incident that had been reported on the 9 o'clock news. When I asked one of the officers what had happened, he told me the father of another officer whom I knew very well had been shot dead at a gospel meeting in South Armagh. A short time later the full horror of what became known as the 'Gospel Hall Massacre' began to filter through.

It was just another Sunday evening gospel service in the Mountain Lodge Pentecostal Church, a small prefabricated building on the main Keady to Newtownhamilton Road, near Darkley and less than half a mile from the border. The congregation, who worshipped regularly in that lonely part of South Armagh, had just gathered into the hall and had started to sing a hymn while waiting for the 6 o'clock service to start. The sixty or seventy worshippers were singing the hymn: "Would you be free from your burden of sin?" And it was as the final verse of the hymn was being sung that, without warning, the sectarian death squad struck.

Arriving at the front porch of the hall as darkness fell, two of them opened fire with automatic weapons at point blank range on the three church elders, who were standing in the porchway welcoming members of the congregation, before directing them to their seats. As two of the elders collapsed mortally wounded to the floor, instant pandemonium erupted in the congregation. A third elder who had also been shot staggered through the inside porch door as worshippers dived for cover. The wounded man managed to stagger, with blood pouring from his face, on towards a side door that led into an ante room, where he too collapsed and died within seconds.

At this point the murderers turned their attention to the terrified gathering, and calmly walked into the hall. There was another burst of automatic gunfire as they sprayed the inside of the hall with bullets. One parishioner threw himself over a seven-month-old baby to save its life. By now the congregation were petrified with fear, as children were screaming hysterically and men and women were sprawled on the floor among bloodstained pews, prayer books and Bibles. As the people pleaded for their lives, the gunmen turned, stepped over the two dead men, and went outside where they reloaded their weapons and sprayed an outside wall of the building with another hail of bullets.

Apart from the three dead elders, seven people were seriously wounded three women and four men. The murder gang fled in a waiting car, and they headed straight for the border less than a mile away. The first person to raise the alarm was Mrs Barbara Bain, daughter-in-law of Pastor Robert Bain. Pastor Bain was the minister of the church and he was to take the service. Mrs Bain ran to a neighbour's house about a half-a-mile away. where she raised the alarm and the police were called. As news of the massacre spread around the Province, a fleet of ambulances rushed the dead and injured to Craigavon Area Hospital, about 20 miles from the scene.

The bravery of the congregation was later recounted by a local doctor, who arrived at the Gospel Hall only minutes after the shooting and attended the injured. He later described the "calmness" he found at the scene. Although it was a tragic event, with two men lying dead at the front door and another inside, one couldn't help but notice the calmness that had descended on the scene. The initial shock of the attack was ended and everyone was quiet. There was order instead of chaos and none was hysterical, even the children were now calm. People were upset but, even in obvious pain, some of them directed the doctor towards others whom they believed were in greater danger and in need of medical assistance. One man had lost so much blood he was put on a drip because there was a danger of him dying before he got to the hospital.

Police and ambulance men were horrified at what they found when they arrived at the church. Bloodstains splattered the floor and saturated prayer books and Bibles. Paper tissues and handkerchiefs that had been used to cover the wounds, as temporary dressings for the injured, were scattered all over the floor. Nine bullets had ripped through the double wooden doors at the front of the building, through which the gunmen had first fired, whilst the pews, seat covers, walls and windows were also riddled with bullet holes. The congregation included 24 children, all under 14 years-of-age. None of those killed or wounded had any connections with the security forces, nor was the Gospel Hall used or attended by members of the security forces. It was the worst sectarian attack ever to take place in Northern Ireland, an assault on the most sacred right - the right to worship.

In the follow-up hunt for the murderers, police in the Republic found the getaway car. It was a hijacked taxi, which had been seized on the

Castleblaney Road shortly before the massacre took place. The vehicle was found burnt out at Castlebellingham, south of Dundalk. The driver had picked up four men in Dundalk and was driving them towards the border, when one of them produced a gun and the driver was hooded before being taken out of the car. He was ordered not to report the hijacking for four hours, but for fear of his life he did not report the incident at all.

Responsibility for the slayings was later claimed by the Catholic Reaction Force, a flag of convenience for the INLA. Police forensic experts later discovered that one of the weapons used in the attack had previously been used by the INLA, when two policemen were murdered at a security barrier in Markethill, a year before the massacre at the church. The same weapon was used six months earlier in a shooting incident at a security barrier in Dungannon, and it was used again in August when, in an ambush on the security forces, two INLA men were shot dead. The atrocity was a naked, sectarian act and it was carried out with one objective in mind - to destabilise the Protestant population in South Armagh. In fact it was so horrendous that even the PIRA, in an attempt to distance themselves from the murderers, took the unusual step of issuing a statement branding the attack as 'blatantly sectarian', and making it clear they had nothing to do with it.

Two days after the murders, on Tuesday afternoon, the congregation of Mountain Lodge Pentecostal Church claimed the victory over the grave, as they sang hymns at the graveside of the first of the three church elders to be buried. The funeral of 39-year-old Mr Victor Cunningham brought back horrific memories to those who had been in the church on the Sunday night before, when the first shots rang out in the hallway of the little wooden building. The minister of the church, Pastor Robert Bain, told the hundreds of mourners who were gathered at the funeral, of the murdered man's love for his church. "Victor's better off today than his killers," said the Pastor. "He's in the presence of the Lord, whom he loved and had in his heart: we sorrow today but we know that in the morning we will meet him again." A poignant photograph of the scene appeared in a local newspaper, as the dead man's widow, Edna, closed her eyes and raised her hands to heaven, her wedding ring glistening in the dying winter sunshine, as she and the large crowd sang, "In the sweet bye and bye, we shall meet on that beautiful shore."

Pastor Bain was assisted by the Rev Harvey Shaw, Pastor David Greenow, Rev R A McMullan, and Pastor Jack Richie, who closed the service by saying, "the gun does not kill the Christian but promotes him to glory, where he will see the face of the captain." The funerals of the other two elders, Mr Harold Brown and Mr David Wilson, took place later.

Chapter 16

On the 27th November the chief of staff of the INLA, Dominic McGlinchey, admitted in a statement that the organisation had been involved in the Pentecostal church massacre. McGlinchey was the most wanted man in Ireland at the time, and he was described by police as a 'pathological killer'. His only motivation was to kill, kill and kill again.

The Irish National Liberation Army was formed in 1975, as the terrorist wing of the Irish Republican Socialist Party. The initial membership of the organisation came from a section of the official IRA who was disaffected by the split in the organisation after which the provisional IRA had been formed. The INLA gained further recruits from the PIRA, after it declared a cease-fire late in 1975. The first assassination to be carried out by the INLA, which effectively established it as a ruthless terrorist organisation, was the cold-blooded murder of a former Belfast Commander of the official IRA, Billy McMillen. McMillen was shot dead in the Lower Falls area of Belfast, while he was shopping with his wife.

The INLA drew most of its membership from south Londonderry, the Lower Falls and the markets area of Belfast. Members of the organisation established themselves as the most sadistic killers in Ireland, after numerous attacks on members of the security forces. When they murdered the Conservative Northern Ireland spokesman Mr Airey Neave at Westminister in March 1979, surprisingly the INLA was only then proscribed, and after, the House of Commons was informed it had developed links with terrorist organisations in other parts of the world. The INLA were responsible for the murder of 17 people, 11 of them soldiers, in the bombing of the 'Droppin Well' public house and disco at Ballykelly, County Londonderry, on the 6th December 1982

The organisation's neurotic leader was born in the village of Bellaghy, in south Londonderry, in 1955, and joined the IRA when he was 17 years of age. Along with his schoolmate Francis Hughes, who later died on hunger-strike in the Maze, and another schoolmate Ian Milne, their photographs appeared on police posters throughout Northern Ireland. They were dubbed the three, most wanted men in Ireland. They were the entrepreneurs of terrorism. During a court case in the Irish Republic to extradite him to the north, McGlinchey absconded, but after a shoot-out with the southern police he was recaptured on the 17th March 1984. Obviously too hot a brick for the Irish authorities to handle, within hours of his arrest he was handed over to the RUC. McGlinchey made history because he was the first Republican prisoner to be extradited from the south to face terrorist charges in Northern Ireland. Previous to this case, the Republic's courts had always refused to extradite people on terrorist-type charges, if they claimed they were political offences.

McGlinchey was remanded in custody at the Belfast court and he arrived in the Maze, where he was immediately put on 30 minute observation

24 hours a day. This effectively meant that the wing class officer had to record in the journal every half-hour, that he had seen the prisoner McGlinchey. This '30 minute Obs' was also rung into the ECR. The routine was kept up day and night as long as he remained in the Maze. Each time he had to appear at court in Belfast, a major police and army operation was put into effect, which was under the control of the security chief officer out of the Maze. McGlinchey was put into a prison 'cell-van', and as we left the prison main gate, we rendezvoused with a unit of the RUC's Special Patrol Group (SPG) in their Land Rovers, as well as military police in their vehicles, and the whole convoy headed off for Belfast. The entire escort was supported by five or six police outriders on motorbikes, who sped ahead of the line of vehicles to stop traffic merging from side streets and to ensure a clear passage for the police convoy. In their own inimitable way, the NIO went over the top in characterizing McGlinchey and some of the other paramilitary leaders as 'super terrorists'. I often thought it would have been much easier to put these cons in an unmarked police car and take them to court without all the hullabaloo.

McGlinchey was tried for the murder of a Toomebridge grandmother, Mrs Hester McMullan, who was shot dead in 1977. Mrs McMullan was a 63-year-old postmistress and mother of a part-time reserve policeman. She was shot dead in her own home after gunmen, having failed to murder her son, turned their guns on the elderly woman. McGlinchey was sentenced to life imprisonment, but the sentence was overturned at the court of appeal on the 8th of October 1985, and he was re-extradited to the Republic to face further terrorist charges regarding a shoot-out with the Gardi. He was found guilty and sentenced to 10 years in Portlaoise prison. It was during his time in jail that a major feud broke out between the IN LA and a breakaway faction, the Irish People's Liberation Organisation (IPLO). The bitter vendetta started when two leading members were shot dead in a pub in Drogheda in the South of Ireland. Over the following months, 13 members of the organisation were murdered, including McGlinchey's wife Mary, who was shot dead while she bathed her two children at her home in Dundalk.

Mary McGlinchey - who it was believed was a leading member of the organisation - was shot seven times through the head and body, by two gunmen who opened fire at close range. They had broken into the house through a back door and dashed upstairs to the bathroom. The Justice Department in Dublin refused permission for McGlinchey to leave the prison to attend his wife's funeral, which took place at Mrs McGlinchey's family home at Bellaghy, County Londonderry.

When Dominic 'Mad Dog' McGlinchey-nicknamed by the media-was eventually released from prison, he went to live in Drogheda and it was here that his violent past finally caught up with him. It was Thursday night the 10th February 1994, when three gunmen, armed with one pistol and two shotguns, punched him to the ground and blasted him ten times. He was shot in both legs before bullets from the pistol ripped into his head and chest. It was near his home as he was making a phone call from a public kiosk that the gunmen struck! McGlinchey's son Dominic, who was 16 years of age at the time, was sitting in his father's car and witnessed the murder. Dominic Junior had also witnessed the murder of his mother only 7 years before. In an interview shortly after the Pentecostal church massacre, McGlinchey admitted his involvement in the murders, particularly with the Ruger semi-automatic rifle that had killed the three church elders.

After some delay the much awaited, Hennessy report was finally published on the 26th January 1984. Despite the high profile of the inquiry it was only relevant to a limited area of the circumstances surrounding the escape, and therefore laid most of the blame on the prison staff. The first casualty of the aftermath of the inquiry was the Governor, who was now allowed to resign. Remarkably, at the same time, the Secretary of State announced that there would be no ministerial resignations since the report showed 'no policy failures'. Clearly the Governor was the sacrificial lamb, doomed at the altar of political expediency. Four days later the Northern Ireland Prison Governors' Association supported by the Prison Officers' Association. Made a statement to the effect that the political restraints imposed on the prison service by the Prison Department and the NIO, after the 1982 hunger-strike, were responsible for creating the 'liberal' regime that made the breakout possible. The two associations also accused the NIO of pursuing an appeasement policy between the end of the hunger-strike and the escape. As expected, the Prisons Minister, Mr Nicholas Scott, rejected the criticism.

On leaving the responsibility for the escape at the door of the Governor, Hennessy went on in the report to praise him for his 34 years of service, ten of which were as the No. I Governor of the Maze, during the various crises that arose in the prison from time to time, like the disturbances over segregation and the hunger-strike. According to Hennessy he had high personal qualities, he showed sensitivity and understanding and he was hard working and conscientious, but his experiences were from a time when the Northern Ireland Prison Service was less demanding. The 41 members of the Prison Governors' Association were so disillusioned by the way the Governor was treated that they issued a statement in which they said they had constantly warned the NIO of the inevitability of a serious problem at the Maze. The report made 73 recommendations for the improvement of security at the Maze, most of which concerned the physical structure and design of the jail. The inquiry was scathing on the decision to make McFarland and some of the other top IRA men in H7 orderlies, and it recognised that for the escape to be successful it was vital that these leaders had freedom of movement and ease of access to all parts of the block. Their employment as orderlies provided them with the means of distributing the weapons, when the time came for them to launch their plan. Moreover, the use of such high-risk prisoners as orderlies was totally against prison rules, which clearly stated that orderlies should be low-risk prisoners in the last weeks of their sentences and unlikely to attempt to escape or become violent.

The report had a great deal of praise for the Director of Prisons and Operations who took over the position in 1982. It described him as a dedicated, hard working and conscientious officer who was very well thought of by the Under Secretary and who enjoyed a high reputation throughout the service. But ultimately - the report went on - he did not appear to appreciate the extent of the many security weaknesses in the Maze, and therefore he must be responsible for some of the shortcomings. At no time did the inquiry address the question of who was responsible for prison policy. Had this been done, the entire tapestry would have been in danger of unwinding.

The Hennessy report was debated in the House of Commons on the 9th February. During the debate the Secretary of State, Mr Prior, paid tribute to the Governor and made reference to the fact that, as he was close to retirement when he resigned, he would not suffer as far as his retirement pension was concerned. He spoke of the Governor "holding the poisoned chalice," and praised him for the honourable public service he had given in very difficult circumstances over the years.

Some time after the report was published Sir James Hennessy was interviewed on an Ulster television documentary programme. He was asked his opinion of the Maze when he arrived to conduct the inquiry. He said:

"*I would refer to the Maze prison at the time as being rather like not having been there at the time-a Colditz during the war, an impregnable fortress in which was kept a lot of prisoners. And the Maze, when we first went there looked rather like that. And for those prisoners to have got control of their block, the H7 Block, from which the 38 escaped in a matter of, I think it was twenty minutes, was absolutely staggering! And so I think for anybody to achieve that, I must regard it as a matter of congratulations!*"

As I watched the programme, I was absolutely shocked. Gross naivety was in his every word. To even relate the IRA to prisoners of war, and to compare the Maze prison to Colditz, was absurd. The Maze prison contained prisoners who had been sentenced in Courts of Law. Some of them had been found guilty of some of the most sadistic murders of the 20th century. There were no mother and baby rooms in Colditz, or photographic studios where family portraits could be taken. There were no free education courses, vocational training classes or a prisoner's welfare department. For the Chief Inspector of Prisons to congratulate the IRA on their success was beyond belief! Such flippant remarks showed a total lack of understanding about the terrorist situation in Northern Ireland, and to come from the Chief Inspector of Prisons was deeply insulting to me and my colleagues at the Maze. I have to say it was a bitter blow to me personally, and it did much to sour my remaining years in the service.

The most serious aspect in the escape was the presence of guns. In any escape the gun is the equalizer. It matters not what security precautions are in place. If a gun is smuggled into the prison, all the security measures are inconsequential. So the guns and ammunition were central to the IRA's plans: indeed without them the escape could not have taken place. The question that presented itself was how the guns could have been smuggled into the prison. In practice, there is no prison so secure that contraband articles cannot be smuggled in. In most of the prisons in the U.K, for example, money, drugs and escape tools are found from time to time. However, the introduction of guns into the Maze was not unique to Northern Ireland's prisons, as there had been similar incidents before. Guns that had been smuggled into the Crum were used in an escape of IRA men in 1981. But it is the vigilance of prison staff, and the meticulous searching of visitors to the prison, that is paramount in ensuring the security of any prison.

Of the five guns recovered during the escape, according to police forensic experts, one had been used in the 1981 escape of IRA men from the Crum, and another one had been used by the IRA in a previous incident. The guns were very small, about $3^{1}/_{2}$" x $5^{1}/_{2}$ in size, and each one weighed no more than ten ounces. There were four semi-automatic pistols and one automatic, which meant they could easily have been broken down into their component parts. The plastic pistol grips had been removed from four of them to make them even lighter and smaller, and all the sharp edges had been smoothed off them, clearly to allow them to be carried close to the body. Of the five weapons recovered and there was probably the same number not recovered - three were .25 'Titan' semi-automatic pistols, one was a .25 'Raven' semi-automatic pistol and the fifth was a .22 'Sterling' automatic pistol. Of the ammunition recovered, three rounds were in the magazine of one of the pistols, four in another, five in another and six in another. Two weapons were empty.

Thus the guns were central to the escape plans, but their concealment in the block was equally important. The weapons had to be hidden in safe places and kept concealed until they were needed. It was vital for the success of their plan that none of the weapons or ammunition should be found by the various search teams that operated in H7. There were three different kinds of search procedures in the blocks. These included daily cell searches of three or four cells, which were carried out by the wing staff and included the searching of the inmates as well as the cells. There were special spot searches of individual cells and the prisoners who occupied them. There were also wing searches, which were of a more thorough nature, when every cell and every prisoner in the wing was searched. Simultaneously, the dining hall, ablutions and hobbies room were searched, and a team of officers searched the sterile areas and exercise yards surrounding the wing. Even the roof of the Block was searched by trades officers, who checked the guttering and down-pipes that channelled the rainwater from the roof.

The wing search was a large-scale search and was carried out by the pre-night-guard staff, which numbered about 40 or 50 officers. This major search was occasionally extended to the entire block, in which all four wings were searched at the same time. The pre-night guard search team were independent of the block staff, who had to work with the prisoners on a day-to-day basis. 'B' wing in H7 had been given a full and thorough search by the pre-night guard staff on the 25th August, only four weeks before the escape and seventeen individual cells were given a spot search on the 13th of September, only twelve days before the escape. All these searches produced nothing of significance, but after the escape when H7 was searched by specialist search teams which were brought in from other prisons in the Province, it was discovered that the legs of the cell tables had been hollowed out and were possibly used to hide ammunition. In the ablutions a triangular, plywood box partition was fitted to the top of the wash-hand basin unit, with a mirror attached to it over each basin. When this was searched, it was discovered the mirrors had been removed and a hole cut in the plywood behind each one, giving the prisoners access to the cavity, then the mirrors were replaced. Other possible hiding places were identified in the block.

Hennessy made reference to the poor performance of some staff and weaknesses in procedures and organisation of the ECR. Some of the closed circuit television (CCTV) monitoring equipment was defective and there was no general alarm system to alert the staff in and around the prison in the event of an escape. The report recommended that all these failures should be examined urgently. It also laid great emphasis on the communications system in the Maze, and the increased use of CCTV surveillance equipment.

The report also highlighted the lack of a riot squad in the Maze and suggested that this failure be remedied by the introduction of a permanent quickreaction force. Although there were times when a riot team was set up during particular circumstances, the assistance of such a team was badly lacking immediately prior to the escape. Within days of the publication of the report, a start had been made to the establishment of such a force. It was called an 'Instant Reaction Force' (IRF), which was a more acceptable name than riot squad. One of the now-disused workshops was cleared out and prepared for the IRF base. Although the report suggested the use of staff normally employed on other duties, when the IRF was established it was made up of officers who were on permanent standby. They were supplied with the latest in riot equipment and trained in self-defence, unarmed combat, and how to react in riot or hostage situations.

What was drama on the world's TV screens was the life that members of the security forces had lived for years. I often thought the almost celebratory comments in the media about some terrorist murders were so abhorrent. 'A well planned ambush', described a couple of gunmen hiding behind a ditch, waiting to murder a policeman. 'A highly sophisticated device' -this described a piece of metal pipe, rammed full of explosives with a detonator and a piece of fuse wire. Sensational statements like these, and the role of the media in the troubles, were discussed by a representative of the Independent Broadcasting Authority at a meeting in Belfast in 1984. The discussion centred on the deaths of PO

Dessie Irvine, who was murdered in 1977, and Assistant Governor William McConnell, who was killed in March 1984. Both murders had taken place after they had given filmed interviews on television.

Governor McConnell was murdered on the morning of Tuesday the 6th March (Shrove Tuesday), as he was leaving home to go to the Maze prison. He was 35 years of age, and I had known him since I went to work in the H Blocks in 1976. It was about 8.15 when he said goodbye to his wife Beryl and his three-year-old daughter Gail, at their home in Hawthorden Drive, near the Belmont Road, in Belfast. As he walked to his car, which was parked in the driveway, two gunmen dashed in through the gates and opened fire. Mr McConnell died instantly in a hail of bullets that struck him in the head and face. The murder gang then made off in a small car they had taken from an elderly couple whom they had held hostage since the night before.

Governor McConnell was no ordinary, soft target. He was the Secretary of the Prison Governors' Association, and had been in a bitter dispute with the NIO since the publication of the Hennessy report. He had 'gone public' over prison policy in the Maze and the way in which responsibility for the escape had been unloaded onto the staff by his political masters. I was on duty at movements control that morning and was detailed the pedestrian gate. It was a bright March morning, and shortly after the murder, the police contacted the prison about Mr McConnell's death, and the news filtered through to the main gate area. Soon afterwards the No. I Governor arrived at the gate, and as I let him in I said to him, "We've just heard the news, Sir, that Governor McConnell was shot dead this morning." He was astounded, and said, "What!" He immediately turned and ran into the tally lodge to speak to the Governor in charge.

Mr McConnell had a premonition of his own death because he had spoken out a few weeks earlier on a television programme, and although he was silhouetted to protect his identity, his name was displayed at the bottom of the screen. He knew he could be signing his own death warrant by appearing on the programme to voice the Prison Governors' dismay with the Hennessy report, but he was convinced he had to speak the truth. His fears were disclosed in a letter that was read out to a packed church at his funeral. Mountpottinger Baptist Church in Templemore A venue was packed to capacity long before the service started, and crowds gathered outside. The Rev David McGaughey, cousin of the dead man, read out the letter to the mourners and told them that Bill had written the document on the 3 February, the day after appearing on the TV programme.

He gave it to Mr McGaughey and requested that it be read out at his funeral if anything happened to him. The letter was headed, 'To cousin David, for his use'. And it was addressed to 'All in attendance', on the subject of 'My Demise'. It went on:

'I have decided to write this statement since I have come to the conclusion that the public interest is best served by knowing that whatever happens to me, I spoke the truth. I did not take the decision to go public on the matter of the Hennessy report lightly. I realised the danger I was placing myself and others in, when, in consultation with my colleagues on the committee of the Prison Governors' Association, I agreed to act as their spokesman.

Some will be gathered today asking questions which only a full investigation of the facts will reveal. Clearly, in attempting that process to continue, someone has decided that I should play no further part in the proceedings! I feel sorry for them, and can only pray that their part in the story will one day be revealed. My wife Beryl has been supportive of all I have done. I would commend her and Gail to your keeping and prayers.

Finally, let no one be alarmed as to my eternal security. In March 1966 I committed my life, talents, work and actions to almighty God, in sure and certain knowledge that however slight my hold upon Him may have been during my years at school, university and the prison service, His promises are sure and His hold on me complete. Nothing can separate me from the love of God in Christ Jesus our Lord. At our marriage ceremony we sang the hymn, 'My hope is built on nothing less'. Please, sing it today, and may God be with you all'.

(Signed) Bill McConnell

In his statement Mr McConnell had written more between the lines than was written on them. He had joined the service in 1971, after leaving Queen's University with a BA Degree. He was a man of deep convictions and had the courage and honesty to speak out, characteristics he always displayed in the Maze. He paid the price. The truth cost Bill McConnell his life.

The IRA later claimed responsibility for the murder, and within a short time the murder gang was rounded up. Surprisingly, a 63-year-old civil servant, who lived only a few hundred yards from the McConnell home was arrested and charged with complicity in the murder. He worked with the Department of Agriculture, and during questioning he admitted working with the IRA over a period of five years. During this time he had monitored members of the security forces living in the east Belfast area, and correlated information about their movements. During the trial, evidence was given that, as well as providing a safe house for the murder gang, he disposed of the murder weapons, wigs and gloves that they had used. A few days earlier he had bought razor blades so they could shave themselves in an effort to change their appearance before leaving the area. He received a life sentence for what the trial judge described as his despicable role in the murder. He later turned 'Queen's Evidence' and testified against the other I RA men.

On Monday the 4th June I was detailed 8 o'clock start in the visitors' car park reception. Driving through Dollingstown on my way to the Maze, little did I know but that I was driving past a place that within an hour would be the scene of a brutal murder and an attempted massacre of the security forces. As I was to find out later, it was the murder of a friend whom I had known many years before. His name was David Chambers and we were reared in the same neighbourhood and went to the same school. David was a part-time soldier in the Ulster Defence Regiment, which he had joined in 1977. He was on his way that morning to his work at the Boxmore container factory just outside the village, when he was ambushed and shot at point blank range by the IRA. It was about 8.10 am as he was riding his motorbike along the Inn Road, only a few hundred yards from the factory gates, when the IRA man opened fire. David was shot several times and died instantly, and as his work-mates who were also on their way to the factory rushed to help him, the police were notified.

Within minutes police checkpoints were set up in the area in an attempt to catch the gunmen. Forensic 'Scenes of Crime' experts sealed off part of the road which was close to a derelict house. They had collected a number of bullet shells and were still searching the area for further clues, when shortly after 9 o'clock a huge bomb that had been concealed in the derelict house exploded, showering police and forensic detectives with shrapnel and masonry from the building. Miraculously, no one was seriously injured and only one policeman and a soldier were slightly hurt in the bomb trap, but pensioners' bungalows on the opposite side of the road were wrecked with the blast. As ambulances took the injured men to Craigavon Hospital, about twenty families were accommodated in a nearby school until about 6.30 that night, when the area was declared safe.

The murder and bomb trap were intended to be a carbon copy of an attack which took place at Narrow Water near Warrenpoint on the 2th August 1979. A 500Lb bomb in a truck laden with hay was detonated by the IRA as an army convoy drove past, killing six members of the Parachute Regiment. Shortly afterwards a second explosion in a derelict house damaged a helicopter carrying members of a 'quick reaction force', and a unit of men from the Queen's Own Highlanders, killing twelve soldiers including their commanding officer, LtColonel David Blair. A gun battle then broke out between the army and the IRA ambush gang, who were firing from the southern side of the border on the opposite bank of Carlingford Lough, where it narrows between County Louth and County Down. The Narrow Water ambush was the army's greatest loss of life in a single incident since the IRA's terrorist campaign started. Thankfully the Dollingstown bomb trap did not cause a single death, although a large crater was left where the house had stood and large stones littered the road.

David had been due to celebrate his thirteenth wedding anniversary the following day. He and his wife Carol worked in the same factory where they had first met, and where he was a supervisor. She had started work on an earlier shift about an hour before her husband and knew nothing about the shooting, until she was told her husband had been in an accident. It was not until she arrived at Craigavon Hospital that she heard what had happened. Thirty-four year old David lived with his wife and two daughters, Julie and Lynn, at Glenfield Road in the Mourneview area of Lurgan. Two days after the murder

Wednesday the 6th June was his youngest daughter's birthday, but instead of celebrations, Lynn with her mother and sister Julie were grief-stricken as they attended the funeral of her father. Sometime later two IRA men by the names of O'Dowd and Murray were sentenced to life imprisonment for David's murder. During their trial the sentencing Lord Justice recommended that O'Dowd should serve at least 25 years for the murder.

The brutal murder of David Chambers took an ironical turn some fourteen years later. It was on Monday the 12th October 1998 that Julie Chambers - who was only ten years old when her father was shot dead on his way to work-was working in a shop in Lurgan. When she overheard a group of people planning a welcome home celebration for an IRA man called 0' Dowd, a name that was engraved in her mind since that dreadful morning in 1984 when her father was murdered. It was only after she heard about the planned welcome home party that she learned her father's murderer had been released from the Maze. Both men had been released from the Maze under the terms of the Belfast peace deal, O'Dowd on the 2nd October and Murray 7 days later. The release of prisoners who had been sentenced to long terms of imprisonment was bizarre. It was a wilderness of mirrors, where lies were the truth and the truth, lies; and the prison staff were left suspended between the two.

In an interview later, Julie said, "I just felt physically sick, I couldn't believe dad's killer was out of jail. I just ran straight home and told my family." Julie's mother complained bitterly that she thought when her husband's killer was given a recommended sentence he should not have been released under the Belfast deal and that the family hadn't even been informed that the two IRA men were to be released. This illustrated the coldness of the NIO, and their uncaring attitude towards members of the security forces and their families who have suffered so much over the years.

In July 1984 the personnel chief officer sent for me and told me I would be assigned duty in H Block 3 from that date. He said the staff in the block were under such pressure it was decided to have a periodic staff change to help them cope with the tension of the place. I was on the move again, this time to H3, and on Friday the 6th July I started duty in the block. Access to H3 was through segment gate 4, the second segment gate from the admin area into the phases. By now many of the Hennessy recommendations had been put in place, and at each of the two segment gates a watch tower had been built, along with a vehicle airlock, similar to that at the main gate complex. The design of these two segment gates had come in for particular criticism in the Hennessy inquiry, especially the fact that each gate had been manned by only one officer. The report read:

"An officer acting alone cannot safely and effectively search vehicles while retaining control of the gate. He should either be supported by a second officer who can keep him in view at all times from some secure point, or the gates should be opened by remote control, once the officer has given satisfactory proof that he is not under duress. If a double-gate airlock is to be retained, and there are strong security reasons why it should be, the construction should be modified to enable both gates to be closed when a vehicle has entered the airlock. There is also a need for better communication between the ECR and the gate staff manning the gates, and for an effective method of raising the alarm."

The tower was built very high and it not only overlooked the airlock, but from the top you could see the entire prison complex as well as much of the surrounding countryside. The segment gate and the inner fence gate were automatic and were operated by the officer in the tower. A hydraulic ram on each gate was electronically operated, and they could be opened or closed at the press of a button. An over-ride mechanism ensured that both gates could not be opened at the same time, and one gate had to be firmly closed before the other one could be opened. Bolts and locks on each gate ensured that when it was closed it could be locked and secured in that position.

A similar procedure was in place at the pedestrian gate, to the side of the segment gate, with an airlock walkway and gates that were also operated by the tower officer. Each tower was equipped with a general alarm button and a halogen spotlight on each of it's four sides. The tower officer had a radio transmitter (RT), and the tower was fitted with a landline intercom, through which the officer had direct contact with the ECR. A second officer in the vehicle airlock searched all vehicles entering or leaving the blocks and secured the gates when there was no movement. During the night guard period the search officer was stood down and after 10 pm when the prison was sealed, the segment gates were controlled by the tower officer. From the tower at night the symmetrical lines of lights and 'S' wire seemed to stretch for miles, and as the army towers on the perimeter wall were silhouetted against the night sky, it gave an eerie atmosphere to the place.

H Block 3 had effectively been divided in two, to appease the paramilitary organisations. 'A' and' B' wings were occupied by Republican prisoners and in 'C' and 'D' wings the Loyalists were in control. But I found a major change since my last stint in the blocks. An empty cell in each wing had been made into a hobbies room, and what was the hobbies room had been transformed into a small gymnasium with a fully-equipped multi-gym. Socialist, collective-type, shopping systems had been established in the wings by the prisoners' use of their weekly tuck-shop allowances, firstly by the IRA and then by the loyalists. The prison tuck-shop allowed the prisoners to buy chocolate bars, tobacco and other light refreshments from their own personal cash accounts. But instead of each prisoner buying the articles for himself, one prisoner would spend all his allowance on one product. For example, an inmate would spend all his allowance on tins of Coke, another on tins of Fanta and another on Mars Bars. Tobacco, cigarette papers, crisps and other chocolate bars were bought in the same way. All the supplies were placed in a cell, which basically became a walk-in larder for all the inmates in the wing. Purchasing their tuck-shop items in this fashion did not mean they got any more than they would if they had bought them singally. But the object was, it was a psychological chip against the establishment, an ongoing game of one-upmanship, through which they were trying to create an advantage over their keepers.

A double cell in each wing had been converted into a TV lounge, complete with easy chairs and cushions. On Sundays this cell was used to hold the wing Mass when, to my surprise, no more than five or six prisoners would take part. This was a far cry from the early days in the Maze when every RC inmate attended the Mass. The wing orderlies were detailed by the wing commanding officer (CO) of whatever organisation happened to occupy the wing, either Loyalist or Republican, and not by the prison staff. More and more control of the wings had been given over to the wing CO's. Although officially the prison authorities did not recognise the paramilitary command structure, there is no doubt that the organisations were in charge of the wings in everything but name. However, it has to be said, the orderlies carried out their work as normal, and everyone knew what work had to be done and the wings were kept clean and tidy.

The exercise period was at 9.30 each morning, as it always had been, when the yards were unlocked and the cons engaged in some kind of recreation. Jogging was probably the favourite pastime, with a number of inmates running at a leisurely pace around the exercise yard. Sometimes a football match would be played between two teams from the wing, and at other times the prisoners would occupy their time in a boot-throwing contest, in which they would throw a wellington boot to see who could throw it the furthest.

Since I had last served in the blocks, when the prisoners' half hour visits entitlement was rigorously adhered to, the practice had now been relaxed and it was down to the discretion of the visits PO if each visiting period were to be extended. As a result the visits procedure had developed into an absurd ritual in which the prisoners could remain with their visitors as long as the visiting cubicle was not needed for another visit, and some of the visits continued for two or three hours.

The new liberal prison regime arrived at its ultimate level of absurdity, when a Republican inmate applied to his Block Governor for permission to have a Bodhran drum allowed into the jail. He claimed he wanted to learn to play the instrument as part of his Irish cultural studies. The Governor's inexperience in dealing with such matters manifested itself when he authorised the request without realising he was opening a door that would not easily be closed.

When the Loyalists heard the drum being played, they too applied for instruments to show their cultural identity, and soon the block resounded to the sound of flute music. Their ingenuity and inventive talent showed itself as they made drums out of empty plastic disinfectant containers, and uniforms out of coloured paper that had been glued and pinned together. Ultimately, a full size flute band was formed, complete with a drum major and a bannerette carried on a brush shaft that was painted for the occasion. The exercise yard was used as a parade ground, and sometimes as I watched the spectacle it made me wonder what was going to happen next in the Maze.

Chapter 17

Of all my friends and colleagues killed over the past 40 odd years, the one killing that had the most profound effect on me was the murder of my very good friend and colleague Pat Kerr. I first met Pat on night guard duty in the compounds, shortly after I joined the service in 1975. I served with him all the time I was in the blocks, particularly when I worked in the tally lodge and he was the PO in charge.

Pat was shot dead on the steps of St Patrick's Roman Catholic Cathedral in Armagh, after attending the 10.30 morning Mass on Sunday the 17th February 1985. He was walking down the steps towards his car when two gunmen came up behind him, and fired three shots into his head from a pistol at point-blank range. As their victim fell to the ground, the two gunmen fled on foot, down a grassy slope at the side of the pathway in the direction of Cathedral Road. Later two men were seen speeding away on a high-powered motorbike. Pat's two youngest children, who were with him, screamed with horror as their father lay in a pool of blood, and a doctor who had been in the congregation rushed out to the scene of the shooting, but he said that Pat had died instantly. He was given the last rites by the same priest who had celebrated the Mass only minutes earlier.

Pat was very security conscious, and the fear of crossing the border into the Republic produced a cruel twist of fate that cost him his life. Early on the Sunday morning of his death he had decided not to travel south to attend a family funeral in Castleblaney. However, his wife Maura and their ll-year-old daughter Deirdre did go to the funeral, and Pat, accompanied by his son Gregory, who was 8-years old, and his 5-year-old daughter Kristin went to Mass instead. As all members of the security forces were aware, it was dangerous to cross the border, and Pat was no exception, as he already knew he was a prime target for the IRA after his home was raked with machine gunfire five years before. He was awarded the British Empire Medal about two years earlier, for distinguished service and exemplary conduct.

As the two hysterical children and other worshippers were taken back inside the Cathedral, police were on the scene and soon a team of about twenty detectives set up an incident centre near the Cathedral and started door-to-door inquiries in the surrounding neighbourhood. About 800 people were at the Mass, and there were scenes of pandemonium when the murder happened. It was later stated by the police that their investigations had come up against a wall of silence, for despite the fact that Pat had been gunned down as dozens of worshippers were streaming out of the Cathedral, not a single eye-witness came forward with information. In fact the fear that had been instilled into the shocked community had caused a totally negative response, and as a result the inquiry turned into one of the most difficult the Armagh police ever had to investigate. They could only appeal to anyone who saw the speeding motorbike or knew of its whereabouts to get in touch with them.

As the children's grandmother Mrs Margaret O'Hagan was still in the Cathedral when the shots were fired, the two children had run on ahead of their father towards the car. Gregory, who was dazed by what he had seen, and his hysterical sister were quickly ushered back into the building. Meanwhile Mrs Kerr, along with her daughter, was at Pat's uncle's funeral when the news of the tragedy was broken to them, and they were quickly driven back across the border to their home.

Pat had decided to take two days' leave and look after the young children while his wife and Deirdre travelled south. At the church, because his mother-in-law had only recently been released from hospital after treatment for a heart condition, he had parked the car close to the Cathedral steps. After the murder the Roman Catholic Primate, Cardinal Thomas O'Fiaich, who was in his residence only a short distance away when the shots were fired, ran to the murder scene but Pat was obviously dead. The Cardinal said later, "Can anyone conceive a greater crime than to murder a man in front of his own family as he was coming from worshipping God?"

On Tuesday morning, the 19th February, accompanied by hundreds of my colleagues from the Northern Ireland Prison Service, I walked behind the coffin of my great friend Pat Kerr as the funeral made its way from the family home at Folly Park to St Patrick's Cathedral about a mile away. The mourners were led by Mrs Kerr and the family, as we made our way along the streets of Ireland's ecclesiastical capital, to the Cathedral. The Cathedral, which holds 2,500 people, was packed to capacity and many had to stand outside. A poignant photograph appeared in the press of eleven-year-old Deirdre, looking up into her mother's face as her daddy's coffin was taken out for burial in the adjoining cemetery. Another sad twist of irony to the brutal murder was that Sunday the 17th February 1985 was Pat's 37th birthday.

Police later discovered that the IRA murder gang had stalked their victim for weeks and finally planned their assassination to take place at the Mass, although it was well known that Pat was not a regular churchgoer. Information received by the police indicated the murderers attended the Mass, where they identified Pat, and made their move as the congregation were leaving the Cathedral. In a statement the IRA later admitted responsibility for the murder.

The Emergency Control Room (ECR) staff came in for particular criticism in the Hennessy Report, and it suggested that urgent action should be taken to improve the effectiveness of the radio communications system in the prison. At the time the largest section of the radio traffic was taken up by the transport department, because every driver had to carry a radio transmitter and notify the ECR of all the vehicles' movements. At busy times this resulted in the radio communications network being jamed up with radio traffic and the ECR staff were overwhelmed. As a result it was decided to set up an independent radio communications system for all the vehicles in the jail. This was called 'transport locations', and it basically monitored the movement of every vehicle from the moment the driver came onto the network in the morning until he left it at night.

The mode of operation-for example-was that when a van picked up a prisoner at a block, the driver radioed transport locations and informed them the name of the inmate and his destination. The officer in the locations would then move a magnetic tag, bearing the call sign of the van and the name of the prisoner, on a metallic board from the block to the destination. The metallic board was effectively a large map of the Maze prison. The procedure was very effective, particularly in monitoring the movement of the meals-truck. Each time the lorry was leaving the kitchen, the driver was given a fixed route, and as he was entering or leaving a block he radioed his location, therefore any deviation from the route would have been noticed immediately.

At the time there were altogether 36 prison vehicles in or connected to the Maze. These included eight minibuses that were used to convey the prisoners from their blocks to the visits complex. Another five minibuses were used to convey visitors from the visitors' reception car park to the visits complex. A fully equipped ambulance was used to bring ill or injured inmates from the block to the prison hospital, and an outside hospital van was used to collect drugs and supplies from the stores at the Royal Victoria Hospital. A bin lorry was used to collect the rubbish bins from the blocks. About 16 or 20 bins were collected twice a week from each Block, and the hydraulic mechanism pressed the contents to the front of the truck. The same lorry collected the rubbish in Maghaberry prison, and each day when the lorry was full, it was brought to the Maze and the rubbish was tipped into a large skip and then taken to be dumped.

This process was adopted after the escape of a prisoner from the compounds in the early 1970's. He was Brendan (Darkie) Hughes and he had escaped after being thrown into the open backed garbage lorry, and driven out of the jail. At the time the only type of security device for searching the bin wagon at the prison main gate was an officer prodding the rubbish with a pointed broom handle, a procedure that could hardly be described as the ultimate in efficiency for the largest most modern prison in Western Europe. Hughes hid himself in the rubbish and later made his getaway when the contents of the lorry were emptied into a landfill site, some miles from the jail. He was taken across the border and given a completely new identity. He came back to Northern Ireland, and about six months later, after masquerading as a cuddly toy salesman, he was arrested in the upper middle class Malone Road area of Belfast. When the house was searched, a large amount of bomb-making equipment was found, including detonators, fuse wire and explosives, along with street maps of Belfast and plans for bomb attacks.

The transport pool also had three, large buses that had been bought from the London Transport, and were used to convey prisoners to and from the workshops, when the workshops were in operation. A van was assigned to the central stores to carry supplies to the blocks twice per week, and the education

189

department had a van for conveying teachers and equipment throughout the jail. A minibus was allocated to the prison chaplain's office to convey the prison chaplains and all visiting clergymen to the blocks. This vehicle was nicknamed the 'Pope mobile', because on certain religious days it was packed full of priests. A van and a tractor and trailer were allocated to the landscape gardeners, who cut the lawns and attended the flowers and shrubs that grew along the sides of the blocks and throughout the admin area. The rest of the vehicles in the prison were attached to the trades department, the tuck shop, the laundry and, of course, the kitchen. The' Instant Reaction Force' had a large truck with a grille attached to the front, to be used to smash through gates etc. if a situation so required. This wagon was nicknamed the 'WarHorse', because it was used to convey the riot squad to the scene of an emergency.

As I started to get into the wing routine once again, I was amazed to see the changes that had taken place since I had worked in the wings previously. Whilst the prison staff had some control over the prisoners, the place was run like a five star hotel. Complete with lunch menu for the midday meal, and in the event of a complaint about food, the Principal Officer in charge of the kitchen had to meet the prisoners and take note of their complaints.

The place had become so lax that the cons were indifferent to both the staff and the establishment. This was brought home to me one evening when I was on association duty in the wing. All the prisoners were in the dining hall watching TV, and it was approaching lock-up. I walked to the dining hall grille and shouted, "Right, lock-up!" They all just looked round at me and, in what was obviously a rehearsed lack of concern, I got a rendering of 'Okie from Muskogee', which went:

"We don't smoke marijuana in Muskogee, We don't take our trips on LSD, We don't burn no draft cards down on main-street, We like livin' and being free" Suddenly, and as abruptly as it had disappeared, sanity returned after they had sung the first stanza, and they started to move to their cells.

The Block Senior Officer was a Welshman by the name of Ford. A likeable character, he had an officer's gift of leadership and a logical and ordered mind, which made him a first class boss. When he spoke, he had a soft voice with a lilt of the Welsh valleys in it. He was on the move all the time and did not sit in his office but rather, just strolled around the circle supervising all movement. Sometimes I would banter him about the Irish Regiments and the various battles they were engaged in but he would always make the witty reply, "What about the South Wales Borderers and the 11 VC's before breakfast?" This was the battle at Rourke's Drift, Natal, in 1879, against the Zulus when 11 soldiers of the South Wales Borderers won the Victoria Cross.

But it was during the evening association period in the wings that the main activity took place. One evening I was on duty at the dining hall grille and the place was a hive of activity with a card game in progress at the first table. A well-built con in his forties suddenly lifted his head and squinted my-optically over his glasses at me before his attention was taken up with his hand of cards again. He was almost bald, his fat face was unshaven and the bristles grizzled and grey.

As I looked at his jeans and T-shirt, which were particularly ill-fitting and uncared for, I could see the Maze was still no fashion parade, even though they were allowed to wear their own clothes. Out of the corner of his mouth protruded a short, cigarette dog-end that seemed to have gone out hours before, as the tobacco stained paper was too wet to be lit. He glanced at me suddenly, his face splitting into a grin revealing a set of badly damaged teeth that were the same colour as the dog-end, except for a few strands of yellowish saliva that joined the two rows together. He puffed enthusiastically on the dog-end and, to my surprise, its end ignited into a gush of flame and clouds of smoke poured from his mouth. He threw back his head and roared with a raucous laugh, "Hi, Killer, is my lolly-pop sticks up from the car park yet?" The volume would have been more akin to a match at Wembley in support of the national team. I assumed he was a little bit deaf. He was as refined as a bucket of coal. I moved my head slightly from side to side, indicating his lolly-pop sticks had not arrived, and that I wanted no conversation with him.

Some of the prisoners, especially married men, seemed to be tired of the whole thing and only wanted to serve their time and get home again to their families. However, there was a core of fanatics who were dedicated to the cause, and who saw any acceptance of the prison regime as a sign of weakness or surrender to authority. One such prisoner who had served 16 years, and was entitled to parole and home leave, refused his entitlement by saying; "When the 'Brits' release me for good, I will go! But I am not leaving this place to come back again." I often wondered how he felt when he was finally released, and discovered that life had gone on without him, and all his mates and friends were now married with families.

A game was in progress between two cons at the snooker table, one of whom was giving a running commentary on the perfonnance to his mate. He moved with quick, bird-like motions, as if he were perpetually in a hurry or on the verge of dealing with some urgent business. As I watched the game, I noticed that one of the cold taps in the ablutions was running, so I went over and turned it off. As soon as he heard the water had stopped running, the one who was doing all the talking spun round and scurried towards me, like a spider across its web. He said, "Hi, mister, would you turn that water back on? I want it to be nice and cold before I put it in my water-gallon at lock-up." As I looked at him, I could see his face was pinched with tension, and stress was written all over him. So I decided to take the easy way out and do what he asked. I walked over and turned the tap on again, and as I stepped back to the grille he said, "Thanks, mister," and returned to the snooker table.

Early in 1985 a notice appeared on the announcements board in the admin building, inviting applications for the position of Weapons Training Officer - Armourer at the Maze. I applied on a half sheet for the post, and within a few days I got a letter inviting me to a selection board in Dundonald House.

The interview was set for 12.20 pm on Friday the 16th August, the venue was Room 305 and I was instructed to produce my warrant card at the front door, where I would be directed to the interview room. The day arrived and I made my way to Dundonald House, took the lift to the third floor and walked along the long corridor. A secretary sat at a desk outside one of the offices. I gave her the interview letter and she asked me to take a seat as she lifted the phone, and in a moment directed me into the office.

I knocked the door and. a voice called, "Come in!" I opened it and walked into the small, spartan room. Three figures sat behind a desk that seemed to take up the entire width of the room, and partially blocked the little light that was getting in through the single window. I instantly recognised two of them; one was the chief officer from the Maze and the other was the security governor, also from the Maze. Like the chief officer beside him, the security governor was not a popular figure in the prison-a dour, uninspiring man with a distant and offputting authoritarian manner. Born and brought up in the Republic of Ireland, he talked through the side of his mouth, which caused him to acquire the nickname'Mick-the-lip'. I have to confess I never liked him but, then, few did. He would try to adopt a Cambridge accent, but his southern Irish brogue would break through from time to time, which showed he was making an even bigger fool of himself than nature had already achieved. Every time I heard him speak I thought of the old adage: 'You can take Paddy out of the bog, but you can't take the bog out of Paddy'.

The third interviewer was from the Prisons Department, a person I had never seen before, who had been slotted into the top of the service without ever making contact with the ordinary officer on the ground. The customary chair was strategically placed in the centre of the room, so that its occupant would feel isolated and insecure, and as I sat down I felt like a felon in the dock. They each in turn asked me a number of questions about my career in the service, and my knowledge of ordnance supplies, which I answered as best I could. I couldn't help but think, how grotesquely out of step with reality the three of them were as they sat there, in that small office, asking me questions about a subject they knew very little about. The interview ended and I left the building knowing I had no chance of being successful because, experience had taught me, before most of these positions were advertised, they were already filled by the nudge and whisper-brigade.

Since I became a Christian in 1979, there is one 'Gospel meeting' in our church I particularly enjoy. It is the watch-night service that is held on the last night of each year and continues for a few minutes into the New Year. It is always a poignant service for me, and creates a moving, spiritual atmosphere in the building.

I attended the watch-night service on Tuesday the 31 st December 1985 and on my way home from the meeting I heard the news that a bomb had exploded in Armagh, killing two policemen and seriously injuring a third constable. It was not until the following morning that I learned one of the dead constables was someone whom I had not seen for many years, and had I met him in the street I probably would not have known him. He was Drew McCandless, whom I had known as a boy when we attended the Union Street Gospel Hall together. I felt sad when I recalled those happy days, so long ago, but sadly I had lost contact with Drew and many other childhood friends since that time.

Drew was 38 years of age and had joined the police in 1982. He was stationed in Armagh, which was convenient for him as he lived with his wife and two children in Portadown only a few miles away. The three constables left Armagh Police Station on Tuesday night to patrol around the centre of the town, checking shops and lock-up premises. It was only seconds into the New Year, when they were walking along Thomas Street, when the 5lb bomb exploded. The device had been concealed in a litter-bin which was attached to a traffic sign, and as revellers in the pubs throughout the town were singing' Auld Lang Syne', it exploded. Drew and his colleague, 24-year-old Reserve Constable Michael Jonathan Williamson, who were closest to the bomb, died instantly. Constable Williamson had only joined the police a year before. Immediately after the blast, police sealed off the area, and the third constable, who received senous leg wounds, was rushed to Craigavon Area Hospital about 10 miles away.

In order to create maximum confusion after the bomb blast, the gunmen opened fire down the street with machine-guns. As the gunfire rang out, frightened revellers in two nearby public houses dived for cover, each crowd believing it was under attack by the rival factions. In Anderson's public house in Linenhall Street a piper had just stopped playing-in the New Year, when the explosion went off and the shooting started. The scene was the same in McKeown's at the bottom of Thomas Street, close to where the bomb was placed.

Police investigating the murders discovered the bomb had been detonated by remote control, with the firing point in a house across the street, where a couple and their three children were held hostage for several hours by the murder gang.

Drew took a keen interest in charity work and work with young people.

He played football and stood-in as referee from time to time. In fact, as Mid Ulster League referee he was due to officiate at a match on the very day he was murdered. The IRA, in claiming responsibility for the attack, said, "It was intended to show that our campaign in 1986 would be carried out with increasing effectiveness"! Drew was survived by his wife and son Andrew, who was aged 12 years, and his daughter Kathryn, aged 14.

By early 1986 I was on the move once again and I found myself detailed the admin gate. This was another area of the prison that came under serious criticism by the Hennessy inquiry, because at the time of the escape, there was only a single gate dividing the administration area from the main gate complex. However, since the publication of the report and its recommendations that major improvements should take place to secure the admin area, a double gate vehicle airlock had been constructed. In order to allow room in the airlock for the large buses and lorries, the distance between the two gates was about 30 yards, by about 10 yards wide, and a 25 foot high fence ran round the vehicle lock, which was attached to posts about four yards apart. An electric light was attached to the top of every second post, and a large halogen light on the four corner posts shone into the vehicle lock.

Beside each of the two vehicle gates there was a pedestrian gate, and all four gates were manually operated by an officer inside the airlock. As each pedestrian was admitted into the lock, the officer locked the gate and then walked the 30 yards to the second pedestrian gate to let him out. Given the numbers of staff who were in the Maze at the time, the gate officer was almost continuously on the move.

On Tuesday the 11 th February I was assigned my first duty at the admin gate, which, as I soon discovered, was the busiest post in the jail. I was 8.00 o'clock start, and from the moment I relieved the night guard officer, the place was like Piccadilly Circus. All the vehicles entering the prison, as well as all the staff, had to come through the admin gate. As a result no sooner had I let a van through, than a queue of staff appeared at the pedestrian gate, and when they were admitted, there was a queue of vehicles waiting. A small, wooden sentrybox that was fitted with a gas heater sat in the corner of the airlock, but even in inclement weather it was impossible to use the box. A second officer manned the inner fence gate and controlled movement into the reception area. It was also his duty to search all vehicles leaving the prison, and when each one was checked, he called to me and I opened the gate and allowed the vehicle into the airlock. Each morning and afternoon a third officer was detailed from the nearby visits complex to act as a relief officer to the gate staff.

On the 14th March I was told there was a letter for me and some of the other officers who were involved in the escape. It was in the personnel office, so I reported to the office in the admin building. I was handed a sealed envelope and asked to sign a receipt for the letter. I thought this was somewhat unusual, and when I signed the receipt, I was handed the envelope. I opened it and was amazed to see it was an official document headed: Northern Ireland Office, Dundonald House, Upper Newtownards Road, Belfast. The letter was dated the 13th March 1986, and read:

Commendation

'I am very pleased to inform you that in recognition of your bravery at the time of the escape from HM Prison Maze (cellular) on the 25th September 1983, it has been decided that you should be officially commended by the Minister Mr Nicholas Scott MP. It is intended that a Certificate commending your actions will be presented at a special ceremony. The arrangements for this event have not yet been finalised; however, as soon as the details are known, I will write to you again. In the meantime please accept my personal congratulations on the award you are to receive.'

The document was signed by someone called Thompson, whom I had never heard of before. But I have to say I was delighted that they were finally going to recognise what we had done, and I couldn't wait to get home to tell Delta I was going to get a commendation for bravery.

Two weeks later 1 received another official document from the personnel office. I opened it and it read:

Maze Escape 1983-Staff Commendations.

I am very pleased to invite you to Stormont Castle on Friday the

4th April 1986 at 12 noon when the Minister Mr Nicholas Scott MP, will be presenting Commendation Certificates to some members of the Northern Ireland Prison Service. You are also invited for drinks and a buffet lunch after the ceremony.

As a recipient of a Commendation Certificate you may, if you wish, be accompanied by not more than two guests for this special occasion. Please let me know as quickly as possible if you will be attending and also the names of your guests if appropriate. If you require to park your car at Stormont Castle please also let me have the registration number. It will be helpful if you could arrive at Stormont Castle approximately 20-30 minutes before the ceremony is due to commence.

This time the document was signed by someone called Watson, whom I also had never heard of. However, a few days later on Friday the 4th, Delta, Joanne and I headed off to Stormont for the commendation ceremony. By coincidence we had been invited to a wedding in Bangor that same day. It was the wedding of Delta's second cousin, and it was to take place in Bangor Abbey in the afternoon.

The ceremony was held in the original Stonnont Castle, a few hundred yards from the Northern Ireland Government Buildings, and as I parked the car we were directed to the venue by the police who were on duty. At the entrance to the building we were met by the man who was currently the Number One Governor at the Maze, who showed us into a large reception room where we met some of the other officers and their families. There were eleven of us altogether and we were dressed in uniform for the occasion. At one end of the room there was a table where waitresses served tea, coffee and biscuits while we waited, and it was here, to my surprise and with some disdain, I saw the Number One Chief Officer. What he was doing at a bravery commendation ceremony I will never know. Obviously, the past had been exorcised and he was in full control once again. Perhaps it was, after all, just a three-card trick.

We were ushered into the main hall, which had been set out with rows of chairs for the guests. As we filed in, the officers who were to receive the commendations were shown to their seats at the top end of the hall beside a lectern. After a few minutes Mr Scott and some officials from the Prisons Department filed into the hall and sat opposite us, as one of them walked to the lectern to welcome everyone to Stormont. He said how pleased he was to be taking part in the ceremony, and after a few more pleasantries he introduced the Prisons Minister. Mr Scott stepped forward to the lectern, and after welcoming everyone he said how delighted he was to officiate at the occasion. He went on to tell the gathering how he was at his London home, watching television on the afternoon of Sunday the 25th September 1983, when his step-son burst into the room shouting, "Nick! Nick! Some prisoners have broken out of the Maze!" He immediately lifted the phone and rang the NIO, and was briefed on the situation, and he remained in direct contact with the Prisons Department throughout the rest of the night.

When it was time for the Commendations to be handed out, one of the officials stood up, called out the name of each officer from the Certificate, which was set in a gold-rimmed frame, and then handed it to the Minister. As the officer stepped forward, Mr Scott shook hands with him, handed him the Bravery Commendation, and congratulated him for the courage he had shown during the escape. As he ended the ceremony, the Minister invited everyone outside to a large patio area that had been set out with tables and chairs, where a scrumptious buffet was prepared. From the Castle grounds we had a good view across a large part of east Belfast, and could see the imposing shipyard cranes as they rose towering to meet the blue skyline. We had our photographs taken with the Minister, and the early spring sunshine made it a beautiful day.

We were the first to leave Stormont, as we had to drive to Bangor to attend Ruth's wedding, and as we left the Castle grounds, we were all in agreement that it had been a most enjoyable day. As we arrived at Bangor Abbey, the wedding ceremony had ended and the photographers were busy at their work. We took some photographs and met the other guests, and when everyone was ready, we headed off to the reception, which was held in a hotel at Groomsport. The wedding reception and the splendid seaside setting of the hotel brought to an end a truly memorable day.

To ensure that the admin gate was manned 24 hours a day, seven days a week, there was a squad of seven officers who were assigned to the various duties throughout the week-night guard, evening duty, long day, straight day and to cover the association period. 1 knew the other six officers and had worked with them at different times before, as we all had a few years' service and were experienced in the job.

As the front of the education building was only about 20 yards from the admin gate, we had our tea breaks in the small kitchen just inside the front door of the building. Here I got to know some of the teachers and the education officer, who had recently retired from the army. That same year I sat the promotion examination again, but the Senior Officer's rank had once again eluded me. When the exam results were posted on the notice board, it only stated the names of those who had passed. The members of staff who had failed were not mentioned. So when I examined the list and couldn't see my name, I realised I was unsuccessful again. I have to say it was a matter of great disappointment to me, particularly after all the studying and preparation that I had put in before the exam. I wanted the job, and in truth I felt I had earned it.

I had done my best to prevent the escape and to recapture the prisoners and could quite easily have lost my life in the effort. So when I was turned down for promotion, it was a bitter blow. I thought that at least I had earned a degree of respect and trust.

One day I was having a cup of tea in the education block when the education officer came into the kitchen, and we began to chat about the education facilities that were now available to the inmates. As I told him I had failed the promotion exam, he suggested that I should start an '0' Level course in English Language. He explained the curriculum and how it would be organised through the education department in the Maze. Similar to a correspondence course, one of the teachers would be my tutor and mark each assignment and give me relevant advice about the course. I was 47 years of age at the time and I thought I was rather 'long in the tooth' to be starting back to school, but on reflection I decided to give it a go, and over the following year I became engrossed in the course studies. The actual lessons took the form of a number of written essays, which the teacher would set by giving me a subject to describe or write about. Then my work was marked and the process was repeated. And so the study course continued until the end of the year, when I had to sit a final examination.

One day I was speaking to a colleague about the course and I was surprised when he told me the Prisons Department would assist in paying the exam fees, and I would be allowed time off duty to sit the exam. So I applied through the Personnel Governor for funding, and a few days later 1 received the relevant forms from the Prison College at Millisle. As I filled the forms in and sent them off: I didn't realise it at the time, but it was the start of a long and quite successful period of study in further education.

On the day of the '0' Level exam, a small room was made available in the education block. As I walked in and sat down at a desk, one of the teachers, whom I did not know, was the adjudicator and she set the exam papers in front of me and said, looking at the clock on the wall, "The time starts now!" I immediately turned the paper face-up and started to read the question! Throughout the $2^1/_2$ hours the exam lasted, the teacher sat at another desk and marked some papers. A couple of minutes before the end of the set time, I stood up, shuffled the papers together and handed them to her. The exam was over, and as I left the building to resume my duty on the admin gate, I was content that I had answered all the questions, but I wasn't sure if what 1 had written would be enough to achieve success. However, I went back to my work and put the whole thing out of my mind. Moreover, of all my educational accomplishments over the following years, I would always remember, with a little bit of pride, that first '0' Level in English Language.

One morning several weeks later, I was on duty on the admin gate. It was about 10.00 o'clock and the morning's mail had been delivered to the prison a short time before. My attention was drawn by the education officer who was calling my name, as he walked from his office. He had a document in his hand

and he called out, "Billy, you got that exam". I didn't quite understand what he was talking about, and I asked, "What did you say, George?" His reply took me totally by surprise as he held the slip of paper up so that I could read it, and said, "You passed that '0' Level exam!" The document was headed by the name of the Belfast College that marked the exam paper, and the grade and pass mark were alongside my name and examination number. I was delighted with my success and thanked him for his help and advice.

In the days that followed, every time I went into the education block, the teacher would suggest that I should start another course. One day 1 was in the main office and a sociology course book was on the desk. As I lifted it and started to leaf through the pages, I was struck by its explanations of the development, functioning and classification, of human societies. I decided to do a General Certificate of Secondary Education (GCSE) on the subject. After the 12 months course I was successful and passed the final exam. This was followed by a Royal Society of Arts (RSA) in English Language and Maths. I also completed a course in physiology. I was now strongly advised by my friends in the education department to go for a Degree, and at the beginning of the academic year 1992/1993 I applied to the Prisons Department for funding for a Degree course. When it was granted, I started the course, which was through the Open University.

It was a six-year course and the first year's study was at foundation level, but then each year got more difficult as the curriculum progressed. Tutorials were held in Queen's University Belfast for guidance in the academic study of the curriculum. The tutorials were held one evening per week and the tutor was an Open University lecturer. One night I was driving down to Belfast to the class when I was stopped by the UDR. A Greenfinch asked me where I was going and I told her I was on my way to Queen's University, at which she replied, "Are you a lecturer in Queen's?" "No", I replied, "Not quite. I'm an Open University student." She obviously thought I was rather old to be a student. The course required me to attend Summer School classes at Stirling University in Scotland, and at Sussex University on the south coast of England. But I have to say it was all worthwhile, because I achieved a Diploma in Applied Social Science, and at the end of all the studying I had a Bachelor of Science (Honours) Degree. Ironically, I achieved the Degree in my last year in the Prison Service; and on the day of the conferment ceremony, which was held at the Waterfront Hall in Belfast on the 12th June 1999, 1 had been retired from the service for three months.

Chapter 18

The scene at the Lurgan War Memorial on Remembrance Day is the same as in any city, town or village in the rest of the United Kingdom, when the nation meets to remember the dead of the World Wars and other conflicts. I parked my car and made my way to the town centre to watch the parade of police, UDR, regular army and other organisations. After the two minutes silence was observed, wreaths were laid at the Cenotaph. As the ceremony ended, I made my way back to the car and went to the normal Sunday morning service in our church.

Sunday the 8th November 1987 was my 48th birthday and as the church service ended and I drove home on that beautiful, crisp November day, I was not aware of the shattering events that had taken place in the west of the Province earlier on that Remembrance morning. When I walked into the house, I was taken aback to see Delta, who had been preparing the Sunday lunch, crying and in a very distressed state. When I asked her what was wrong, she said, "A bomb has exploded at the War Memorial in Enniskillen and a lot of people have been killed." A shiver ran down my back as I thought of the horror of such a thing happening. As we listened to the news and the death toll started to mount, anger gave way to sadness as we began to realise the full extent of what had happened. Eleven people were killed and 63 injured when the IRA bomb ripped through the former St Michael's Primary School and demolished the gable wall of the two-storey building. Rubble and masonry were hurled over the footpath and across the road, burying many of those who had been waiting for the Remembrance Parade to arrive. It was what became known as the 'Poppy Day Massacre'.

The Enniskillen Cenotaph stands on a traffic island at a road junction, at East Bridge and Belmore Street, an isolated area of the town. On previous years a crowd of people would gather at the nearby end wall of the school, which provided shelter on stormy days and was a good viewpoint to watch the wreathlaying ceremony. As the Queen was about to lay a wreath on behalf of the nation at the Cenotaph in Whitehall, crowds had gathered in the most westerly county town of the United Kingdom to pay the same homage to Enniskillen's fallen of two World Wars. Suddenly the bomb exploded, sending clouds of dust and smoke into the air over the ruins of the former school. Panic gripped the area, as people ran screaming in all directions, with blood pouring from head and leg wounds. As men, women and children were staggering around in the street, shocked and dazed, they were soon being helped. Members of the Ulster Defence Regiment who had been assembling at the front of the Fermanagh College of Further Education, ready to parade with their band, dashed to help in the rescue operation.

Soon the UDR men and members of the RUC were working alongside firemen and ambulance crews, trying to clear the rubble to get to those who were buried underneath. The air was filled with cries and shouts of pain as seriously injured people were lifted out of the debris. As more firemen and ambulances arrived at the scene, rescue workers tore at the masonry with their bare hands. Parents were looking for children and children were looking for parents, as young UDR women in their uniforms knelt with the injured and dying, and helped to lift them into police cars and ambulances. As more police arrived, they eventually started to move spectators away from the scene of the worst sectarian carnage that had ever been witnessed in County Fermanagh.

The following morning police headquarters issued an official list of all those who had died in the atrocity, and as I read through the obituaries, I was deeply saddened to see the name of a man I had known many years before. He was Samuel Gault, now a retired RUC Sergeant. I had known him when I was mobilized off the Specials in the early 1960's. I was stationed in Bessbrook and he was in Forkhill. A cruel irony to the death of Samuel Gault was that, exactly 25 years to the day, he had been shot and wounded by the IRA in the ambush at Jonesborough in South Armagh. Constable William John Hunter died in the ambush and another two of my colleagues from Bessbrook were wounded. Though Samuel survived that ambush a quarter of a century earlier, he became a victim of the Provisional IRA as he stood near the cenotaph at Belmore Street in Enniskillen on that fateful Sunday morning. When he left school, Samuel joined the police in 1958, serving in South Armagh and Belfast before moving to Fermanagh, where he spent the remainder of his service. His work at various stations in the County included instructing young constables in the Police Depot in Enniskillen. For 18 of his years on the police he served as a Sergeant.

The youngest victim of the 'Poppy Day Massacre' was a 20-year-old student nurse, Marie Wilson, who died in hospital holding her mother's hand. The death of Marie Wilson brought a tear to the nation. Her mother, Mrs Jean Wilson, wept as she described the scenes in the Erne Hospital, as a surgeon told her he could do no more for Marie. "She was still just barely alive, so I took her hand and said goodbye," said her grief-stricken mother. Marie's 60-year-old father, Gordon, who was also caught in the bomb, told how he held Marie's hand as they both lay buried under several inches of rubble. Mr Wilson said, "The rescuers were trying to get through to us and Marie kept telling me she was all right. Then she said, 'Daddy, I love you very much', and those were her last words." Gordon Wilson was discharged from hospital on Sunday evening, after being treated for a dislocated shoulder and cuts and bruises.

Two weeks after the atrocity, Sunday the 22nd November was a bitterly cold and showery morning, and as Britain and the world shared in the sorrow of Enniskillen, the local branch of the Royal British Legion finally held its annual Remembrance ceremony. But it was no ordinary Remembrance ceremony. The Prime Minister, Mrs Thatcher, and Mr Tom King, the Secretary of State, along with thousands of people from all over the United Kingdom, gathered at the Cenotaph, not only to remember the dead of two World Wars, but to remember the 11 people who had been murdered by the IRA only two weeks earlier. About 180 Royal British Legion Standard Bearers marched behind

Ballyreagh Silver Band, while the pipes and drums of the 4th (Fermanagh) Battalion UDR lead the military part of the parade. About 2,000 ex-servicemen and women, police officers, members of the UDR and members of various services, including the British Red Cross, St John's Ambulance Brigade, youth organisations and school pupils, also attended the memorial service.

The final chapter of the Poppy Day Massacre at Enniskillen ended for one family on the 28th December 2000, when the death took place of Mr Ronnie Hill, who had been seriously injured in the explosion. Mr Hill fell into a deep coma two days after the IRA bomb blasted the gable wall of St Michael's School on top of him, on the 8th November 1987. The former Principal of Enniskillen High School never regained consciousness. He was cared-for by his wife Noreen. Who showed her undying love for her husband over the thirteen years since the 'Poppy Day Massacre'.

In the autum of 1987 Joanne saw an advert in the 'Truth for Youth', a young people's magazine of the Free Presbyterian Church. The advertisement was for a tour of the Holy Land in March of the following year, which would be a special visit to the land of Israel on the 40th Anniversary of the Foundation of the State. We talked it over and Delta decided that she wouldn't go; however, I decided to find out more about it. I rang the tour leader, the Reverend Trevor Baxter, who was the minister of the Dungannon church at the time, and asked him to put Joanne and myself down for the tour.

A couple of weeks later we received an invitation to attend a meeting for everyone who was going on the trip, arranged for 8.00 pm on Monday the 11th January 1988. I was glad of the opportunity to meet all the other people who were going on the 14-day holiday, and the second tour leader, the Reverend Reggie Cranston, explained that we would be flying out on the 4.30 pm shuttle from Aldergrove to Heathrow on Saturday the 5th March. We would then board the Israeli plane for an overnight flight to Ben-Gurion International Airport in Tel Aviv.

The day for departure soon arrived and there was great excitement as we all met at Aldergrove for the first leg of our journey to London. We managed to get some sleep on the six-hour flight to Israel, which took us across France, Spain and then the Mediterranean Sea till we touched down in the land of Israel. By now daylight had broken and the rays of the early morning sunshine welcomed us to one of the most unforgetable experiences of our lives, when the cabin doors opened and the Middle Eastern heat blew gently into our faces. We claimed our luggage, boarded a coach and were soon on our way to our hotel in Jerusalem. After breakfast we had a short walking tour to the Garden Tomb, where we had a communion service. The Tomb, situated north of the old walled city of Jerusalem, is believed to be the place of crucifixion and resurrection of Jesus Christ. A rocky, limestone hill with contours that resembled a human skull, locally known as the 'place of the skull', was described as the true Calvary. The presence of the nearby rock-hewn tomb from the first century gave Scriptural significance to the site. But its simplicity and beauty gave a peaceful atmosphere to the Garden Tomb and made it a pleasant and poignant place for prayer and meditation.

In the following days we visited Bethlehem, the Mount of Olives, the Garden of Gethsemane, the pool of Bethesda and we walked along the Via Dolorosa and visited many other Biblical sites in the city. On the sixth day of the pilgrimage our air-conditioned coach took us to Bethany, where we visited the Tomb of Lazarus, then on through the Judean Wilderness to Jerico and Qumran, where the Dead Sea Scrolls were found in 1947. The manuscripts, some dating back to 100 BC, illustrated early Biblical history and are now exhibited in the Museum of the 'Shrine of the Book' in Jerusalem. We also spent some time swimming, or rather floating, in the Dead Sea.

We then visited the Rock Fortress of Massada about $2^1/_2$ miles from the shore of the Dead Sea. Cut out of a mountain range by deep gorges which surround its base, the mountain-top stronghold was constructed in the middle of the second century BC by Herod the Great, and used as a residence in case he was removed from his kingdom by Mark Anthony. After a breathtaking ascent to the top by cable car, we enjoyed the panoramic view of the Dead Sea and the Jordan Valley.

The following day we left Jerusalem and proceeded along the Jordan Valley to Mount Carmel, renowned as being the scene of the contest between monotheism and paganism, as the prophet Elijah challenged the prophets of Baal. Caesarea, the capital of Roman Judea, was our next stop, then on to the plain of Meggido, or (Armageddon), site of the last battle. Meggido strategically joins Egypt and the countries to the south with Syria and the northern nations and the area stretching to the coast of the Mediterranean. In the 10th century BC, Solomon rebuilt and fortified the city, which became one of his cities of chariots and a bulwark for the defence of his kingdom.

We spent the remainder of our Holy Land tour in Tiberias, on the Sea of Galilee, where we visited Capernaum, the City of Christ. We sailed across the sea to a kibbutz on the slopes of the Golan Heights, on the opposite side of the Galilee. For me, the highlight of the pilgrimage came when we visited the kibbutz of Yardenit on the River Jordan, where a baptismal service was held. It was Tuesday afternoon, the 15th March, and with some other members of the group I was baptised at the same place where Christ was baptised. The Reverend Baxter officiated at the ceremony, assisted by the Reverend Cranston and the Reverend Derek Ervin. On the final day of our tour of Israel we left Tiberias and drove across the lower slopes of Mount Hermon, the highest peak in Israel, believed to be the site of the Transfiguration of our Lord.

Our next stop was Caesaria Philippi. Built by Herod's son Philip as the capital of his territory, he named it Caesaria in honour of the Emperor. But in order to distinguish it from the other Caesaria, it was called Caesaria Philippi. Our journey took us back to the Mediterranean coastline, where we visited Acre, Haifa and Jeffa before arriving at Tel Aviv, where we got our flight back to the UK. As the plane circled over Ben-Gurion Airport and took its course across the

Mediterranean, I began to reminisce on my holiday to Israel. As I reflected on my experiences of the 14-day tour of the Land of the Bible and the places I had seen, I couldn't help but think of my father and mother, who had been Christians since early in life. How throughout the years they had read the Scriptures and studied God's Word about the places I had seen, and I had walked on the very ground the Lord had walked on. But because of their humble background, the very thought of ever visiting the Land of Israel, I am sure, never crossed their minds. As I thought of them, I was sure, that if through some extraordinary circumstance someone had offered the fare for one of them to go and visit the Land of the Bible, the answer would have been. "No, I'll not go but let one of the boys go in my stead." It was these thoughts and reflections that made my trip to Israel so poignant a pilgrimage.

When I returned to duty in the Maze, I realised how important it was for me to have had a holiday in the first place, because day seemed to follow day in an endless repetition in which the days of the week appeared to run together in one uninterrupted succession of regular procedure. When I thought of the prisoners, whom in truth, I hadn't much sympathy for, and when I reflected on my experiences in Israel and the places I had seen, I felt for them, because in the two weeks I had been away they had seen no further than their cells, wings, blocks and their two, half-hour visits in the fortnight.

I soon got back into the day-to-day routine at the admin gate, where the banter among the staff helped to break the monotony. One member of the gate guard squad was a stout, low-set man with a fat face and a temper as short as his stature. He was easily wound up and was well known for his short fuse, as he would suddenly burst into a fit of violent rage over something so insignificant that a normal person wouldn't have taken it under his notice. His nickname was Grizzly, which said a lot about his bearing and mentality. One day we were on duty together, 1 on the admin gate and he on the inner fence gate. Each time I unlocked the inner fence gate to let a vehicle through, Grizzly opened it out by keeping control of the gate and then closed it again. Earlier that morning we had a slight difference of opinion about a change of duty a few days before, but by now Grizzly was getting wound up as if the self-destructive impulse that always ran deep in him had suddenly taken over. He started waving his arms in the air, his face went red with rage, his eyes bulged wide open and the sinews on his neck stood out like ropes. He was shouting obscenities and calling me names. If anyone had ever suspected Grizzly of having half a brain, his performance as he rose to total loss of control would have convinced them he hadn't even that.

I walked up to him, and as he was still blasting away, I quickly switched my weight from one foot to the other and, pivoting on my hip, I whipped my right fist round in a tight arch of a right hook. The blow struck him fairly on the edge of the chin, and as he staggered back, he collapsed to the ground. He lay still for a moment and then gave a slight groan. A couple of officers who saw the escapade stood shocked at the spectacle of Grizzly lying on his back in the vehicle airlock. As he started to move, one of the officers went over and helped him onto his feet again. He was a bit dizzy for a few moments, but he soon came to his senses and went quietly back to his post. The news of the incident quickly spread around the staff grapevine, and the banter and wisecracks soon followed. At lunchtime I was relieved by the evening duty officer, and as I was going out through the tally lodge, the staff behind the counter started to cheer. One of them shouted, "Hi, Killer, carry him around for a few rounds, the crowd's complaining about not gettin' their money's worth!" As I went out through the main gate, making my way towards the officers' mess, someone shouted, "Hi, Killer, pick on somebody your own size!" Just then, another officer shouted, "Hi, Killer, the bigger they are, the harder they fall!" And so the waggery continued. Weeks later they were still at it. One morning I was walking past the admin block and somebody in the duty office shouted out through the window, "Killer, golden gloves! Golden gloves!" The whole episode became a jail joke, as everybody joined in to have a good laugh at poor old Grizzly.

Since the phasing out of special category status on the 1 st March 1976, the prisoner population in the compounds gradually decreased as more and more inmates were released after serving their sentences. As a result, in 1988, there were less than 100 prisoners from all the factions in the compounds, and the decision was taken that the Compound Maze would be closed. All the remaining prisoners were transferred to H Block 1 and H Block 2, and the compound staff were dispersed throughout the other prisons in Northern Ireland. The link gates that divided the compounds from the blocks were finally closed for good. The entire Compound Maze, with its 22 compounds, three football pitches, three separate gymnasiums, eight inside observation towers and the many other ancillary buildings. Some of which were replaced after the fire in 1974 with portacabins and caravans, were left to disintegrate in the winter storms of the following twelve years. The compounds of Long Kesh had served their purpose, after containing some of the most sadistic murderers of the 20th Century for almost three decades.

In proportion to the type of prisoners who were held in the compounds, the few who succeeded in escaping were minimal. This fact will stand as a living testament to the courage and conduct of the prison officers who served in the Compound Maze, not only the Ulster staff, but the men from their home stations in England, Scotland and Wales. With the sudden outbreak of terrorism in the Province, the unique situation that developed effectively meant that most of the training as prison officers was done on the job. It is with this consideration that I have to give a special mention to my colleagues in the Northenl Ireland Prison Service. Not only did they have to contend with the volatile situation in the compounds, but they and their families also lived under a continuous threat from the IRA murder gangs.

On the 26th November 2000 the army closed down the military base that had stood guard over Long Kesh and the Maze for almost three decades. The final closure of the camp became a certainty when the Maze was closed in the summer, following the release of the last wave of inmates under the terms of the Belfast Peace Deal. The Royal Irish Regiment had been responsible for running the base since the previous February, and it was a fitting tribute to the former Ulster Defence Regiment that they should be the last Guard Force Regiment to serve in the camp. The following morning, on the 27th November, civilian workers moved into the 90-acre base to demolish all the buildings, the last of which were the two former aircraft hangars which dated back to Long Kesh's use as a wartime RAF airfield. As I watched the last soldiers to leave the camp on Ulster TV news, I thought of the nostalgic aspect of the place as thousands of soldiers had served in the camp through some part of their careers over the past 30 years, and had worked as the Guard Force to one of the most famous jails in the world.

My mother's health was declining and in 1987 she decided to go into a residential home at Finaghy in south Belfast. I drove down every other day at lunchtime, and in the evenings, to see her and she was visited frequently by other family members and friends. She was also visited by a family whom we had known for many years. Keith and Beverly Dowey visited her with Beverly's mother, who was our neighbour when we lived in Hill Street so many years ago. Beverly was about the same age as Joanne, and the families remained good friends over the years. My mother enjoyed her time in the home. She was a devoted woman of faith, and the residence was run on that basis.

My mother's health worsened, and at the end of February 1990 she was told by the doctors that she was terminally ill. The news devastated me. It was probably made worse by the fact that she was 88 years of age at the time, and it was so unexpected that she should take this disease at this stage of her life. When I spoke to the doctor, he told me there was no reason why she should not live out her normal life span. But this was not to be, because her health further deteriorated and she looked very ill, but was still smiling and in good spirits, thanks to the painkiller morphine. However, on Monday the 2nd April 1990, in the afternoon and only five weeks after being told she had the disease, she finally passed away. I was with her all that day and had the privilege of talking to her right up until death. I thought it was bad when my father died, but when my mother died I was overwhelmed with grief. It was the lowest point in my life.

In my disciplined world of uniform, rules and regulations, love and emotion were almost a sign of weakness. There was no place for such sentiment. Yet I have to say I loved my parents dearly, and they returned that love to me. We shared a deep and caring relationship, and I am thankful that I could be with them in their declining years. I never thought I had achieved much for them to be proud of me, but my mother was delighted when I was awarded the Commendation for Bravery in 1984. I was grateful to have had the opportunity to be with both of them to the end. Sometimes I wonder what would have happened to me if my parents had not provided such a compelling atmosphere of faith during my early childhood years.

It was about seven months after the death of my mother, when I heard the terrible news that Keith Dowey had been murdered by the IRA. It was Saturday the 10th November, and it was not until the evening time that I heard of the brutal murder of four Protestants at Castor Bay on the shores of Lough Neagh. The four men were David Murphy, an RUC Detective Inspector, Tom Taylor, who was a Reserve Constable on the RUC, Keith, and Norman Kendall. The murders of the four men had an unexpected twist, in that two of the victims, Tom Taylor and Norman Kendall, were my schoolmates when we were at Carrick School some 40 years before. The four were members of a gun club that had exclusive access to a stretch of the Lough Neagh shoreline, and were part of a wildfowling syndicate who were regular visitors to the Lough. They had prearranged to meet at their normal rendezvous place, Morrows Point, and arrived in three cars just before 7.00 o'clock after driving through a DOE Water Service Depot, where two security guards were on duty. They signed their names in a book before entering the property, the gates were opened and they drove through.

Minutes later the IRA sectarian death squad struck, as the four men prepared for their early morning expedition. One of the security guards later reported seeing a masked man drive away from the scene but, unaware of the loughside slaughter, he didn't challenge the man. Gunfire was always heard in the area after the duck shooters had arrived, and they often wore balaclavas. Fears for the four men were aroused when they failed to return from their expedition, and it was not until about three o'clock in the afternoon when the bodies of the four friends were found. One of the bodies was still inside the car, two were lying outside on the ground and the third was lying near the water's edge. A Citroen car belonging to one of the men was later found partially burnt out at Brownlow Terrace in Lurgan.

Within minutes of the alarm being raised, police sealed off the area and a major investigation was started. Scenes of Crime Officers found evidence of a struggle and they believed one of the victims tried to fight off his attackers, as his jumper was ripped as if he had fought with the gunman. They also discovered the shotguns belonging to the wildfowlers were still in their carrying cases, and were not loaded. Detectives interviewed the security guard who saw one of the murderers, still wearing his mask, driving the car away from the scene. Police also discovered that the murder gang made their escape in a boat and crossed the lough under the cover of darkness. Fifty-year-old Inspector Murphy had served in the police for almost 30 years, and had been commended on eight occasions. He was the holder of the RUC Long Service Medal, and was married with a son and daughter. After joining the RUC in 1962 and serving in County Armagh, he had been attached to the Special Branch in Lurgan up until a few months before his murder, when he was transferred to Cookstown. He was a keen sportsman and a crack shot as he represented the police at clay pigeon shooting competitions.

Tom Taylor had joined the Police Reserves in 1974 and was also stationed in the town. He was 49 years of age and was married with three children. He lived in the Mouneview area of Lurgan. Norman Kendall was 44 years of age and he worked as an electrician for the Northern Ireland Electricity Service. He was also married but had no family. Keith Dowey was 30 years of age and worked with the Water Service. Keith and Beverley lived in Ann Street in the town with their two children Kyla and Aaron.

On the following Monday, Tuesday and Wednesday I attended the funerals of the four men. Keith on the Monday, Tom Taylor and David Murphy on the Tuesday and Norman Kendall on the Wednesday. At Keith's funeral the former Presbyterian Moderator Dr Matthews described how the Ulster people were tired of statements from the Government about their determination to win, whilst at the same time showing sensitivity to those who gave latent or overt support to the IRA sectarian death squads.

It was slightly less than ten years after the murders of Keith and his three companions, in late October 2000 that newspapers reported the death of the man who had led the IRA murder gang who carried out the Castor Bay ambush. The articles alleged that the man was the main gunman in the attack and that he had died of cancer. Never having been brought to justice, death notices in some of the papers described him as a 'courageous soldier' and 'comrade'.

But to the families of the four men who were murdered in the frenzied attack, he was a psychopathic murderer, whose only interest lay in fighting for the cause. He was alleged to have been the leader of the gang and he was supposed to have gone 'berserk' on what was meant to be the kidnapping of the Special Branch Inspector. It was a case of poetic justice, for one who did not show an ounce of compassion for his four fellow human beings at Morrow's Point on the 10th of November] 990.

Since the murder of the Chairman of the Prison Officers' Association, Dessie Ervine, in 1977, members of the Trade Union Committee were replaced periodically, and by 1988 my friend and colleague Brian Armour was the Vice Chairman of the POA at the Maze. He had been elected to the Association a few years earlier. I first met Brian shortly after I started to work in the blocks in 1976, although we never actually worked together as we were on duty in different phases in the jail. He was 48 years of age, a married man with two children, and had also served in the army. Brian had been warned that his life was in danger after an IRA communication was intercepted on its way out of the prison three months earlier. Although we all lived in danger of IRA assassination, members of the POA Committee were under particular threat because the IRA perceived that by attacking our representatives they would intimidate all the staff.

Brian was murdered on Tuesday the 4th October 1988, when a booby-trap bomb exploded under his car killing him instantly. It was about noon when he was driving his Montego car along Abetta Parade off the Beersbridge

Road. He touched the brakes and the car's sharp jerk dislodged the mercury tilt-switch, the electric circuit was completed and the two-pound Semtex, high-explosive device detonated. The car continued out of control along the road for about 50 metres, before crashing into a small river at the side of some garden allotments. The murder of Brian Armour, and the investigation surrounding the crime, would later reveal a conspiracy of treachery, murder, and collusion with the IRA death gangs that would stun the United Kingdom Prison Service. The unrepentant traitor was another former colleague and friend in the Maze whom I had known for many years, Christopher John Hanna.

Hanna was born and brought up in the Donegall Road area of Belfast. He left secondary school when he was 14 years of age, and spent the next 10 years working as a shop fitter, before joining the Prison Service in 1971, when he was posted to the 'Crum'. I got to know John Hanna after he had successive postings to the Maze. He was then posted to Hydebank Young Offenders' Centre, but in 1982 he was posted back to the Maze on promotion to the rank of Principal Officer, eventually being detailed as PO in Charge of H Block 1. I never actually worked in HI with him, but I did serve on night guard duty when he was the PO in charge. This duty gave him access to the keyroom and the ECR, in the admin building that was the nerve centre of the prison's security system. Like all prison staff, John and his wife and family had suffered their share of risks, both on and off duty. He was forced onto five weeks' sick leave after being injured while helping to foil an escape in the 'Crum', and in a separate incident he, his wife and three young children had to move out of their home on the outskirts of Belfast. They were moved under army escort after he had escaped an IRA murder bid when he managed to slam the front door of their home in the faces of two gunmen.

In what became known as 'The Mata Hari Betrayal' (after a Dutch dancer in France who was executed as a German spy during World War 1. (original name Margaret Gertrud Zelle), Hanna, who was 45 years of age at the time, was arrested by the police in June 1988 and charged with passing on information to the IRA, which led to the murder of Brian Armour. He was also charged with passing on the names and addresses of several other prison officers, and information regarding the security of the Maze prison. He later described to police the role he was to play in a potential, mass breakout from the jail. The plan was that guns would be smuggled into the prison, to be used to take over the ECR and the keyroom. The mass breakout was to take place in Phase 2, which housed H6, H7 and H8, and the plan would have been activated when a vanload of explosives would be detonated outside the perimeter wall.

Shortly after the murder of Brian Armour, a Maze Governor and his wife had a narrow escape when they found a similar type of device under their car, which was parked outside a Lisbum supermarket. The Governor, nicknamed 'Mick the lip', was later transferred to the mainland.

Hanna's slide into treason, obscurity and death began when he parted company with his wife. But since he joined the service, certainly since he first came to the Maze, he had the reputation of being a bit of a playboy, drinking in pubs and clubs around Belfast.

One night in September 1988 he was drinking in a hotel bar on the outskirts of the city when he met an attractive brunette. She was a would-be actress from Twinbrook called Rosena Bruce. But she was not the well-spoken lady he thought she was. She was an IRA spy. By coincidence she had come to the attention of the police a year before, and the Special Branch were closely monitoring her movements. She began to lure Hanna into a web of intrigue and treason that would illustrate the IRA's skill in manipulating people for their own purposes. The 'chance' meeting ended innocently enough with Hanna taking her home and dropping her off in west Belfast, but before they parted he gave her his phone number in the Maze. A few days later she rang him and asked to see him, so he suggested a rendezvous at Blaris Cemetery, only about half a mile away from the jail. However, Hanna's car was kept under surveillance by the high, closed-circuit TV monitor at the extern gate, and Special Branch Officers secretly photographed the couple. A few days later the Special Branch monitored a second meeting of the pair in the graveyard. They met at other prearranged places, and it was during these encounters that Bruce started to ask him about his work in the Maze and about the security of the prison. This in itself should have been a warning to Hanna that there was a more sinister side to the illicit meetings.

Hanna was arrested in May 1989 and charged with complicity in the murder of Brian Armour. Evidence was given at his trial that he had passed on details about Brian to the IRA. Although it was confirmed that he was suffering from multiple sclerosis, the Court accepted psychiatric evidence that he was not suffering from the disease at the time he passed on the information. He was convicted and sentenced to life imprisonment for aiding and abetting in the murder of Brian Armour.

Hanna's counsel immediately appealed the Court's decision on the grounds that insufficient weight had been given to the medical evidence. But the sentence was upheld by the three appeal judges, who stated that the trial judge had the benefit of seeing Hanna as he gave evidence in the witness box for seven days, and he did not seem to be mixed up or confused.

Little surprise was expressed by the staff in the Maze during his trial, when psychiatric evidence was given that he had a 'grandiose' opinion of himself and believed he was playing a 'shrewd game' with the IRA. The Court heard a psychologist explain in evidence that Hanna's perfonnance in specific intelligent tests was only slightly better than that of a mentally-handicapped person. After such evidence about his mental ability, the question asked by many members of staff in the Maze was: "How on earth could such a character have ever been promoted in the Service, and be in charge of an H Block in the Maze prison?" The question was inunediately lost in the all-embracing answer:

"No comment for security reasons!"

After serving the first two years of his sentence at Maghaberry prison, Hanna's health worsened and he was eventually transferred to the secure Block at Musgrave Park Hospital, known as Ward 18. As all the patients in Ward 18 were sentenced prisoners, and although it was a ward in the hospital, it was under the jurisdiction of the Prison Service and effectively part of the prison. By that time I was attached to the Transport Department at the Maze, and we were detailed two evening associations per week on visits at the hospital. The visiting periods were from 7.00 to 9.00 on Tuesday and Friday, and the process was exactly the same as in the Maze, in that the visitors had to be searched on arrival and then escorted to the prisoners. The officer stayed in the ward and observed the visit until the half-hour was up and the visit was terminated.

On Friday the 11th December 1992 I was detailed Ward 18, and when I reported for duty, the PO assigned me to Hanna's visit. I waited for a few minutes until the visitor arrived, and when I collected the visiting pass, I was surprised to see that the visitor was his wife. When she arrived at the reception, she was passed through the female search and into the waiting room. I escorted her to her husband's small single ward. We walked in, and she sat down on a chair at the bedside and started to sob. I sat on a chair near the door, as he asked her about their children, and between long gaps the conversation became sparse and the half-hour was a forlorn visit. When the visit was over, she got up, said goodbye to him and I followed her as she walked out of the ward. At the door I turned and said, "Cheerio, John." He looked at me and said, "Thanks, Killer." His tone was filled with despair, and the expression on his face indicated his surprise that I had even spoken to him. Since he was sentenced, he had been ostracized by the staff in both Maghaberry and Ward 18, who refused to speak to him, but I felt there was no harm in speaking to him, because it was not all his fault. It was a trap that showed the sinister skill of the 'Provie Godfathers' in manipulating someone with a weak personality, and showed the professionalism of the organisation. As we walked along the corridor, he called her name a couple of times. She didn't look back, but burst into tears and, crying bitterly, she walked on into the waiting room. It was the last time I saw John Hanna. Two weeks later he went into a coma and died on the 27th December.

It was when Hanna was arrested and undergoing interrogation by the police that they became particularly interested in his accomplice. Not that they wanted to charge her for her part in the crime, but they wanted to use her as an informer, to collect information about her godfathers. Hanna was willing to help in the plan, clearly seeing the opportunity to, in some way, make amends for what he had done. He immediately offered to turn Queen's evidence against the woman. However, when the Special Branch arrested her and confronted her with the evidence they had compiled against her, she refused to disclose her IRA contacts, and the plan to turn her into a double agent collapsed when she refused to co-operate. The police had to release her, because they realised the evidence they had against her would not have been strong enough for a conviction. They would have had to rely on Hanna's testimony, and as it was his word against hers, they knew who would be the best witness in court, as the officers who interrogated her described her as a 'cool customer' .

It was some nine months after Hanna's death that the would-be actress played her final role, and on Friday the 10th September 1993 she was sentenced to 20 years for her part in a booby-trap bomb plot similar to that which killed Brian Armour. Her final performance occurred when she was arrested near Larne on the 18th April, 1992, transporting a bomb in her car, and she was jailed along with two fellow conspirators, both from Belfast. But the ironical twist to the Special Branch operation was that it had all the hallmarks of being set up by an informer, she had finally been snared by someone in a role that could easily have been her own. Even when she drove into the trap, the ageing actress tried to give her best performance, but the act collapsed when she pulled off her white, woollen hat to speak to the detective and her ill-fitting, ginger wig came with it. The joke was over!

The Hanna episode came as a rude awakening to the Prison Department, only a few years after the escape and the Helmessy Report, which was designed to improve training of prison staff, and create a greater awareness to the dangers of prison officers allowing their guard to relax, not to mention the major security improvements that the report had recommended, most of which had already been put into operation. Here was an escape plan, which had it materialized, would have surpassed anything the IRA had ever done before in the Maze. It has to be said, however, that much of the inadequacies the Hanna affair brought to light were understandable. Since the blocks were opened in 1976, both the staff and the prison had come under an unrelenting barrage of propaganda from the IRA. Inside, the prison staff were engaged in a constant struggle to keep control throughout the dirty protest, the hunger-strike, the escape and, in the years following the escape, the incessant programme of appeasement. Staff were so discouraged that the very thought of running the Maze as a normal prison was 'out the window'. The officers were totally demoralized. These were the unsung heroes of the IRA campaigns, and they received precious little support or recognition from the Government.

Chapter 19

Christmas 1988 saw the greatest reduction in the prison population in the Maze since the phasing out of internment in 1977. One hundred and three prisoners were released on Christmas parole. The release of so many prisoners was the first sign of a new set of priorities that were being established by the Prison Department. A few weeks later I spoke to one prisoner who had served 17 years in the compounds and the blocks, and it was the first time he had been out of prison in all that time. I asked him what he found most unfamiliar on his few days' freedom, and he explained that the most remarkable experience he had was walking up a hill or going upstairs. As the Maze is built completely on the flat, I could understand his feelings after almost two decades in the Maze.

In August 1989 the first female prison officer took up duty in the Maze, and she was followed soon afterwards by others. It was a clear indication that the prison regime was entering a new phase.

By the end of the decade, new regulations giving prisoners even more say in the running of the prison had come into force. Coupled with cutbacks, these resulted in the demands on the Prison Department's slender resources being impossible to fulfil. Consequently, reduced manning levels in the prison created more pressure on individual officers, particularly those in the blocks, and the situation became almost intolerable. The Chief Officer rank in the service was abolished, and replaced by a new rank of Governor 5. The No. 1 Chief Officer in the Maze was transferred to the Department where he became a member of another new group that had recently been formed, 'The Operational Assessment Team'. The object of the team was to assess the duties of prison staff and evaluate all duties in the prison.

The Chief Officers were absorbed into the new Governor rank, which further lowered morale amongst the staff. As the Chief Officer rank was the highest discipline rank in the service, it was always held in high regard by the officers on the ground. Conversely, the rank of Assistant Governor was generally made up of men who had joined the service at that grade, although there were some who came up through the ranks. Some had arrived at the Maze straight from Queen's University and hadn't a clue about the running of a prison. These were a symbol of the new breed of enlightened prison official, who seemed to have the perception that all the inmates in the Maze were victims of circumstances, who came from a deprived background. And who only needed a wee hug or someone to buy them a puppy dog or some sweets and they would be good little boys. But when the psychological pressure was put on them by the paramilitary leaders, they soon found it unbearable, some of them cracked up, and others resigned from the service altogether.

I enjoyed my spell of duty on the admin gate, mainly because I was out in the fresh air. There was always plenty of stir when it was busy and there was a lot of movement in and out of the prison. Amongst the many visitors to the prison throughout the year was a delegation from the International Red Cross.

The organisation based in Geneva, Switzerland, was made up of representatives from all European countries. A group of four or five members would visit the Maze twice a year to inspect the jail, and scrutinize the conditions under which the prisoners were held. They inspected the prison hospital and all the medical care that was administered to the inmates.

The educational facilities and the prisoners accommodation were also inspected. They visited the Cell Block and interviewed any prisoners who were being held under the Code of Discipline. The circumstances under which they were charged were also looked at. Sometimes the noise and commotion in the wings was so bad that the cons couldn't stand it, and there were occasions when the pressure got so bad they would deliberately breach the prison rules to get a spell in the 'chokey', to get their 'heads showered'. The group also visited the POA Office and spoke to the staff representatives. They investigated complaints from the prison officers regarding their conditions of employment etc. But most of the staff gave them the cold shoulder and regarded them as a bunch of 'space cadets' . The delegation usually had one and sometimes two Germans making up their number. I often thought it was a bit rich, that Germans should be coming here to scrutinize the conditions in a British prison. After all, they weren't so kind to their prisoners when they gassed six million of them in the holocaust during the war.

The prison hospital was always deemed by the paramilitary organisations to be neutral territory, and the hospital staff were treated with a degree of respect by the prisoners. The hospital officers still realised they were in danger of assassination by the IRA and tried to take precautions, particularly those living in isolated areas. Therefore it came as a blow when my colleague John Griffiths was murdered. He was a hospital officer in the Maze and was killed when his car was booby-trapped at his home near Loughgall on Thursday morning the 4tb May 1989.

John was 37 years of age and a native of the north of England. He came to Northern Ireland in the early 1970's when he was a soldier with the Royal Engineers. Here he met the girl who later became his wife. They were married in England but returned to Ulster in 1973. He became a full-time member of the Ulster Defence Regiment when he joined the 2nd County Armagh Battalion shortly after returning to Northern Ireland. In 1978 he left the UDR and joined the prison service, when he was posted to the Maze. He trained as a hospital officer and was later attached to the prison hospital. He was transferred to the hospital wing in Maghaberry for a short time, but returned to the Maze where he remained until his death.

As John left home at ten past seven on the Thursday morning, he got into his car and had only driven about 50 yards when the bomb, which contained two pounds of Semtex, exploded. It had been attached to the floor under the driver's seat and detonated when the mercury tilt-switch activated the device. After the initial explosion, there was a small bang and the car burst into flames. John hadn't a chance, as the car was an inferno within seconds and was completely destroyed in a very short time. On hearing the blast and realising the worst, his wife dashed from the house to find her husband trapped in the car, that had been ripped apart by the blast. Her horrific screams shattered the morning silence as she watched helplessly as John died in a ball of flames. Neighbours, after hearing the explosion, rushed to the scene only to find Mrs Griffiths and her 16year-old daughter screaming hysterically. As they made daring efforts to rescue John, they were repeatedly driven back by the fierce flames from the ignited petrol tank. Realising their efforts were hopeless, they eventually persuaded the mother and daughter to return to the house. John with his wife, 16-year-old daughter Wendy and their 7-year-old son John, had lived in the village until they moved to the bungalow about two miles from Loughgall, a year before.

Two days later on Saturday the 6th May, a bunch of flowers marked the spot where John died. The simple floral tribute had been placed on the scorched hedgerow in the laneway to the Griffiths' family home by his wife Annabel, shortly before the funeral of her murdered husband. In bright sunshine, over 1,000 people gathered outside the house where a private service was held, before the cortege left for the burial service in the village churchyard. A large contingent of uniformed men and women from the Prison Service marched in ranks immediately behind the family mourners, and relays of officers carried the coffin. Grief-stricken, Mrs Griffiths and her daughter led the mourners along the narrow, country road, whilst her son remained at home, still cared for by family friends. Her husband's coffin, draped in the Union Flag and bearing his prison officer's hat and black gloves, beside a wreath of red roses from his wife, was carried by family relatives including John's father and brother who had flown over from England for the funeral.

At the scene of the murder, the cortege paused for a moment before continuing on towards the village. Officials of the Loughgall Darts Team, of which John was a member, paid their respects and the funeral once again paused outside the village Football Club, where on every other Saturday afternoon John could have been seen in support of the village team. A young police constable came to attention and saluted the coffin outside Loughgall Police Station where, two years earlier, eight IRA men died when they drove into an ambush by a unit of the Special Air Service. The IRA men were caught in the act as they launched a bomb attack on the village police station. At the church a guard of honour was mounted by the prison staff, as hundreds of mourners filed into the building for the funeral service. Later a similar guard stood silently around the grave, as a lone piper played a lament. As a final tribute, the cushion of red roses and two wreaths of carnations from the dead man's daughter and son, were placed on the grave.

A few weeks after John's murder I was talking to a colleague who was a member of the Prison Officers' Welfare Committee who visited the home from time to time and kept in touch with the family. He told me a touching story about a litter of rabbits that were being reared in a shallow warren not far from

John's home. His son found the warren and was keeping a watchful eye on the young rabbits, when one day he discovered the mother had been killed on the road. He collected the litter in a cardboard box and brought them home to rear by feeding them with a milk bottle and a teat. When his father saw how young the rabbits were he thought they would need to be fed during the night, so he told his son he would get up and feed them in the early hours. It was Wednesday night the 3rd May, and by bizarre coincidence, at the very moment John was feeding the little rabbits to keep them alive, the IRA murder gang were placing the bomb under his car outside his house.

One day a circular appeared on the notice board requesting applications for drivers in the transport pool. A few days later I was talking to the PO in charge of the Transport Department and he suggested that I should put my name down for the driving course. I was interviewed for the post and about a week later I received notification that I had got the job, and on Monday the 4th September 1989 I started my new detail in the transport section. After reporting to the PO that morning my first assignment was on Lima 19, that was the radio call sign of the education van. All the vehicles in the Maze transport pool had a numbered call sign, prefixed by the word Lima. I delivered books and equipment to the blocks from the Education Department, to be used by prisoners who were engaged in further education classes, and generally ran errands around the jail for the teachers.

Each morning and afternoon a mobile book library and audiotape collection was brought to one of the blocks, and the inmates could swap books and cassettes. The books were in racks on a wooden trolley that had to be wheeled onto a large, four-wheeled trailer. There were six or eight trolleys altogether, and a tow-bar was fitted to the back of the van that allowed the trailer to be towed around the blocks. Some mornings I had to collect some of the cons and take them to one of the old workshops that had been converted into a classroom where art classes were being held. Then they had to be collected again about lunchtime and returned to their blocks. One day a couple of months earlier, when I was on the admin gate, a well-dressed man whom I had never seen before, was being escorted into the prison. Later on I saw the officer who had escorted the visitor and I asked him who the day-tripper was. He turned to me and said, "0 that's a male model; they were taking him down to the art class to pose for the cons." I thought I'd seen it all in the Maze prison, but this was unbelievable. At a time of cut backs in the National Health Service, the Prisons Department could afford to employ someone to pose for an art class of terrorist prisoners in the Maze. The lunatics had finally taken over the asylum.

I always enjoyed driving at the 'front of visits'. Effectively this was conveying the visitors from the reception at the visitors' car park to the visits complex inside the prison. There were always plenty of wisecracks and banter from the staff in the car park, and sometimes the visitors joined in too. The form of transport used was three, large, electrically-operated vans called 'Cramptons', each of which held about 20 passengers in the back. They were painted light blue and white, and looked like furniture removal vans with no windows in the sides. But the roof of each van was high enough to allow people to stand up, and it was made of transparent fibreglass that allowed plenty of light into the passenger department. The vans had to be put on electric charge each night to charge up the batteries for the next day. Sometimes, particularly on a Saturday evening after the visits had been very busy and the vans had been on the go all day, the batteries would start to run down. Occasionally a van would stop on the road with flat batteries and it had to be towed back to the loading bay where it was garaged and put on the charger. If there happened to be visitors on the vehicle when it broke down, they would be transferred to another van to continue their journey.

The only time one of the Cramptons was allowed into the phases of the prison was when there was a wedding and it was used to convey the bride and the guests from the visitors' car park to the small church. One of the inside vans would collect the inmate-groom and the best man at their block and bring them to the church for the wedding ceremony. The service was always conducted by the prison chaplain, of whatever religious persuasion the group belonged, and when the wedding ceremony was over the chefs in the prison kitchen supplied a wedding cake, sandwiches, pastries, tea and orange juice for the reception. The church vestry was always prepared beforehand for the wedding reception, which was conducted with the normal toasts, speeches and had the usual jovial atmosphere of a similar celebration outside.

At the back of the visits complex on the inside of the jail there were six or seven vans to convey prisoners from their blocks to the visits area. It was a convenient duty for me because at slack times when the visits were not so busy, I had the opportunity to study my OU Course. It was an 'Introduction to Psychology', and as I would pick up my course book I was soon lost among the theories of Freud, Eysenct, Piaget and B F Skinner.

Sigmund Freud was renowned as the father of phychoanalysis, a method of psychotherapy based on the exploration of unconscious mental processes that affect human behaviour. I often wondered what Freud and those other famous figures of psychology would have made of the Maze Prison and its residents. At the heart of Freud's theory was the idea that people's behaviour is driven by unconscious mental forces, which are beyond their awareness or control. However, there is one certainty. He would have had plenty of clients to study and observe, in order to formulate his theories.

During the 1980's negotiations took place about staffing levels in the United Kingdom Prison Service. These negotiations ultimately brought about the introduction of a staffing system known as the 'Fresh Start', into the service on the mainland. However, the Northern Ireland Service rejected the new system on the grounds that it would not work satisfactorily in the situation currently prevailing in the Province. After lengthy negotiations between the Prison Officers' Association and the NIO, an alternative system was introduced known as the 'Way Forward'. After the arrangement was explained to the staff at a POA meeting in the Maze, a ballot was taken for its acceptance or rejection. I voted against the new system because I thought the whole thing was dreamed up by the Home Office to reduce costs, by cutting overtime and manning levels. Of course any reduction in staffing levels effectively meant handing over the control of some parts of the prison to the paramilitaries and withdrawing the staff from those areas. However, the vote in favour of the new system was carried, and the 'Way Forward' came into force in September 1989. The main changes the arrangement introduced were group working and predictable duty patterns. Before the system came into force, duties could only be predicted up to three days in advance. The system also introduced a 39-hour working week, which was to be phased in over four years and would result in the ending of all overtime. To compensate for the overtime loss, generous new pay scales were introduced, but as we soon found out, the control of some parts of the prison was lost and would never be regained. In fact, the end result of the scheme was the creation of 'no-go' wings in the paramilitary blocks, in which the prison staff were not permitted to enter without the permission of the wing OC.

In September 1991 the first female Governor was posted to the Maze.

She arrived on promotion from the female prison at Maghaberry and was assigned to the Security Department. I was taken unawares one day when I first met her. She was at the desk as I walked into the security office and asked to speak to the Governor, at which she replied, "I'm the security Governor." I stared at her for a moment in surprise at seeing such an attractive, young woman in such a post. Like most of the staff in the Maze at the time, I had reservations about a woman being in charge of a department in the jail, particularly in an important area like security. But as we got to know her, and the staff saw how considerate and helpful she was, they accepted her as a first class Governor.

In the autumn of 1992 Joanne got engaged to be married and the following summer, on the 20th July she was married. Unfortunately the happy occasion was saddened by the death in January of her grandmother. Delta's mother took ill and was admitted to hospital in October. Her health continued to deteriorate and she died on the 30th January 1993, at the age of 91.

Later that same year during Remembrance Week a documentary programme was screened on local television. The programme centred on a family from County Londonderry and the grief and heartbreak they had endured since the murder of their daughter about eight years earlier. Tracey Doak was one of the 299 police officers who were murdered during the 30 years of the troubles. The IRA murdered 277, the INLA and IPLO murdered 12 and the loyalists killed seven. Three were murdered by unknown groups as the organisations responsible refused to accept responsibility for the murders. In addition to those murdered, 8,326 have been injured during the course of their duties. The IRA have bombed and assassinated RUC officers, and in some cases policemen have been beaten to death and even relatives and other civilians have been murdered in the process.

Woman Constable Tracey Doak was stationed in Newry, and on Monday the 20th May 1985, whilst on mobile patrol with three colleagues along the main Dublin Road, a bomb exploded totally destroying the police vehicle and killing the four occupants instantly. It was shortly before 10.00 a.m. that morning, as the armoured police car drove past a trailer which was packed with explosives, that the massive landmine was detonated. The car was one of a two-vehicle patrol which was to have acted as escort for a cross-border money shipment, and as the security van arrived from the Republic, the three vehicles moved off in convoy towards Newry. The four police officers were Tracey Doak, who was 21 years of age and came from Coleraine. She joined the RUC in 1982. Inspector William James Wilson was 28 years of age. He joined the police in 1975 and came from Moira. Reserve Constable Steven George Rodgers was 19 years of age and came from Dunmurry on the outskirts of Belfast. He had joined the RUC less than a year before and was a single man. Constable David James Ronald Baird was 22 years of age and single. He lived in Antrim and joined the police in 1983.

Police later discovered that at about 7.30 pm on the Sunday evening a trailer unit was hi-jacked from a farmhouse on the Dundalk Road outside Newtownhamilton by two masked men. One had a rifle and the other a handgun. Detectives believed the IRA used the unit to tow the trailer-bomb to Killeen, as one of the gunmen stayed with the family and at 11.15pm the second gunman returned with the unit and the two men left the house. The security van was supposed to be carrying cash totalling two million Irish pounds, from Dublin to Belfast and as it drove past the old customs station the bomb was detonated by remote control.

The TV presentation of the Doak family was very poignant to me. Not only did I associate myself with the police woman and her colleagues as fellow members of the security forces, but Tracey was also about the same age as Joanne and she was engaged to be married when she was so brutally murdered. As Joanne was married only a short time before the programme was screened, it brought home to me in a very graphic way the trauma and pain the family had suffered since their loss. The funeral of Woman Constable Tracey Doak took place at Ballywatt Presbyterian Church and after the service, interment was in the adjoining churchyard. Tracey was the daughter of Beattie and Jean Doak, and they both took part in the programme.

Each sweeping decision by the faceless people in the Prisons Department confounded the conventional experience at all levels in the service. All the appeasement in the Maze came to nothing, and by 1993 sporadic incidents of intimidation started again. These culminated in two separate incidents in H3 and H8, when two officers were overpowered and blindfolded, tied to chairs and had their heads shaved. They were then covered in paint and frogmarched out of their wings. They were both loyalist wings and the protests were in sympathy with their fellow prisoners in the Crum, who were protesting about conditions in the jail. About three weeks later, serious trouble erupted in the loyalists Blocks over a prisoner who was refused compassionate parole. It was Friday evening the 27th August when the inmate was told his mother had taken seriously ill, and he immediately applied to the Governor for 48-hours compassionate leave. His parole was granted and he was collected at the block and taken to reception for documentation before being released. However, an Assistant Governor, in his wisdom, turned down the prisoner's parole and sent him back to his block. There was something repugnant about the Governor's decision in the circumstances. But it certainly must have been infuriating for the prisoner. It did nothing to endear the prison staff to their charges. When I heard about the incident I felt disgusted about the whole thing.

The prisoner got back to his wing in a very distressed state and when he told his wing OC and the rest of his mates about the refusal, they threw the staff out of the wing. The incident triggered a disturbance that escalated and became the largest riot ever to take place in the Maze prison. When all the wings that could be locked, were locked, the staff were kitted out in riot gear and all the UVF wings in the jail had to be taken by force, one by one. It was in the early hours of Saturday morning before the staff had taken control of the wings and the riot was quelled. Twenty-four officers were injured in the disturbances, some of them seriously, and seven prisoners were also hurt. In the following days the UVF issued a statement to the effect that more 'appropriate action' would be taken.

The retaliation quickly followed when within hours there were attacks on prison officers' homes in the Newtownabbey, Antrim and north Belfast areas. The cars belonging to some officers were set on fire outside their homes, and shots were fired through the windows of other houses. But we only had to wait five days to see their 'appropriate action'. On Wednesday evening the 1st September gunmen smashed their way into the home of an officer and shot him dead at point-blank range. He was 44-year-old Jim Peacock who lived with his wife and five of a family in the Oldpark Road area of north Belfast. Jim had served with me in the Maze since he joined the prison service, and although we didn't actually work together I knew him very well. He was a tall, quiet-natured man who would have done nobody any harm, and was probably picked out as an easy target because of his gentle character. Jim had been transferred from the Maze to Belfast prison to be closer to home because of intimidation from both Republican and Loyalists. He and his family had been forced out of their home because of IRA threats and at other times the house had been petrol-bombed and the windows smashed.

Jim was in the kitchen of his home when the gunmen burst in through the door and a single shot rang out. The bullet struck him in the back and he collapsed to the floor, bleeding badly from the wound. His 13-year-old daughter Penny was upstairs in her bedroom reading when she heard the sound of glass breaking and then the shot. She dashed downstairs and found her father on the kitchen floor. Jim was barely breathing as Penny knelt down on her knees and cradled his head in her arms. "It's me, daddy. Wake up daddy, it's Penny. Are you alright, daddy?" She asked, willing him to live, as her father lay motionless on the floor. "1 was crying and crying and I just stroked his hair, and for a moment he tried to say something. But he couldn't. I think he knew I was beside him, and it was nice that he knew he wasn't alone," Penny told her mother and the rest of the family later.

J A Peacock-Officer-Belfast- I /9/93, is the last entry engraved on the Roll of Honour on the memorial stone at the Maze. Of the 30 names inscribed, 29 were murdered since 1974. But thankfully, less than a year after the murder of Jim Peacock, the IRA declared a ceasefire, which was quickly followed by a similar declaration by the Loyalists. The sectarian murder campaign of the IRA and the retaliatory violence by the Loyalists had finally created a desire across the political spectrum in Northern Ireland to find a durable peace. The Loyalists, through their spokesman and veteran activist Gusty Spence, expressed unreserved remorse for the 25 years of troubles. But sadly the IRA representatives expressed no remorse whatsoever for their part in the 25 years of carnage. However, it has to be said that the ceasefires and ultimately the Belfast Agreement were the final elements of a strategy commenced by Mr Peter Brook, who was appointed Secretary of State for Northern Ireland in July 1989. The much despised, Anglo-Irish Agreement of 1985 had run its course, and Mr Brook had set about forging a new, triangular relationship between London, Belfast and Dublin. The Anglo-Irish Agreement had given the Irish Government some say in the affairs of Northern Ireland, much to the abhorrence of the Unionist population, a sentiment so strongly held by my former M.P. Mr Harold McCusker that the following words were engraved on his headstone, after his death on 1st February 1990.

"I shall carry to my grave with ignominy the sense of injustice that I have done to my constituents down the years - when in their darkest hours 1 exhorted them to put their trust in this British House of Commons which one day would honour its fundamental obligation to them to treat them as equal British citizens."

Hansard. 18th November 1985.

After a major escalation in the IRA's bombing campaign when they targeted the commercial centres of many towns in the Province. The Secretary of State, on the 9th December 1991, announced a freeze on public spending in several areas, to meet the increased cost of the IRA bomb damage. At the same time the IRA's actions were met by a corresponding increase in Loyalist violence and by the end of 1991 the UVF had killed 19 people, and the UDA and UFF between them had killed a further 15. The cost of damage to homes in the Province by IRA bombs was £2 million more than the total cost for the previous five years. When Mr Brook made a speech in which he said the Government would be "imaginative" in dealing with the IRA if they would suspend their campaign of violence, it was perceived by the terrorists as a signal that the Government wanted to talk, and the stage was set for all-party negotiations, which concluded on Friday the 10th April 1998 with the Belfast

Agreement.

For some years after the escape in 1983 and the Hennessy inquiry that followed it, the whole episode became submerged in my mind under the wealth of changes in the prison regime and the events in the Province in general. But it was never quite forgotten and about ten years later the event suddenly assumed a new significance. The Deputy Governor of the Maze who had been in charge of the prison at the time of the escape, was promoted and posted to Maghaberry where he took charge of the new £50 million jail. I think it was this event, more than anything else, that spurred me on to write down a few notes and record my past experiences.

When work first commenced on the building of the new prison at Maghaberry it was intended it would receive its first committals in 1981. However, due to the continuous fears about security and the many interruptions in the building programme after threats against the workers by the IRA, the completion date slipped steadily behind schedule. The cost increased from £20 million, which was the projected figure at the start, to £50 million in 1986 when the prison was finally opened. The first inmates into the new jail were transferred from Armagh Prison, and the old Victorian Prison in Armagh was closed about a year-and-a-half later. The prison contains a female block which is set apart from the main complex. This female part of the prison also has a Young Offenders Centre for female inmates. Soon after it opened the prison staff showed determination in making Maghaberry the leading prison in Northern Ireland, for which purpose it was designed. In the meantime, Belfast prison was run down and eventually closed in 1996, when the remaining imnates were transferred to Maghaberry. Moreover, the story of Maghaberry prison will no doubt continue because in recent times as a more relaxed regime was introduced, like the Maze a few years earlier, disturbances have increased and there have been some serious incidents. Assaults on staff are now common and there has been a hostage situation when an officer was held captive by armed prisoners. However, all these incidents have been quelled by the customary professionalism of the prison staff.

In April 1995 the Prison Service was established as an executive agency and a framework document was published which described the policies and resources within which the service was to operate. The document also described the key goals and main performances which were determined by ministers, and against which, targets were set in order that the performance of the service could be measured. A year later saw the first squad of auxiliary prison officers detailed to the Maze and from that date all personnel who joined the service were called auxiliaries and were employed on much lower pay scales than those who were in the service before. It was a matter of manning the Maze 'on the cheap'. The Chief Executive would appear on TV from time to time and brag about the way he had reduced manning levels in the jail. In effect, what he meant was that he had handed parts of the prison over to the IRA and the other paramilitary organisations, and therefore needed less prison staff to run the prison. The new Corporate and Business Plan strategy beggared belief.

Early in 1995 the first prisoners to be set free under the terms of the Belfast Agreement were released on licence and within the following year more were discharged. It was explained to each prisoner that if he were to get involved in criminal activity whilst on licence from the prison, he would be returned to the jail where he would complete the remainder of his original sentence. As the numbers in the Maze started to decrease, staff were redeployed, and in the transport department some vehicles were taken off the road. So I found myself on the move once again and I was told that from Monday the 3rd June I would be detailed to one of the blocks. When I saw the duty roster for that day I found myself assigned to H Block 4, which I knew was an IRA block. The Monday and Tuesday were rest days, so I started duty in the block on Wednesday morning and as I walked in through the front grille, I could see it was the same depressing and claustrophobic place. The wings were totally different from those in which I had worked before. In the ablutions a shower cubicle had been converted to take a tumble-dryer that sat on top of a large, industrial washing machine, and the ablutions area was now divided off from the wing by a wooden partition with a door in the centre. The whole construction was painted with emulsion paint.

The staff had been withdrawn from the wings, and the only time officers were allowed to go into the living accommodation, was to carry out headcounts in the mornings and at night. The cell doors were permanently in the locked, open position and even during the night they were not closed. The cell walls were painted in a variety of colours and matching curtains covered the windows of each cell. A power and aerial socket was now fitted in each cell and the inmate was permitted to purchase his own portable TV set, which allowed him to view a selection of eight TV channels. A blanket or curtain hung over the entrance to each cell to give some privacy to the occupant and, in some cases, a sheet of plywood which had been supplied to the con as a bed-board, was placed at the cell entrance.

The complement of staff in the block had been drastically reduced and now comprised of a PO and SO and about 12 or 14 officers. It has to be said that some of the grilles were now electrically operated and CCTV cameras were strategically placed to monitor the movements of prisoners. These were attached to the ceilings in the wings and in the circle and others were placed outside the block. The cameras in the wings were limited to what they could see, by prisoners hanging coats and other articles of clothing on clothes-lines along the side of the corridors. The simple act of opening two cell doors on opposite sides of a wing could also hinder the camera's view. All the monitors for the CCTV cameras were in the block control room where, they were kept under constant observation by an officer. Prisoners were allowed free movement between the wings on each side of the 'H', and a limited number were permitted to cross the circle to associate with their friends on the opposite side of the block. In the small officers' mess, heavy metal shutters were fitted to the wall at the side of each of the two windows. These were installed as protection against an external attack following a major riot, during which prisoners tried to pour burning fluids over staff who were trapped in the mess area. The riot had erupted following a search by prison officers of a Loyalist block and resulted in a number of staff being injured and extensive damage being caused.

Access from the wings to the exercise yards was now through a turnstile which was left open from 8 o'clock each morning until 9 o'clock at night, and was electrically controlled from the Block control room. All electrically controlled grilles and equipment as well as CCTV cameras were overseen by the ECR, who had in place, an override system that allowed them to take charge of the apparatus. The exercise yards on each side of the block were now overlooked by a 'yard watchtower' that had been constructed at the sterile area between the two exercise yards on each side of the block, on 'A' and 'B' side and 'C' and 'D' side. The yard towers were not as high as the internal watchtowers, but they were well placed to observe the yards and were each fitted with an intercom to the control room and lit by the lights on the surrounding fence. The cons in each wing in H4 had their 'officer commanding' (OC), who was the spokesman and represented the wing in any dealings with the Governor. Each wing had its own education officer who organised all educational activities in the wing, and encouraged the rest of the cons to take advantage of all the further education facilities. All the inmates in each wing were given specific jobs and responsibilities by their OC, such as organising tuck-shop lists, the wing laundry, cleaning the ablutions and polishing the wing floors. The organisation ensured a hierarchy whereby every prisoner in the wing contributed to the routine tasks for the smooth running of the wing. The four wing OC's in each block were responsible to the Block OC, who ensured that accountability and discipline were enforced at all levels and that the IRA's views and objections were presented to the prison authorities with one voice. The system of ranking ensured that nothing happened without the OC's consent. I was not long in H4 when I discovered that the Block OC was none-other than Brendan 'Bic' McFarlane, and when in my normal duties we passed by each other, we passed like ships in the night, our exchange of glances telling me he recognised me. I certainly recognised him.

Some of the cons who were on specific education courses were issued with computers by the education department. The computers were used for purposes other than education, as typed lists were made out of inmates who wanted to see the doctor or welfare officer. When the bulk order forms were placed for the tuck-shop, they not only had computerised the forms but they had also calculated the deductions from the individual prisoner's tuck-shop money and the lists subsequently had only to be verified by the tuck-shop staff. The daily lists of names for attendance at visits and football were made out by the cons and handed to the grille officer. The inmates in the wings ran their own additional education classes, mainly in the Irish language and political history. At the latter stages of my time in H4, they decided to form an Irish-speaking wing, when the Irish language was spoken all the time and the only time English was spoken was when their spokesman came to the grille to make a request for the grille officer. By now, when the headcount was called at 8.00 o'clock in the evening, the officers had to go down the wings and search about for the cons in order to count them. Some of the cons would have been in the dining hall, the ablutions and the gym-cell or in their cells reading or listening to the radio. It was a far cry from the days when they had to stand at their cell doors to be counted before lock-up.

Chapter 20

Staff had little or no confidence in the authority of the Governor or senior management of the prison, because the appeasement policy seemed to be endless and the prison regime at times seemed to be getting out of control altogether. Privileges and possessions were allowed by the Govemor without question, and there was no end to what they were allowed into the prison. As a result the prison staff had no idea of the boundary line between what was acceptable and what was not. Some cells were so packed full of personal belongings it would have taken two officers half a day to search one cell. Even exotic birds and budgerigars were kept in cages in the cells and when they allowed them out to fly, it was not unusual to see budgies fluttering around the circle or perching on top of the filing cabinet in the Govemor's office. In the wings, bird seed was placed in front of the CCTV lenses so that at times all that could be seen on the monitors were close-ups of budgies feeding vigorously on the seed. On the one hand it seemed the security department was paranoid about security. There was even a CCTV camera inside the block control room that was trained over the control officer, and on the other hand, the demands for extra food, milk and other supplies were endless. It became the normal practice in the wings that when extra food stuffs were supplied, they were dumped in the rubbish bins. One incident I witnessed in a wing was that the inmates complained about the dinner not being properly cooked. Then when the second meal was supplied to the wing, an empty bin was placed at the side of the hot plate and as each con received his lunch he scraped his plate into the bin without even tasting the food. Sometimes in the clothing department at the prisoners' car park, the staff would find articles of prison clothing - clothing that was supplied to the inmates by the prison department - being sent out on a visit for friends and relatives.

The conditioning of prison staff was unrelenting. The continuous episodes of intimidation, coercion, threats, demands and complaints were interspersed by times when prisoners would come up to the wing grille and chat to an officer and engage him in conversation about some mutual interest. During the dialogue the prisoner would drop a hint or veiled threat to the officer about his behaviour in the block, and in an almost sympathetic tone of voice he would say, "You know, if you continue with these rubdown searches you can't really expect us to be responsible for your safety here!" Very soon the rubdown searches and indeed all the searching stopped altogether as the staff accepted the situation and opted for a quiet life. Following on from this bonding process, some staff were so conditioned and fearful that, if a situation developed, they would side with the prisoners against their own colleagues, rather than leave themselves open to attack from the prisoners.

I was on duty at the wing grille one day when an inmate spoke to me in an aggressive tone. I asked another officer the name of the prisoner and he told me the inmate's name as he walked into the wing. Within a few minutes the wing OC came to the grille and shouted at me, at the top of his voice, "Why are you asking questions about my men? Anything you want to know ask me. I'm in charge here!" The next time I saw the officer I told him what the con had said and asked him if he had told the wing OC I was asking questions about the inmates. He denied telling him, at the same time knowing perfectly well no one else could have told him. Probably the most humiliating feature of the appeasement agenda was walking into the PO's office and finding him sitting at his desk chatting in a very familiar manner to the OC of the IRA, and knowing that the prisoner had been in the Maze for a long time and had even been on the 'streaker protest' 20 years earlier. It was so degrading to the staff to see that he was now accepted on a par with the Block Principal Officer. When I reflect on these events, I think that the most appalling aspect was that the Prison Governors and senior civil servants in the Prisons Department were continually covering up the situation that prevailed in the Maze. Hiding behind the facade that the prison was a high security establishment and everything was under control. The ongoing joke among the staff was, "Well things can't get any worse, but they always do!"

For some time the practice had been established in the Maze that a children's party would be held twice a year for children of prisoners up to the age of 16 years. The object was to strengthen ties between the inmates and their families, and the parties were held at Christmas and in the summertime. These social gatherings were organised through the welfare department and their staff were in charge of escorting the children from the car park to the gymnasium and the adjoining football field. But by 1995, the parties were extended to include the mothers of the children. They were described by the prison department as, an extension of the policy of helping prisoners to maintain and strengthen their family links. However, it was seen by the staff as an extension of the policy of bolstering up the cease-fires. Other concessions were made that introduced card phones to the jail and a telephone cubicle was constructed in each wing. The illegal use of mobile phones that had been smuggled into the prison was rife for some time. In one case an officer observed an inmate standing with his hand up to his ear and his back to the officer. He seemed to be in conversation and the officer thought he was talking to himself, but when he investigated he discovered the prisoner was talking on a mobile phone. The phone was immediately confiscated but to the deep embarrassment of the officer, the phone was later returned to the prisoner. Periods of compassionate parole were extended and renamed Compassionate Temporary Release, and later that year, half sentence remission was introduced.

The Christmas parties were a complete success in 1995 and 1996. But when the prisoners in H8 were being organised for the 1997 festive gathering a few weeks before Christmas, it was found that every inmate in the Block had his name down for the party, even single men who had no children. When the minibuses arrived to take them to the gym they all charged out in one big crowd, making it impossible for the staff to count every prisoner, never mind identify them. The procedure for the controlled movement of prisoners in the block was that they were moved between grilles about six at a time before the next batch was let out of the wing. But the practice had long disappeared due to the rampant intimidation of staff

When the visitors arrived at the reception car park and after they were given the normal rubdown search procedure, they were ferried into the jail and to the gym by the normal transport. Within a short time the scene on the football pitch was like that of a three-ring-circus with everyone joining in the festivities. There were two bouncy castles, a karaoke machine, stunts enacted by professional clowns, three-legged races and pillow fights that were put on by the cons. The number one Governor later described the merriment as he visited the scene, to see that everything was alright and there were no complaints from the guests. He recounted how, as he was near the karaoke machine, some of the inmates shouted, "Come on, Governor, why don't you give us a song." He declined. "Not least because I have a dreadful voice." When we heard this, it was the opinion of many staff in the jail that any prison officer with the slightest idea about prison security would have been fore-warned, by such an invitation to join in the fun, that all was not right. When the party was over the prisoners remained in the gym to 'clean up', whilst the visitors were loaded onto the minibuses to be returned to the car park.

The scene became chaotic with the cons jumping onto the buses to say goodbye to their loved ones and children clambering off the buses to say goodbye to their fathers. As a result, the actual counting of the bodies was impossible and when the vehicles were eventually full, the people were still rampaging about. When the visitors arrived at the main gate complex they engaged in the same antics, making it impossible for the staff to count them there too. Probably the most appalling lack of judgement by the escorting officers was that they allowed the visitors' buses to leave the gym first, and did not ensure that the prisoners were counted and returned to their blocks and secured, before the visitors were allowed to leave. This failure was clearly the result of months and years of the conditioning of staff who had fallen into a languid frame of mind and didn't want any hassle. But to make things worse, almost an hour elapsed between the first bus and the last one leaving the gym.

More confusion was experienced by the staff at the block when the inmates eventually arrived back at H8, and the gate officer allowed the first vehicle into the courtyard. The second minibus arrived, and before the officer could get the gate closed, they all piled out of the vehicle and walked in through the gate.

It was some two hours later when the IRA's Commanding Officer in H8 asked to speak to the Senior Prison Officer in charge of the Block. He walked into his office and told him that one of the prisoners had escaped. It was only then that quick headcounts were carried out and the information was found to be only too true. The prisoner was named as Limn Averill, who was serving a life sentence for a double murder. It was later discovered that during the party celebrations he had dressed up in women's clothing, adorned a wig and make-up and made his escape by mingling with the women and children in one of the buses. In the event of an escape from a normal prison, the staff would feel some shame and regret, even when they were not involved, but the whole sphere of security in the Maze had now deteriorated into a joke - a literal joke.

The following day I was on duty on contractors' escorts at the extern gate. The duty was basically to escort contractors into the prison to carry out maintenance. The escorting staff met in the tally lodge and it was my job to mark off the name of each officer as he reported for duty. A number of staff were already in the office, having a chat over a cup of coffee when an officer came in whose name I didn't know, even though I had seen him before. So I interrupted the conversation and asked, "Excuse me, your name wouldn't happen to be Averill by any chance?" At which the whole crowd burst out laughing.

If the 25th September 1983 was the darkest day in the history of the British penal system when the 38 IRA men escaped, then 1997 must have been the darkest year. The trouble in the Maze started on Tuesday night the 28th January when the authorities decided to have a full-scale search of the prison. I was on night guard that night, and when I drove into the prison at about 8.00 0' clock as usual, I was surprised to see so many vehicles in the car park. There was even a large number of police Land Rovers as the RUC search teams were brought in to assist in the search of the jail. As the night guards took up their posts, the Governor called for volunteers amongst the day staff to stay behind after lock-up to help in the search. But as the staff filed out through the tally lodge and there was not going to be enough to search the jail, he called a 'state of emergency'. In this event, all staff were supposed to obey orders without question and stay behind to continue duty, but at the tally lodge twelve officers still refused to abide by the Governor's instructions and went home. The following morning the twelve were suspended from duty and disciplinary charges were made against them. The staff in the Maze rallied with their support for the men which was one hundred percent, and in a mocking gesture of the whole charade they became known as the 'Maze 12'. Within a few hours a full-blown dispute had erupted between the Prison Officers' Association and the Prisons Department. A POA meeting was called in the Officers' Mess and a vote of no-confidence was passed by the 2,600 membership in the Governor and senior management of the prison-the Chief Executive Mr Alan Shannon and his advisors.

The Prisons Department claimed that the control of the prison was at stake in the dispute, while the POA said the 12 officers were being made scapegoats for the management's incompetence and loss of control of the Maze. In a statement the POA Chairman, Mr Finlay Spratt, said:

"There is a crisis in the Northern Ireland Prison Service and it all stems from the suspension of those 12 officers. The staff have spoken. It's up to the management to restore confidence between them and the officers on the ground.

The prison staff are the people who stand between the public and the terrorists!"

Mr Spratt explained at the meeting that the management had not followed the procedure agreed when the service became a separate Government agency a year before. The POA Chairman continued:

"They're bluffing the public by calling the search an emergency-they hadn't searched the place for almost a year. The Chief Executive didn't follow the procedure and agreements. The Maze is a total shambles. Prisoners can walk from block to block without being searched. They don't even know how many prisoners are being locked up at night-they work on assumed numbers."

The Prisons Department made their all-embracing observation that they refused to comment on operational matters at the Maze. But what the staff found so galling was that over the years there were riots and disorders by the prisoners in the jail, causing millions of pounds worth of damage and not a single inmate had been charged. And here, because they refused to obey an order, 12 officers were suspended and charged. There was one thing we were all agreed on, namely that the whole contemptible affair illustrated the mentality of those who were in charge of the Maze at the time. However, on the 4th March the Prisons Department announced that the disciplinary charges against the 12 men were dropped, no doubt as a result of the no-confidence vote by the staff and the fact that the press had now got their teeth into the whole episode, and the case was receiving a lot of publicity.

The second serious incident of the year took place just over two weeks later on Sunday night the 23 rd March, which was a very wet night as there had been heavy rain throughout most of the day. A dog-handler who was on evening duty patrolling in Phase 2 was relieved by his night guard colleague and went home. Later that night he received a phone call from the duty Governor of the night guard who was speaking from the ECR. The Governor asked him if he had observed anything out of the ordinary when he was patrolling in the sterile area at the back of H7. He replied that he had noticed nothing untoward. The Governor told him that the night guard dog handler had reported to the ECR on his radio that there had been a subsidence in the ground near the fence with 'A' wing exercise yard, and between the block and the perimeter wall. As it was so late nothing further could be done, although the army guard force was informed and extra soldiers were put on patrol duty along the outside of the perimeter wall for the remainder of the night.

Early the following morning a search team was dispatched to H7. What they found surprised even me and I thought that nothing more would surprise me about the Maze prison. In cell 18, the third cell from the bottom of' A' wing on the outer side of the wing, they found a tunnel that extended 32 metres under 'A' wing exercise yard, under the yard fence and into the sterile area. The ground subsidence in the sterile area had been caused when the end part of the tunnel had collapsed due to the waterlogged ground, and the fact that that section of the tunnel roof had not yet been propped up. Pieces of bed ends, lockers, plywood that had been supplied for handicrafts and food containers (hay boxes and dixies) had all been used to support the completed section. The tunnel entrance was a half-metre square hole that had been cut in the concrete floor in the corner of the cell close to the door. The entrance opened into a shaft about a metre-and-a-half deep before turning in a straight line, in the direction of the outer wall. The collapsed section of the tunnel was still about thirty metres from the perimeter wall. When the search officers opened the cell on each side of cell 18, they found the two cells were stacked to the roof with rubble. As each layer of the mud and clay had been placed in the cell, lengths of torn bed sheets were stretched over the top before the next layer was dumped. This effectively caused the rubble and mud to be bound together into a square block the shape of the cell, so that it would not collapse out into the wing when the cell door was opened. At the same time, small toilet disinfectant blocks supplied for the ablutions were interspersed in the mud to conceal the damp smell.

Within a short time the 95 IRA prisoners who occupied the block were moved to another block, and a JCB digger was brought in to open the tunnel from end to end. This disclosed the whole range of props and supports used to keep the walls and roof of the tunnel from caving in, but it also revealed an improvised lighting system. An extension lead, which had been supplied with the computers, was joined to lengths of cable that had been stripped from fittings in the other wings, and wired to the cell light that lit up the one-metre-in diameter tunnel. A makeshift air pump was used to pump fresh air the length of the tunnel. The next day one of the security officers took a video camera and videoed the entire excavation feat. The word was put around that any of the staff could come to the security office and view the trench and the evidence that had been left behind by the nocturnal burrowers. A couple of days later I went round to H7 and saw what was left of the now-opened tunnel and the two cells still filled with rubble and mud. I then called into the security office and saw the video and the improvised tools that had been used to hack through the concrete in the cell floor, and dig out the material. It was generally believed it took them about twelve days to dig, with teams working 24 hours a day. They intended to finish the tunnel and have a mass breakout for Easter.

In the weeks that followed the discovery of the tunnel there was a human outcry, from politicians and the press alike, for the Maze Governor's resignation and for an urgent inquiry into yet another Maze fiasco. The question being asked was, how could such a thing have happened without the prison officers seeing anything suspicious. The answer was that the wings in H7 were now no go areas and the staff were not allowed in there without the permission of the IRA's Commanding Officer. All compassionate, temporary release of IRA prisoners was cancelled indefinitely and prison visits and parcels were stopped. A major crackdown took place and all the cells in the jail were searched. Some Loyalist prisoners in H5, who refused to co-operate with the staff, were moved to H6 to facilitate the searching, but they were later returned to H5. To make things worse for the Prisons Department, the IRA released photographs taken during the excavations in the tunnel. This caused great embarrassment for the NIO, and the Government appointed a senior civil servant and former Director of Prisons to head an inquiry into the affair. In the meantime, protests by Loyalist prisoners about the searches and the introduction of a tough, new regime were beginning to escalate and they warned that if riot squads were used against them 'a price would be paid'. Although the Governor did establish contact with the Loyalists, he refused to negotiate about the new regulations and the more frequent headcounts.

The protests eventually escalated and got out of hand, and by the end of April, the prisoners went on the rampage, and scaled the walls onto the roofs of H I and H2. When this happened the Loyalists' Commanding Officer gave the prison staff five minutes to leave the two blocks, and seeing the situation was hopeless because the staff were completely outnumbered and the prisoners had gained the advantage, the officers took the keys and radios and left. It was at this point that an incident took place that showed the total shambles the prison security was in.

An officer later told me he reported for evening duty that day about 12.30pm, and walked all the way to his block. As he walked into the hall he was promptly seized by the prisoners. Although he was later released unharmed it showed the total failure in security that he was not informed of the situation before he got to the block. As the protesters set fire to one of the exercise yard towers, palls of smoke rose over the jail, and some of the cons who were wearing masks, carried flags and posters complaining about being punished for the IRA's antics because it was they who had attempted to escape. Later that same day, things took a more sinister turn when the LVF Leader, Billy Wright, announced his group were joining the protest. But eventually the Loyalists were encouraged to give up their protest and were moved to different blocks. It was only then that we discovered they had caused hundreds of thousands of pounds worth of damage in H I and H2. In their rampage of destruction they smashed up the ablutions and dining halls, and ripped out the plumbing and flooded their own accommodation.

In March 1997, 37-year-old Billy Wright had been sentenced to eight years, and at the same time he was under a UVF death threat. He was a marked man, and had survived several IRA attempts on his life. As a result, he was held in the segregation unit at Maghaberry for his own protection. At that time, he and his followers were involved in a dispute with the authorities about segregation and the recognition of their Loyalist Volunteer Force as a separate, paramilitary group in the prison. The LVF protest escalated when they threatened to go on hunger-strike, to the death, if their demands were not met. The situation was becoming volatile and it had created a dilemma for the authorities in Maghaberry, particularly for the Governor, who could recall the Maze hunger-strike sixteen years before, when the ten IRA men died.

The NIO were afraid that their 'flagship prison', might be at the receiving end of a malicious, propaganda campaign that a hunger-strike would present. The only alternative was to transfer the L VF to the Maze, but that was also fraught with difficulties not least because there was not an empty block to house them because of H7 being closed for renovations after the tunnel episode. The L VF were now equally despised by the IRA and the other Loyalist organisations, and if they came to the Maze they would have to be segregated from all the other groupings. When the NIO considered all the possibilities it was decided to allocate the LVF to 'C' and 'D' wings in H6, opposite the INLA who were housed in 'A' and' B' wings. This effectively meant that the only two paramilitary groups not on ceasefire were both housed in the same building. The old remand visits complex that had not been used for some years was opened. It went through an urgent programme of refurbishment, and was renamed the L VF visits area. On Friday the 25th April Billy Wright and three of his commanders were transferred to the Maze.

Since the ceasefire had been declared by the IRA, the terrorist campaign in the Province had significantly decreased, but hopes for lasting peace were shattered on Monday morning the 16th June 1997 when two policemen were shot dead in Lurgan. The people of the town were gripped with a deep sense of foreboding after the cold-blooded and brutal murders, for fear of possible retaliatory action by the Loyalists. It was a bright and sunny morning as the two constables patrolled the Wellington Street area in shirtsleeve order. They were nearing the end of their patrol, and were in Church Walk only about 100 yards from the police station, when two IRA men stepped up behind them and shot both of them in the back of the head at close range. The policemen were taken totally by surprise and fell to the ground where more shots were fired into them by the gunmen. As passers-by on the main street recognised the sound of gunfire, the murderers dashed to a getaway car and sped away. The car was later found abandoned and burnt out on open ground in the Kilwilke housing estate. It was later established that the murder gang were both wearing wigs and disguised as women.

Residents in Church Walk reported hearing at least seven shots, and while a doctor was on the scene within seconds, it was clear the officers were beyond help. The two community policemen were Constable Roland John Graham who was 34 years of age and came from Richhill in County Armagh. He was a married man with three daughters aged 2, 7 and 10. Mr Graham joined the RUC in 1983 and was a holder of the Police Service Medal. The second victim was full-time Reserve Constable David Andrew Johnston who was 30 years of age and came from Lisburn. Mr Johnston was married with two sons, aged 3 and 7. He joined the RUC in 1986 and also held the RUC Service Medal. As David Johnston was exactly the same age as Joanne, it was the first time in the 41 years since I first joined the security forces that I felt a sense of consternation about the Government's will to defeat the IRA. They were now starting to murder our children.

As there was fewer staff required for the running of the Maze, some officers in H4 were detailed posts in other parts of the prison each day. On

Saturday the 27th December 1997, I was assigned to the visits complex and when I reported for duty that morning the SO told me I was allocated 'relief officer' and early meals. This effectively meant that I had to relieve some of the officers who were on static posts before going for my lunch break from 11.30 am till 12.30 pm. Then I would report back to visits and take up a dinner 'guard duty' over the lunch period when the visits complex was closed.

The prison had been exceptionally quiet over the Christmas period because about 150 prisoners had been released on Christmas parole and, as a result, the visits area was slack in comparison to an ordinary Saturday morning. When it was time for me to go to lunch I left the prisoners' reception area, and walked through one of the visiting blocks to the visitors' reception area. When I arrived at the outer grille the officer on duty said to me, "Sorry, Killer, I can't let you out. All movement has been stopped. Somebody has been shot in H6!" As I looked at him I thought he was joking, because he was always on the banter about something. "Stop acting the wag, Martie, and open the grille," I said to him, waiting for his joke-line. But he turned to me and said in a more serious tone of voice, "I'm not kidding you, Killer. Somebody's been shot in H6, and all movement's stopped!" At first I could only stare in disbelief, but as I waited we continued to chat, and some officers were walking about the visitors' reception area as usual, but no one seemed to know what had happened or who was shot. A few minutes later we got the word that movement had started again, and as the grille opened I walked round to the Officers Mess for a bite to eat.

I returned to the prison about half an hour later and the first officer I saw was a man I had known for many years. As I walked over and asked him what had happened in H6, he told me that Billy Wright had been shot dead and that the police 'scenes of crime' people were in the block investigating the murder. For once in my career I felt fearful, as much of the inside of the Maze was becoming as dangerous as the outside. The security debacle in the jail was clearly illustrated by the fact that a prisoner had been murdered and the sum total effect on the running of the place was that movement had been stopped for less than half an hour, and then everything continued as if nothing had happened. The prison buzzed with conversation about the murder the rest of the day, but it was the following morning when I got talking to some of the staff from H6 that I began to get a picture of what actually happened the previous morning in the block.

On Sunday the 28th I was detailed the hospital gate, and from there I could see the coming and going of police and prison staff who passed by on their way up to H6. Since the lNLA and the L VF-the only two paramilitary organisations in the Province who were not on ceasefire-were housed in the same block, the situation was volatile to say the least. It was always the practice for the visits escorting officer, when he arrived in the block to collect an inmate for visits, firstly to collect the prisoner's security book from the control room. Then he would call out the prisoner's name to the grille

Officer who in turn would echo the call into the wing. On Saturday morning the 27th December, that call, 'Bill Wright for a visit!' was the signal that set in motion an assassination conspiracy that would rock Northern Ireland and almost push the Province over the preface.

A few weeks before Christmas the INLA devised a plan to murder the L VF leader, and by Christmas the trap was ready to be sprung. They had acquired two weapons and ammunition, a Dillinger and a .38 calibre semiautomatic pistol. It was later discovered that they even test fired the weapons in a cell at the bottom of the wing the night before the murder. Given all that happened in the Maze that year, the staff would not have been surprised if they had found an indoor firing range in the wing.

Although the Governor had been assured by both organisations that neither group would launch a first strike against the other, officers in H6 gave many warnings to the security department of the danger of a pre-emptive strike from the INLA. The exceptional precaution was taken of allowing the visits van into the block forecourt, where it reversed up to the front door, and where the LVF men could not be seen by the INLA in 'A' wing as they passed from the hall guard into the van. The visits vans collected the prisoners at the front gate of all the other blocks. The L VF were very aware of the danger, too. In fact on one occasion they refused to allow the block bumper (floor polisher) to be returned to 'A' and' B' wings for fear of it being booby-trapped.

It was the first time Billy Wright had taken his visit on a Saturday morning, and when his name was called for the visit, a member of the INLA murder gang took up position between grilles on the 'A' and 'B' side of the Block. From here he could see across the circle and had only to wait for his victim to walk through 'C' and' D' grille and into the circle. When Wright was identified by the escorting officer, the circle officer opened the grille and they both walked into the hall guard. At this point the gunman dashed down 'A' wing and out through the turnstile into the exercise yard, where he was followed by his two accomplices. The three then scrambled through a one metre square hole in the sterile fence, scaled the wall onto the roof of 'A' wing, scurried across and dropped down into the forecourt where the visits van was just leaving the front door with Billy Wright on board. The van only travelled about thirty metres when it had to stop to allow the gate officer to open the block gate. One of the gunmen then ran to the side door of the van which could only be opened from the outside, and slid it open. Billy Wright and the escorting officer were sitting facing the door on the opposite side of the van from the gunmen. On seeing the man, Wright jumped to his feet and tried to get out through the back door which was locked, but the gunmen opened fire, hitting his victim eight times as he collapsed and died instantly. The three INLA men then scaled the wall and returned to the wing.

In the days that followed I listened to reports on the staff grapevine, from officers who worked in the block, about the sequence of events that led up to the murder. A pair of improvised wire-cutters was used to cut through the sterile fence and it was believed that this part of the plan was carried out on Christmas Eve. The square metre of wire was then tied in place with shoelaces and concealed behind chairs that were stacked in front. But the ultimate irony was that, on the sterile wall only two metres from where the hole was cut, there was an alarm button. This was originally a static observation point for an officer when prisoners were having exercise, but the post had been stood down some years before, when the inmates were given the concession that the exercise yards would remain open all day.

After an inquiry into the murder it was established that the CCTV camera, on the roof of H6, that monitored the 'A' wing exercise yard area was out of order and had not been functioning for five days. A second 'strange coincidence' was that, on the evening before the murder, the L VF visit sheets were sent down the INLA wing by mistake. This in effect gave the murderers prior notice that Wright was on a visit the following morning. But the final 'coincidence' took place on the morning of the murder, when the officer who was on duty in 'A' and 'B' exercise yard watchtower was ordered to vacate his tower, and report to visits to assist there because of a staff shortage. It was 9.15 am, and we all know there was an agreement between the POA and the Governor that, in exceptional circumstances, officers on some static posts could be stood down to facilitate staff shortages in the jail. But the agreement did not extend to H6 because of the extraordinary regime in that block where the two most ruthless organisations in Northern Ireland were housed in the same place.

When the tower officer arrived in the block he immediately phoned the POA office, and told them about his change of detail, at which point the POA representative confronted the duty Governor and informed him about the agreement. At this stage the tower officer was instructed to return to his original duty in the tower. The whole altercation had taken over a half an hour, and when the officer had walked back to the tower and taken up his post again, he saw the three prisoners on the roof of 'A' wing. They were returning to the wing after committing the murder. It was almost 10.00 am when the ECR received an emergency call from H6 stating that there had been a shooting incident in the forecourt of the block. The riot squad was called, and on arriving at the scene, threw a cordon around the block and the scene of the crime. An ambulance was summoned from the Lagan Valley Hospital, and when the duty Governor arrived in the block an INLA spokesman in 'A' wing asked to speak to him. They immediately surrendered to the authorities and handed over the two firearms and the wire-cutters. The murder gang were arrested by the police, and an NIO spokesman later said the weapons were probably smuggled into the prison over the Christmas period. The INLA prisoners in 'A' wing of H6 were all searched, and transferred to H3. The question that cried out to be asked was, why weren't they moved to H3 a week earlier?

The NIO were anxious to ensure the maintenance of the ceasefires in order to build confidence in the political process, and they had directed the prison authorities to relax security in the jail. There is no doubt that this played an important part in the murder of Billy Wright, the Averill escape and the tunnel, earlier in the year. In an interview on a TV documentary about the escape tunnel, the Governor of the Maze actually bragged about catching a visitor trying to smuggle a dog into the prison. The fact that someone was willing to try to smuggle a dog into the jail showed he thought he had a good chance of success, and he knew that if he were caught he would not be prosecuted.

The circumstances surrounding the murder of Billy Wright would have consequences that would run on for a long time, not least for his elderly father, Mr. David Wright, who strongly believed that the death of his son was the subject of a political conspiracy. I think all the staff agreed it was a devastating event to take place in a once high-security prison, even in the context of the total chaos in the Maze at the time.

On Tuesday the 30th December thousands of people attended the funeral of Billy Wright as the cortege made its way from his home to Seagoe Cemetery on the outskirts of Portadown. As the funeral made its way through the crowded streets, the town centre came to a standstill as shops and businesses closed as a mark of respect to the Wright family. A guard of honour of young men in white shirts lined both sides of the hearse, and hundreds of others walked behind, many wearing sunglasses and black, leather jackets. As the infamous Loyalist leader had survived numerous murder attempts he always feared that some day a Republican murder gang would finally succeed in killing him. It was for this purpose that he had left specific instructions about his funeral, including who would officiate at the service in the home and who would take part in the oration at the graveside. It was later said that Billy often recounted: "I am always conscious that I turned my back on the greatest friend I ever had, the Lord Jesus Christ. "

The murder of the L VF leader provoked the inevitable retaliation, and within a few hours, 45-year-old Seamus Dillon was shot dead and two other men seriously injured. The three men were security guards at the Glengannon Hotel outside Dungannon, and they were shot by L VF gunmen in a Vauxhall car that drove off at high speed afterwards. Dillon came from Coalisland and had been released from prison three years earlier, where he had been serving two life sentences for the murders of a 23-year-old policeman, Constable Stewart Logan, and a 60-year-old Protestant farmer, Mr William Hughes, at Ardboe. In a statement the L VF said further action would be taken later but the murder of Seamus Dillon was only a mark of respect to the memory of Billy Wright. Within the following days there was an upsurge in violence that threatened the ceasefires and even jeopardised the tentative political negotiations designed to bring to an end all the violence in the Province.

Chapter 21

The search for a lasting settlement to the thirty years of trouble in Northern Ireland was depending more and more on the consent of the prisoners in the Maze, both Republican and Loyalist. On Friday the 9th January 1998 the Secretary of State, Mo Mowlam, convened a meeting in the Maze gymnasium, where she came face-to-face with some of the Province's most notorious terrorists. The prison staff looked on at the bizarre spectacle of a Secretary of State talking with sectarian killers who had waged death and destruction on the people of the Province for thirty years. Dr. Mowlam represented the left of the Tony Blair Labour Party and therefore did not appear to have any difficulty in talking to these people.

Her decision to go to the Maze and talk to some of the most ruthless murderers of the 20th century was predictably reviled by politicians and families of the victims alike. She admitted she was taking the greatest gamble of her political life, as she braved the wave of criticism in a bid to rescue the talks process. In an attempt to prepare the ground for her visit to the jail, the NIO in an unprecedented move, opened the gates of the Maze to the UK media. It was designed to show the public the inside of the jail and to give the people confidence that the prison service was in control of the place, following the security disasters of the previous twelve months. But the message the NIO was trying to convey fell on deaf ears as the population now knew that areas of the prison were 'out of bounds' to the prison officers. For years the POA spokesman, Mr Finlay Spratt, had criticized the management of the prison and had even made public denunciations about the regime that had allowed the inmates to take control of parts of the prison.

In order to encourage the prisoners and to copper-fasten their support for the peace process, the NIO consented to allow group visits to take place in the prison gymnasium between representatives of the various terror groups on the outside, and their leaders inside the Maze. In the days that followed, my colleagues and I were subjected to the humiliation of escorting former prisoners who had previously served sentences in the compounds and in the blocks, and were now elevated to the respectable position of peace negotiators. However, their arrogance and abrupt tone of voice masked guilt, and showed their deep contempt for the system. They were still the' Godfathers' and were not afraid to let you know, nothing had changed. It was not only wrong, but it was also an affront to decency. We were caught between the known and the unknown, in that special purgatory inhabited only by prison officers.

In February 1998 I was told to report to the personnel office in the admin building to collect a letter. It was an individual, transcript printout of my career history in the service and it included every detail about me since the day I joined in 1975. It particularly emphasized my periods of sick leave, itemising every single day and the reason for my absence from duty. I had been off duty for one day in 1992, suffering from a stomach complaint and even this one single day was itemised. The curious thing about the document was that there was not a word about the Commendation for Bravery I had received in 1984. It seemed the NIO expected its prison officers to remain loyal to the end, whilst its loyalty to its staff was lost in an endless chase in ever decreasing circles of responsibility, by a black briefcase and white shirt brigade of bureaucrats, whose principal calling in life was to give the appearance of the ultimate in excellence and efficiency.

On Sunday morning the 15th March 1998 H Block 6 was once again plunged into the headlines when it was the scene of a second, brutal murder. At 8.30am the staff went into the wings to carry out the morning headcount. The officer in 'C' wing went to the cell occupied by 23-year-old David Keys, an awaiting trial prisoner, who had been remanded in custody charged with two murders. He found the prisoner hanging from one of the concrete window bars by a length of torn bedsheet that had been twisted into a rope. His wrists had been slashed and he had suffered extensive body injuries, both external and internal inflicted by a snooker cue. As the news about the murder spread around the prison, the way in which David Keys had died that shocked even the experienced and hardened prison officers. It was a grotesque murder and sent a shudder through everyone in the Maze, both prisoners and staff alike, and made everyone more than ever aware of the absurd security situation that now seemed to be going into meltdown.

Keys had been accused of being involved in the L VF murder of two men who were shot dead in an attack on the Railway Bar in Poyntzpass, County Armagh, twelve days earlier. He was remanded to Maghaberry prison but soon after he arrived in the jail, he requested to be transferred to the Maze. The duty Governor in Maghaberry contacted the Maze to find out if the L VF in H6 would accept him into their wing; the organisation's OC confirmed his affiliation and he was moved to the Maze. Police 'scenes of crime' teams were back in H6 and when a post-mortem established he had been strangled before he was tied up to the window bar-apparently to make it look like suicide. All the prisoners were moved to an empty wing in the block and a full-scale murder investigation was started. Two fellow L VF prisoners were later charged with the murder, and almost a year after the crime was committed, the case against them collapsed when the principal prosecution witness withdrew his evidence, and the court ruled that the trial could not continue. For the second murder to have taken place in the Maze within a few weeks was bad enough, but it was the thought that if they did such a thing to one of their own, what would they not do to me or one of my colleagues that was so frightening. This incident, more than anything before, convinced me that the remainder of my career in the prison service should be as short as possible, and I decided to get out at the earliest possible opportunity.

When the Belfast Agreement was finally signed in April 1998 after some two years of negotiations between the British and Irish Govenments and all the political parties in Northern Ireland, it provided for the establishment of a

108member elected Assembly with executive and legislative authority. One section of the Agreement recommended the review of the Criminal Justice System and in a sub-section with the simple title 'Prisoners', it specifically dealt with the issue of inmates held in prisons both north and south of the border.

'Both Governments will put in place mechanisms to provide for an accelerated programme for the release of prisoners, including transferred prisoners, convicted of scheduled offences in Northern Ireland or, in the case of those sentenced outside Northern Ireland, similar offences (referred to hereafter as qualifying prisoners). Any such arrangement will protect the rights of individual prisoners under national and international law.

Prisoners affiliated to organisations which have not established or are not maintaining a complete and unequivocal cease-fire will not benefit from the arrangements. The situation in this regard will be kept under review.

Both Governments will complete a review process within a fixed timeframe and set prospective release dates for all qualifying prisoners.

The review process would provide for the advance of the release dates of qualifying prisoners while allowing account to be taken of the seriousness of the offences for which the person was convicted and the need to protect the community. In addition, the intention would be that should the circumstances allow it, any qualifying prisoners who remained in custody two years after the commencement of the scheme would be released at that point.

The Governments will seek to enact the appropriate legislation to give effect to those arrangements by the end of June 1998.

The Governments continue to recognise the importance of measures to facilitate the reintegration of prisoners into the community by providing support both prior to and after release, including assistance directed towards availing of employment opportunities, re-training and re-skilling, and further education'.

As was required by the Agreement, both Governments introduced a phasing release programme within the two jurisdictions. The UK Government established the Sentence Review Commission, which came into being in July and was jointly chaired by Sir Jolm Blellock, a former senior civil servant at the Northen Ireland Office, and Mr Curran, a South African lawyer and prestigious mediator. Eight other commissioners were also appointed and, as the Act directed, all prisoners were asked to apply to the Commission for early release from prison. Within a few weeks there was 558 applications. At first the gradual release system was put into effect. It was made clear to each inmate that he was only being released on licence and in the event of a breach of the law, particularly in the context of a terrorist act, he would be recalled to serve the remainder of his sentence. Over the following two years there was a gradual flow of inmates from the prisons on both parts of the island, but especially from the Maze where the greater number of prisoners convicted of scheduled offences were held.

When the first prisoners started to drift out of the Maze, the Department offered the prison officers an early retirement package, which they called a Staff

Reduction Programme. The package was based on the length of service an officer had completed, his age and the remainder of years he had left to serve before retirement. So it did not benefit everyone. However, the Prisons Department intended to achieve a target of 750 staff reductions by voluntary means, thereby avoiding the need for compulsory redundancies. In effect, within a year the target of 750 had been surpassed and 910 had actually applied to leave the service. The additional 160 applicants had given the Department a problem, and when they consulted with the POA as to how they could restructure the Service to allow the 160 additional staff to leave, it caused concern. As a trade union the POA was placed in a difficult situation in that, if they did not address the issue, the Government might proceed and make changes that were not in the interest of the staff. If they did negotiate the necessary changes, then their members would criticize them. However, they did eventually negotiate with the Department and all 910 staff were allowed to leave the Service.

I immediately applied for early retirement by filling in the necessary forms and in early January 1999 I was informed that the 30th March would be my finishing date in the Service. I soon discovered that many officers of my own age group had applied to leave and as it turned out, the numbers of staff wanting to leave far exceeded the projected requirements. The scale of staff volunteering to leave their employment showed clearly that morale was at an all time low and they were totally disenchanted with the Service. It was understandable, considering that over the years, prison officers were used and abused by the prisoners and at the same time, denied proper leadership and appropriate resources to do their job. As the officers who were leaving the Service had long service and years of experience in dealing with a volatile prison situation, no doubt their experience would take many years to replace. On a visit to the Province, Tony Blair said that he had suggested a medal should be struck for the officers of the Northern Ireland Prison Service and it was with the Ceremonial Office in London for consideration. However, it has to be said, a medal would not replace a father, mother, wife, husband, son or daughter who have been brutally murdered. Nor would it restore the health of prison officers who had been injured, both mentally and physically. These are the needs that should be addressed, the real problems which had been endured by the prison staff and their families, who had in some cases taken their grief, hurt and anxiety to their graves. Since the Belfast deal was signed we witnessed the absurd spectacle of prisoners' groups receiving over £4 million from the European Peace and Reconciliation Fund, to assist former terrorists to be integrated back into the community. Is it not time the Northern Ireland Prison Service and the security forces in general received a more tangible recognition for taking the brunt, over the past 30 years?

One admirable tribute to the men and women of the prison service was paid by Sir David Ramsbotham, Her Majesty's Chief Inspector of Prisons for England and Wales, by expressing admiration for the extraordinarily difficult work carried out in the Maze prison during the years. He acknowledged that Northern Ireland owes a huge debt of gratitude for the meritorious work of the prison service staff. Sir David went further and recognised the failures of the NIO to honour Tony Blair's promises to treat the security forces generously. "The NIO have not been as understanding as they should have been," he said. Prison officers were the social hygienists of the twentieth century; they were asked to cope with and conceal the unacceptable problems, tensions and social disasters of a complex society that can only be described as being in long-term relative decline. The age of heroes was replaced with the age of mediocrity.

Tuesday the 30th March 1999 was one of my rest days, so Friday the 26th would be my last duty day in the service. I was given the day to 'clear my desk', which effectively meant time to clear up all the final details in the personnel office and the Staff Reduction Unit regarding my entitlements under the SRP, and my retirement pension. Then I would have the disconsolate duty of handing in my unifoml at the stores.

As I left the administration building for the last time, and walked through the admin gate, I met an officer who was a fellow member of the Christian Prison Officers Fellowship. We chatted for a few minutes, then shook hands and parted company. Although the CPOF was organised throughout the Prison Service many years ago, it was revived in the Maze in the late 1970's after my own conversion, when Ken McGee and a few of us started lunch-time meetings in a small office near the transport depot. The organisation developed in the Maze and now has a wide membership across all ranks in the Service. Its members are frequently invited to conduct services in churches and they encourage everyone with the Christian message. Contact is maintained with the retired members and there have been some evangelical tours to the mainland and other countries. The men and women of the CPOF are a group of people who occupy a special place in my heart. These are the people who maintained a flicker of light in a dark place.

I called in at the uniform stores on the way out and met some more of my colleagues who were also leaving that day. We left the stores together and as we bade farewell to the staff in the tally lodge, some of whom I had worked with during all the years of my service, one of them shouted after me: "Cheerio, Killer, all the best. Draw as many pensions as you can!" I just laughed and walked on.

On the 24th July 2000 two years after the signing of the Belfast Agreement there was a mixed reaction from some areas of Belfast when the notorious Loyalist leader Michael Stone was released from the Maze. A hero's welcome greeted him from a group of Loyalists who were gathered in the visitors' car park. He had served 12 years of six life sentences for a hand grenade attack at Milltown Cemetery in 1988. But four days later on the 28th July, the date under the terms of the Agreement when, 'All qualifying prisoners who remain in custody two years after the commencement of the scheme will be released' eighty-six Loyalist and Republican prisoners walked through the turnstile at the car park and were free.

It was an abominable sight as I watched the TV news that evening. The IRA men were being greeted with handshakes from Gerry Kelly, the Old Bailey bomber, and the prisoner who was in the meals lorry before making his dash for freedom in the 1983 mass escape from the Maze, the same Mr Gerry Kelly who is now a 'respected' Sinn Fein Assembly Member and who often comments on the reform of the RUC and law and order matters. Brendan 'Bic' McFarlane, the IRA leader in H7 who planned the escape in 1983 was also there to welcome his comrades and no doubt explain their new-found 'peace strategy'. Among those released was prisoner B1827, Sean Kelly, the IRA bomber who murdered nine people including an expectant mother and a seven-year-old girl, when he put a bomb in a fish shop on the Shankill Road in October 1993. But the most repulsive exhibition came when a delegation, including the man who shot the last soldier to be murdered in the Province, stood in front of the press and delivered a statement from the 'Republican Prisoners of War in Long Kesh'. It reminded me of a similar episode 24 years earlier, when the internees were released in 1976 and Martin Meehan the then, so called 'high Priest' of the IRA, gave a carbon-copy oration.

Perhaps it was an omen of things to come, underlying the foolishness of the Government's appeasement policy and the release of prisoners. As they were freed, news broke about the seizure of a huge arms shipment bound for the Real IRA. The weapons, which included anti-tank rockets, sub-machine guns, commercial explosives and cortex, were seized in Croatia after a major, international police operation. A year before, Scotland Yard had warned that Republican terrorists were establishing new arms supply routes from the Balkans, in preparation for a renewed bombing campaign in the Province and on the UK mainland. As Irish Special Branch Officers flew to Croatia, a man was arrested in Dundalk and was questioned about terrorist crimes. The Real IRA have been repeatedly foiled by undercover police operations and as the weapons seizure in Croatia showed, the police were ahead of the game.

The IRA have always found it difficult to procure and successfully smuggle weapons from foreign countries. In 1987 the supply ship Eksund, carrying a large consignment of weapons from Libya, was intercepted after an operation by British intelligence. But the first, big, Libyan shipment of arms to the IRA was seized in 1973 when the Claudia was intercepted. The operation was a complete success after an MI6 agent infiltrated the Zurich-based organisation that set up the arms deal. After the seizure of the Claudia, Joe Cahill, who was the IRA's director of finance, was arrested. In the summer of 1999 a batch of weapons was found in a Dublin sorting-office. The consignment, which came from America, included ammunition for the Baretta sniper rifle, the weapon used with great effect by the IRA in South Armagh.

It was an absurd coincidence that the day on which 86 sentenced terrorists walked free from the Maze, national newspapers carried a story about a head teacher who had been convicted, two weeks previously, of slapping a disruptive 10-year-old boy. She was spared a prison sentence on the Friday, after a magistrate said she had suffered 'sustained and extreme provocation'. Marjorie Evans had been told there was a possibility of her being sent to jail. She was cheered by supporters as she left Abergavenny Magistrates Court, Gwent, after being sentenced to three months suspended for one year. The court also ordered her to pay costs totalling £2,250.

On Saturday the 30th September 2000, the last three Loyalist prisoners in the Maze were transferred to Maghaberry prison and a Republican was taken to Magilligan jail in County Londonderry. As the four prisoners left the Maze, the gates finally closed for the last time, after 30 years at the centre of Ulster's conflict. It was inevitable, and something that the community in Northern Ireland had looked forward to for a long time.

On the day I retired as I made my way out through the main gate, I felt the weight of the Maze slip from my shoulders. The pleasure of work in the Service had long disappeared. It was a part of my life that was now gone, but not forgotten. I felt some optimism though, as I looked forward to what was to come-my retirement with Delta, Joanne, her husband Robert, and my two grandchildren Martin and Clare, whom I love dearly.

Every time I drive down the M1 motorway past the Maze, with its high, guard force watchtowers, the prison towers beyond and the high, weatherbeaten, perimeter wall that conceals from public view, the now infamous H Blocks. Where all traces of their former occupants have been erased beneath several layers of sanitising paint. Neatly folded sheets and blankets sit on the narrow, steel beds and new, plastic chamber pots and water gallons indicate that hundred of prisoners could again be incarcerated at a moment's notice, in the same cells the Provies held their streaker protest in 1978, their hunger-strike in 1981 and from where the mass escape was launched in 1983. But we should all remember that the Maze prison has played a critically important part in protecting life and limb from rampant, sectarian terrorism in Northern Ireland. Over the course of 25 years, an estimated 25,000 inmates passed through its gates and it held within its walls some of the most evil men on the planet.

As the Belfast Agreement remains in a volatile state and international terrorism has increased on a global scale, where man's inhumanity to man threatens the destruction of civilisation itself. I look to the Lord in whom I put my trust in 1979, and who has kept us safe over the years. As I read my favourite portion of scripture, I thank God for the reassurance of the Psalmist who states: 'He that dwelleth in the secret place of the most high shall abide under the shadow of the Almighty'. Psalm 91. V.I. The Psalms are a concentrated essence of human experience and life, our joy and anger, our laughter and fear and our divine protection and security. They are about life and they are about death. I hope that, through my own spiritual experiences as expressed in this book, I have evoked in the reader an awareness of his individual contemporary and spiritual condition.

I have one abiding recollection of the day I retired when there were 19 Governors of various grades in the Maze. I thought it was rather sad that not one of them saw it worth his while to say goodbye to me and my colleagues who left that day. But as I ran my eyes over the buildings that had become so familiar to me. 1 stopped for a moment at the black marble memorial that bears the names of my murdered comrades, and thought of the lives that were lost and the families that were shattered over the years. However, my health was good and my spirit was relatively strong. But there was something else I was thankful for. I still had my memories.

Glossary

APC	Armoured Personnel Carrier
B Men	Ulster Special Constabulary
B Specials	Ulster Special Constabulary
BA	Bachelor of Arts
BBC	British Broadcasting Corporation
BEM	British Empire Medal
CCTV	Closed Circuit Television
CID	Criminal Investigation Department
CO	Commanding Officer
CPOF	Christian Prison Officers ' Fellowship
CS	Crime Special
DOE	Department of the Environment
DUP	Democratic Unionist Party
ECR	Emergency Control Room
GCSE	General Certificate of Secondary Education
HMP	Her Majesty's Prison
HMS	Her majesty's Ship
INLA	Irish National Liberation Army
IPLO	Irish People's Liberation Army
IRA	Irish Republican Army
IRF	Instant Reaction Force
IRSP	Irish Republican Socialist Party
JP	Justice of the Peace
LSD	Lysergic Acid Diethylamide
LYF	Loyalist Volunteer Force
MP	Member of Parliament
NATO	North Atlantic Treaty Organisation
NIO	Northern Ireland Office
OC	Officer Commanding
ODC	Ordinary Decent Criminal
OIRA	Official Irish Republican Army
OU	Open University
PIRA	Provisional Irish Republican Army
PO	Principal Officer
POA	Prisons Officers' Association
PTI	Physical Training Instructor
RAF	Royal Air Force
RC	Roman Catholic
RSA	Royal Society of Arts
RT	Radio Transmitter
RUC	Royal Ulster Constabulary

RUCR	Royal Ulster Constabulary Reserve
RVH	Royal Victoria Hospital
SDLP	Social Democratic and Labour Party
SIC	Security Information Centre
SOSP	Secretary Of State's Pleasure
SPG	Special Patrol Group
SRP	StafT Reduction Package
TAVR	Territorial Army Volunteer Reserve
TV	Television
UDA	Ulster Defence Association
UDR	Ulster Defence Regiment
UK	United Kingdom
USA	United States of America
USC	Ulster Special Constabulary
UVF	Ulster Volunteer Force
VC	Victoria Cross
VCP	Vehicle Check Point
VHS	Very High Speed
YP	Young Prisoner

CONSPICIOUS

BRAVERY

I will always consider it the greatest

priviledge of my life to have served

with the men and women of the

Northern Ireland Security Forces.

I am delighted to have this

opportunity to pay my personal

tribute to them.

My only regret is that I could not

start and serve another

43 years with them.

I will never forget them

as long as I live.

W. McKane